With Best Wishes
Francis Spear
10th May 2013

Games We Play

History of J.W. Spear & Sons

Helmut Schwarz / Marion Faber

Games We Play
History of J. W. Spear & Sons

Publications of the Nuremberg Toy Museum, Volume II

Nuremberg Municipal Museums / Toy Museum

Acknowledgements

The authors would like to acknowledge the cooperation, assistance and encouragement
of the following persons:

Anne Bradford, Hans Danzer, Anneliese Dupont, Manfred Eder, Gunther Friedrich (State Archives
Nuremberg), Rudi Hoffmann, Gerhard Jochem (City of Nuremberg Archives), Elisabeth Kaufmann,
Erika Kaußler, Annette Köger (Deutsches Spielkartenmuseum Leinfelden), Herbert Kreppner,
Peter Lemcke (Deutsches Spielemuseum Chemnitz), Willy Lippert, Klaus-Erik Lohse (Nürnberger
Spielkarten-Verlag), Georg Meidenbauer (J. G Schrödel Ideal), Dieter Mensenkamp,
Erna Mißbach (Library of LGA Bayern, Nuremberg), Helmut Richter (Fürth Municipal Archives),
Rudolf Rühle, Petra Schaaf (Deutsches Spielearchiv), Lothar Schmid, Herbert Spear,
Helmut Steiner, Lotte Stumpf, Betty Suthau, Heidrun Teumer (Library of LGA Bayern, Nuremberg),
Norman Thompson, Reinhold Weber, Adolf Wustmann

This book was published in conjunction with the exhibition:

Games We Play
History of J.W. Spear & Sons
Nuremberg Toy Museum
November 22, 1997 – April 19, 1998

Cover illustration: Stefan Kübler, Dresden
Back of cover: Motif from a Spear advertisement by Irma Graeff, around 1930

Published by the Spear Charitable Trust in association with the Spear's Games Archive Trust
Roughground House, Old Hall Green, Ware, Herts. SG 11 1HB, England
Copyright © 1997
All rights reserved.

Concept: Helmut Schwarz and Marion Faber
Text editors: Helmut Schwarz, Francis Spear
Translation: Janet Christel, Ulrike Seeberger, Nuremberg
Design: Heinz Glaser and Helmut Schwarz
Photography: Christiane Richter, Nuremberg; Photo Richard Krauss, Nuremberg

ISBN 3-921590-51-5

This book is also available in German under the title
Die Spielmacher
ISBN 3-921590-50-7

Printed in Germany by W. Tümmels Buchdruckerei und Verlag GmbH, Nuremberg

Contents

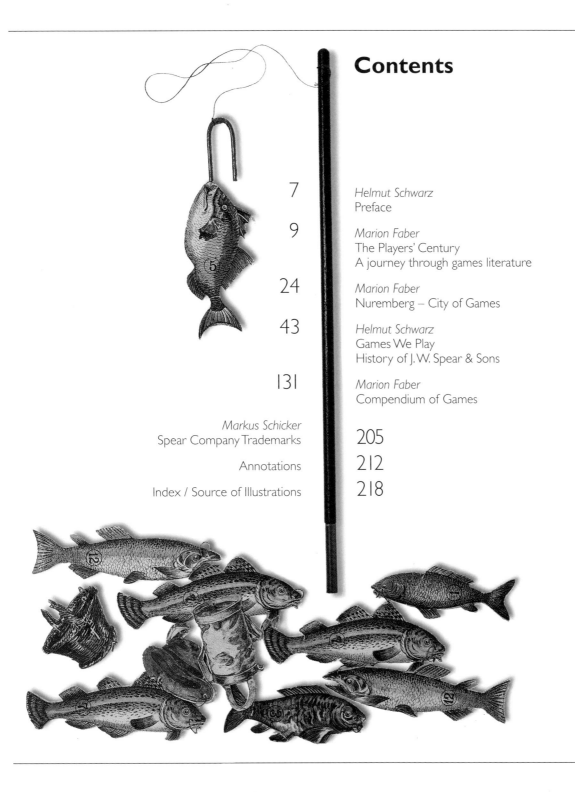

Box label print for "Safety First",
a traffic game that Spear
put on the English market in 1938.

Preface

"Spear" is one of the really big names in the history of games in the industrial era. The company was founded by Jacob Wolf Spear in Fürth in 1879 and developed from modest beginnings to being one of the most important companies in the games sector world-wide. For more than a century, Spear's successfully developed high-quality products – parlour games, activity games, games of skill, children's books, card games, handwork kits and conjuring sets, not to mention numerous outdoor games. "Scrabble" is without doubt the most famous Spear's game – a crossword game which has attained the status of a games classic and has been a source of fascination for millions of enthusiasts all over the world for more than forty years.

This book was published in conjunction with an exhibition presented by the Nuremberg Toy Museum. Exhibition and book complement each other in setting out to illustrate the development of a company which accounts for an important chapter in German and British games history. What makes Spear so special is the fact that the company not only had a very international outlook right from the start, but that for more than fifty years it even had separate production facilities in England and Germany. This fact is, however, also very closely linked to the darkest chapter of German history, since it was due to insane National Socialist racial policies that many members of the Spear family had to seek exile in England and were at the same time robbed of their Nuremberg factory by so-called "Aryanization" measures. We took particular care in giving a detailed description of those shameful actions, which affected many Jewish families in Germany at that time. We believe that we owe this debt in particular to the eleven members of the Spear family who were murdered in German concentration camps.

The first article takes you on a journey through games literature. It aims to show the higher status given to children's and adults' play, from the late 18th century, looking particularly at the "players' century", the 19th century. The second article examines Nuremberg as "a city of games". A wealth of information shows that right from the beginning of the industrial age Nuremberg, already the city of toys, was also very fertile ground indeed for publishers and producers of games. Highly qualified craftsmen, the superior skill of local printers, etchers and lithographers, and the international connections of enterprising merchants were all factors which paved the way for the development of a surprisingly extensive games industry during the last third of the 19th century, in Nuremberg and its neighbour Fürth. The article entitled "Games We Play" then documents the development of J. W. Spear & Sons and its rise to becoming one of the major international games producers. And, last but not least, the games themselves come into their own. A "Games Compendium" introduces the wide Spear range – subdivided into categories and supplemented by numerous colour illustrations. The appendix, apart from giving an index for reference purposes, also lists all Spear trademarks registered in Germany and thus provides valuable help to collectors in pin-pointing the dates of individual Spear's games.

Neither this book nor the exhibition would have been possible without extensive support granted by Francis and Hazel Spear and the Spear's Games Archive Trust established by them. They permitted the Nuremberg Toy Museum unrestricted access to their comprehensive games archive and to valuable company and family documents and furthermore gave material and financial support in realising this project. We owe them our heartfelt thanks for their wonderful co-operation.

"The Players' Century"
New Year gift
by Wiener Theaterzeitung
Coloured copperplate, 1838
Drawing by Theodor
H. Alconiere (1798-1865)
Etching by Andreas Geiger
the Younger

Marion Faber

The Players' Century
A journey through games literature

To this day, games hold a great fascination for humanity. Children work out the meaning of the world in play and would be unable to survive without it. The older they get, the more they have to submit to the rules and regulations determining the life of adults. Adults convey to children that the world is not a game and that school and work denote the serious side of life. That is why when children grow up they often lose the ability to play. The creative, inquisitive energy for play is sometimes only regained when adults have children of their own and discover play anew, and in a new way.

But what is it that makes games so popular, loved or even necessary that hardly anyone at some stage in their life can do without them? There are games theories galore. The main reason must surely be that most games simply are fun and offer freedom to try out new patterns of behaviour. Educationalist Johann Christoph Friedrich Gutsmuths also saw it that way: "Games spread merriment and delight, joy and laughter amongst young folk."[1] In his book, published in 1796, he asks the question: Why do we play? He points out three useful aspects of games: entertainment to prevent boredom, perfection of mental skills and relaxation from work. He says that a person can best relax when prolonged mental activity is followed by an active game, and conversely when after hard physical work a quiet game is played.

On the basis of the contrast between rest and movement, Gutsmuths developed a classification with exactly 106 games, which was intended mainly as a guideline for educators. He himself was also a teacher and worked for several decades until 1837 at Christian Gotthilf Salzmann's famous educational institute in Schnepfenthal, his subjects being physical education and geography.

Among "active games", Gutsmuths includes *ball games* such as hand ball, cricket, badminton or a German-English ball game based on the rules of baseball, *games using smaller balls*, such as billiards, ball-throwing or Scottish golf, *skittle games* of all kinds, post and *ring games* such as quoits, *winter games* in snow and ice or *parlour games* such as blind man's buff. With quiet games in the home he distinguishes between games requiring observation, attentiveness, memory, aesthetic perception, reason, imagination and wit. In addition to well-known games such as cup-and-ball, yo-yos, construction and wooden pattern games, Chinese rings, chess, and mikado, he recommends a whole string of contemporary "games innovations". The "Geographical Card Game" brought out in Brunswick by J. H. Campe, and the "Historical-Chronological Game" published by P. F. Catel in Berlin are just some examples. Gutsmuths would have liked to add several more such current games to his book, but his publisher did not want it to exceed a particular size. This must have pained him, since he still possessed "quite a supply" and therefore intended to deliver supplements, in order gradually "to create a games library such as no other nation possesses".[2]

"Bell and Hammer" Illustration for box lid, from a picture book. Coloured etching, around 1830/40

Apart from their strong educational purpose, however, a rather romantic perception of games also appears in Gutsmuths' book, culminating in the emotional statement: "Games are ribbons of flowers forever binding one to youth."[3] For him games become a preliminary, a rehearsal for life as an adult and a promoter of the qualities needed later on. They allow teachers and tutors to get to know the young people, to get close to them and win their trust.

At the end of the 18th century adjustment to children's needs was in no way a matter of course. Even for philanthropists such as Johann Bernhard Basedow or Christian Gotthilf Salzmann, who in the course of the Enlightenment called for the natural and rational education of young people, play in the sense of free development was rejected and in its place "productive" crafts or physical activities were given priority. Permitting play to a limited extent was regarded

more as an educator's elegant trick to achieve what needed to be conveyed in lessons anyway. There were no games without a purpose. The keenness and the seriousness which characterised Basedow's and Salzmann's educational institutions, inevitably gave their efforts a slightly tense note.[4] Gutsmuths' principles must be valued all the higher in this context. He expressed for the first time that entertainment and relaxation in play are of educational importance until adulthood, and this makes him one of the co-founders of leisure-time education, which of course only became relevant in the industrial society of the 20th century.[5]

Printed collections of games had appeared in great numbers in the 18th century before the publication of Gutsmuths' book[6], though they mostly tended to have a philological-historical or practical content. No games book containing more than information on the origin, history or method of play of games and none giving priority to their refreshing and educational aspect can be found before his time. Gutsmuths is also the first to go beyond the common moral assessment of games, and to subject new games to constructive criticism. He finds fault with the intellectual content of the cards and the poor quality of the paper in the "Geographical Card Game". On the "Historical-Chronological Game" he remarks: "The invention is well thought up; it couches useful knowledge in a clever manner in the guise of a game."[7] Gutsmuths knew what he was talking about and thus the teacher from Schnepfenthal can be seen as the father of games criticism in the modern sense.

Gutsmuths' ideas on play contributed to the enrichment of the educational theory of play, and his main thoughts have remained meaningful right to this day. Editions of his book appeared continuously in Germany throughout the whole of the 19th century.[8] Certainly for some time they provided a scale of educational values which games manufacturers could only ignore at the risk of their products being spurned on moral grounds by strict parents and educationalists. This especially concerns Gutsmuths' rejection of card and dice games and games of chance normally played by adults, which in his opinion children were to be kept away from.

Adult pastimes have always been seen from a somewhat different viewpoint than child's play. In middle class circles a game in convivial company was considered part of the enjoyment of a good life. The man or woman of the world had to be experienced in the art of games in order to be popular in good society. The games enjoyed on such occasions can be seen in Julius Cäsar's "Spielalmanach" (Games Almanac), which appeared in Berlin in at least twelve editions from 1797 to 1831 and later in three reprints[9] under the title "Talisman des Glücks" (Good Luck Charm).

As is to be expected, all possible sorts of card games are listed here, from l'Hombre to Whist, Boston, Casino, Imperial, Tarot, Piquet, Tresett, Commerce, Alliance and Pharo. Readers could teach themselves the various card games using the information given in over 260 pages, whereas chess, billiards, skittle and ball games take up barely 140 pages.[10] Unquestionably l'Hombre must have been one of the most popular games of the time, for its rules and variations take up one quarter of the book. The game is normally played by three players, with forty cards. Completely forgotten today, l'Hombre had spread across Europe starting in the 17th century and had only slowly gone out of fashion in the 1840s. It originated in Spain, the name meaning "man", referring to the player who in the game competes against two opponents.

Since l'Hombre managed to remain socially acceptable for over two hundred years at an international level, it even lent its name to a whole genre of German language games literature which used the popularity of this game as a "leader" for all sorts of collections of games.

"Military Draughts"
Illustration for box lid,
from a picture book.
Coloured etching,
around 1830

Books entitled "L'Hombre" went through as many as eighteen editions from 1697 to 1846. "Royal L'Hombre", as it was often called, because according to contemporary opinion it belonged among the noblest and finest of card games, was for a time also the favourite game at the Prussian Court, until it was replaced by Whist.[11] In the foreword to the 17th edition, of 1837, the editor was still enthusing: "No game has so consistently survived the violent changes in fashion, or has won, up to now, so much new admiration as this, the favourite game of our ladies and gentleman of the aristocracy and of the middle classes."[12]

An Alliance of Reason and Chance

Education and entertainment were basic cultural needs of the rising bourgeoisie in the first half of the 19th century. In a society which in spite of all educational efforts still consisted predominantly of illiterates, the middle classes provided the majority of readers. Numerous publishers tried to the best of their ability to satisfy the desires of their growing and eager reading public. Technically, this was made possible by the introduction, in 1820, of machines for paper production and, in

1823, of high-speed printing presses, which dramatically increased printing capacity.

Light fiction dominated as reading matter at this time, meeting the wide-spread need for distraction from the problems of everyday life.[13] Books on parlour games counted among this trivial literature, gaining more and more importance up until the middle of the century in all countries keen on games – above all in Germany, Austria, Britain, the Netherlands and France. Often they restricted themselves to mere instructions for learners and a listing of rules for reference purposes. More important from a cultural history point of view are books of games touching on more or less all areas of the parlour game, thus giving a clear picture of an entire epoch's games culture.

One of the more sophisticated works of this genre bears the title "Archiv der Spiele oder fortlaufende Beschreibung aller Spiele der Vorwelt und Mitwelt" (Games Archive or Ongoing Description of all Games Past and Present). This three-volume work with its encyclopaedic approach was published by an unknown author in Berlin between 1819 and 1821. It was intended to become a treasure trove for historical researchers, inventors of games and writers – a compendium offering everything on games. Each volume is divided into four categories: games involving physical movement, reason, chance and mixed games. The author only managed to collect 56 games in total, though. Others were supposed to be published in the series, as the author learned of them one by one, concluding with an index for reference purposes. Had the "Games Archive" been added to on an ongoing basis, an impressive collection might have resulted. As it is, it remained merely a rarity on the antiquarian book market.

In Vienna, elegant capital of the Habsburg Empire, games and books on games fell on particularly fertile soil. Here, above all, four publishers had dedicated themselves to games literature: Johann Georg Edler von Mößle (later J.G. Ritter von Mösle's Witwe und Braumüller), Franz Tendler, Anton Mausberger and the Verlag der Carl 'Haas'schen Buchhandlung (Carl Haas Bookshop Publishers). From one of these publishing houses comes a book on games which appeared under the poetical name of "Verstand und Glück im Bunde" (An Alliance of Reason and Chance) in 1830.[14] Even the title formulated that fundamental difference between games of reason and of chance which distinguished games literature of the time. On one side there were always board games, such as chess or draughts, and the more demanding card games, and on the other, dice and simpler card entertainments. The games book in question is no exception, either: It presents a little cosmos of those board and card games which Viennese society had devoted itself to in the idyllic Biedermeier epoch. Even if chess was recognised as being the most sophisticated and most difficult intellectual exercise, there was no way it took first place either in the view of the public or in that of the unknown publisher. Whist, Piquet and especially Ecarté, were named as those parlour card games which were particularly popular in the drawing rooms of the city.

Almost all Viennese games books emphasise Whist as being a sophisticated game of English origin which was played right across the civilised world. The fact that players and spectators had to keep so very quiet in order to direct their attention fully to the game must also have been appreciated. For a young man it was considered good form to be able to shine in society as a skilled Whist player. The Spanish l'Hombre and French Piquet were held in similar high regard. Another Viennese "Spielbuch", of 1829, maintains that there is nothing to beat these three card games for training the mind: "Each of these is unique and shows in its various nuances an enormous depth, an incalculable number of combinations and material worthy of the most careful reflection."[15]

Most games books of the time have one thing in common: the disapproval of games of pure chance, including dice games, lotto, and games at try-your-luck stalls. Of course, there were warnings also in the Viennese games books not to get involved in cards or billiard entertainment in public houses, because "there are card-sharps everywhere who cheat using marked cards, weighted balls and other tricks."[16] There were even organised gangs of gamblers, known in France under the name of "Grecs", who made a habit of haunting the public gambling houses of the capitals and spa towns. "It is not the game itself, however, that is reprehensible", the editor of the Berlin "Spielalmanach" sums up, "but the way of playing, which determines, whether the good or the bad influence, the beneficial or the damaging consequences will predominate."[17] How right he was …

La Cligne-musette.   Blinde Kuh spielen.   Blindman's-buff.

"Blind man's buff"
From a broadsheet
Coloured lithography,
around 1830/40
Verlag G. P. Buchner,
Nuremberg

The Players' Century

A typical trait of middle-class life between 1815 and 1848 was a companionable home life, embracing science, literature, theatre, or music. The decades between the Congress of Vienna of 1815 and the failure of the bourgeois revolution of 1848 was an epoch which on the one hand was shaped by the growing sense of importance of the bourgeois and by an idyllic lifestyle, and on the other hand by the struggle for liberal and democratic rights. As the result of restrictive censorship of every type of liberation and reform movement, the citizens retreated into domestic life with family and friends, where they hoped to find true happiness.

The desperate political situation of the time is reflected even in casual cultural evidence such as games books. Ben Israel, whose ancestors had emigrated from Galicia to America, but then returned to Europe, wrote in his 1834 autobiography: "Politics is frowned upon today, literature is becoming stultified, the scholars are asleep …

and the sands of time have buried the great minds of the German nation — they look down from their ethereal heights in indignation … Playing is all that is left in social circles, and that is why I have devoted myself to it; it always forms the best entertainment."[18] Ben Israel's father had lost all his worldly goods as a result of reckless gambling, which is why his son in his recollections outlines how to wander through life while playing in an honest way. If he is to be believed, he succeeded in this endeavour on his expedition through the gambling houses of Europe, for he became a wealthy man and could take his family to England and then to America, which ultimately became his second home.

In the 19th century in European capitals such as London, Paris and Vienna, a refined way of life developed in much-frequented social meeting places: at the theatre, the opera or in the coffee house. The coffee house was ideally suited to fulfilling the citizens' need for social intercourse,

though for a long time it was restricted to men only.[19] Artists and writers, ordinary citizens and passionate gamblers gained inspiration from an invigorating drink or from newspapers, relaxed with a game of chess or billiards or risked a round of cards.

"Board and Similar Games" Illustrations by Julius Vogel from: Marie Leske, Illustrated Book of Games for Girls, Leipzig 1865

The link between coffee house and chess has become almost legendary. By the 18th century Old Slaughter's Coffee House in London and the Café de la Régence in Paris were the best-known meeting places for the most famous chess masters of the time.[20] Frenchman Philidor, one of the best chess players of the second half of the 18th century, was at home in both those coffee houses and celebrated his greatest successes in Paris and London. The American Paul Morphy also celebrated overwhelming victories, beating his opponents in simultaneous blind matches at the Café de la Régence in 1858.[21] Chess also became extremely popular in Viennese coffee houses during the 19th century.

Serious players, however, withdrew more and more to the numerous chess clubs which started up in the first half of the century. With the increasing need for exchange of information, the first chess periodicals such as "Le Palamède" in Paris in 1836, "The Chess Players' Chronicle" in London in 1841 or the "Schachzeitung" in Berlin

in 1846 were published. With the increasing number of competitions between leading chess masters, the competitive side of the "Game of Kings" became more important, leading to the first international chess tournament in London in 1851. The modern tournament chess calendar began with this competition, which was largely organised by Howard Staunton.

In addition to card games, it was billiards which particularly attracted the coffee house guests. It was held in similar high esteem to chess and was regarded as ideal physical and mental relaxation, even allowing much gracefulness in some of its poses.[22] Billiards had been highly successful since as early as the 17th and 18th centuries, above all in France, not only at court, in aristocratic and upper-class circles, but also increasingly among ordinary people. It is known that Wolfgang Amadeus Mozart was a passionate billiards and skittles player.[23]

After 1800, billiards became enormously popular in the coffee houses. Usually there were separate billiard rooms, which towards the end of the century were extended to billiard halls. In games literature billiards is almost always dealt with at length in all its variations, so that it is possible to speak of an uninterrupted tradition right up to the present day. The 19th century was, however, of decisive importance for billiards, because several technical improvements were made in its manufacture.[24] The ivory balls were increased in diameter, the side cushions on the tables were no longer made of cloth but of rubber, and the holes were omitted from the tabletop. This elegant ball game developed into a sport and spread right across the world as a consequence of the perfection of its equipment.

It is thus certainly no coincidence that the "Wiener Theaterzeitung" (Vienna Theatre Gazette), taking as its motto "The Players' Century", offered its loyal subscribers a copperplate etching showing a billiard player, as a New Year's present in 1838. In pre-Cubist manner "The Players' Century" is embodied in a symbolic figure whose anatomy consists of balls, skittles, dice, draughts and chess pieces, playing cards and games boards.[25] Games buffs of the time must certainly have been just as enchanted by the aesthetic charm of the classic game of billiards as today's observer who witnesses a game between really good players.

The Wiener Theaterzeitung, a fashion trend-setter of its time, put its finger on the immense popularity of games in general and billiards in particular with this collage, in a brilliant artistic interpretation by artist Theodor H. Alconiere. There were hardly any more "compulsive gamblers" than the subjects of the Vormärz (run up to the March revolution of 1848). The manner in which the time was passed in all social circles with flippant games and games of forfeits expresses a certain simplicity of mind which is hard to understand today.[26] Blind man's buff and sack races counted among the preferred entertainments of adults and children alike.[27]

A high status was attached in particular to blind man's buff, as can be seen in its frequently being chosen as a topic in paintings and prints from the 18th century on. All over Europe young people amused themselves playing, chasing each other.[28] There is no shortage of descriptions of the amusing and harmless game in sophisticated circles and as children's entertainment. Even Napoleon played blind man's buff after Saturday dinner with the Bavarian Crown Prince Ludwig, who was his guest in the Tuileries.[29] Among the rural population, the adults also played "childish games". There the farm girls and farm hands who were kept in patriarchal dependence, played blind man's buff and other similar games on summer evenings.[30]

Other games with blindfolds were also popular, involving a greater number of participants who could get up to all sorts of mischievous fun.[31]

"Ball games"
Illustrations by Julius Vogel
from: Marie Leske,
Illustrated Book of Games
for Girls, Leipzig 1865

"Brüderchen, wer klopft?" (Who is it, little brother?) is a game which is frequently mentioned: Two people sitting back to back on chairs are blindfolded and the remaining company dances around them in a circle. Those seated have to guess who is knocking them on the head.

Games of forfeits were particularly popular, when gentlemen and ladies played together. In "ABC der Liebe" (ABC of Love) one of the company begins with the question: "How is your love life?". The others must then answer, in sequence, with a word beginning with the letter A. Whoever fails to think of one must pay a forfeit, and then the game is continued with the next letter. Redeeming of forfeits presented the players with a welcome opportunity of tender advances to other players, as for example in "giving a convent kiss"[32], where the person paying the forfeit has to choose a person of the opposite sex, embrace them and kiss them through the spars of a chair back. If, however, the chosen forfeit was "picking parsley", a lady redeeming her forfeit had to go to all the gentlemen and distribute kisses, which presumably was equally popular the other way round.

Such innocent games belonged to the lifestyle of a middle class which had achieved affluence and

cards.[33] Sociable games with riddles, rhymes, or forfeits, where the circle of guests can stay together, are recommended. In no way, however, may someone be "ordered to play a parlour game", for there are, the book claims, a lot of people, especially gentlemen, who "hate certain games and feel uncomfortable playing them".

Work and Play

In the mid 19th century educationalists – above all the father of the kindergarten, Friedrich Fröbel – began to discover the importance of children's education at pre-school age. Early childhood was given a completely new status as a formative period in life. Fröbel was not only the first to declare toys to be the most important educational aid, but also started to develop them himself from an educational point of view. He regarded the ball as a child's first toy, and he derived his construction sets from simple cubes. The activity games he developed at that time such as paper-weaving, cutting out, pasting and sewing formed the basis for a wealth of kits involving manual skill which could still be bought after the First World War.

Educational games literature from the second half of the 19th century based itself on Friedrich Fröbel's theoretical approach, considerably extending Fröbel's group of activity games. Hugo Elm's "Spiel und Arbeit" (Work and Play), published in 1874, was one such book.[34] In the preface, Hugo Elm, a teacher at the School for Young Ladies in Gera, deals with the phenomenon that most shop-bought toys for children soon become boring, as soon as the novelty wears off, and that they are therefore also quickly broken. After the initial pleasure "the wooden menageries, the tin soldiers, the sheep farm, the hunts or whatever all these things are called that Nuremberg and Sonneberg flood us with every year, lie in well-packed disorder in their cases and boxes" and wait in vain to be unpacked again.

social standing, a lifestyle in which good manners towards the ladies, external appearances and table manners were top priorities. In the rooms which were the centre of everyday life, cherished objects were put on show in display cabinets and on étagères. One went for a stroll, met friends in the coffee house and enjoyed a country outing in cheerful company or a party with friends, setting riddles, playing charades, and performing conjuring tricks, or playing the piano. Games on long winter evenings and on outings in summer formed a natural part of everyday life and were also played on festive occasions. What is so special about this distinctive games culture is above all the fact that it was adopted by a broad section of the adult world.

Two generations later, we no longer find this casual, almost child-like attitude to games. One collection of parlour games proclaims that it is not considered good manners for gentlemen after dinner to play only chess, dominoes or

Scene from a Billiard Hall
Coloured lithography
France, around 1870

Hugo Elm, on the other hand, demands that play material can be (re)shaped and formed, such as for example building bricks and the doll, which can be changed again and again.

Following the example of his educational master, Hugo Elm is more interested in play material of paper, card or wood, which come along in an "unassuming guise" and appear, at a first cursory glance, to offer little appeal because they are not colourful enough. But, he maintains, it is just these unprepossessing things, stimulating the child's own creativity, that children enjoy playing with most after a very short time. For a first, great "evening of work", therefore, all that is needed is a pair of scissors and coloured paper, penknife and glue, in order to make little boxes and other lovely things. In addition to paper work and the use of needle and thread, the basic range of Fröbel activity games included building with specially developed wooden bricks and placing of little wooden sticks to make letters, figures or shapes.

Fröbel's principle, that the purpose of a child's doing something lies in the activity itself, is quite in keeping with the 19th century middle class educational ideal of considering work ethic and self discipline to be life's most important virtues. Domestic activity games in this sense are rather work exercises which admittedly show a certain repetitive pattern. With their help children learn dexterity, patience, perseverance, powers of imagination and ability to express themselves. They increase their knowledge of materials and their feeling for form, and heighten their self-confidence.[35] Whole generations of children have come into contact with these games in kindergartens, schools or in the family. And manufacturers of games such as J. W. Spear & Söhne have gladly followed Fröbel and have for decades brought out painting and drawing games, sewing or embroidery kits, picture or basket weaving sets, construction kits and jigsaw puzzles.

Home Play

According to Fröbel's discoveries, toys should above all be simple, in order to stimulate imagination and creative powers and furthermore, to combine work with play, and entertainment with instruction: "A little girl who has sat in school in the morning with her books and completed other work should be allowed to play with her doll or in the open air in the afternoon." It is with these words that Marie Leske begins her "Illustrated Book of Games for Girls"[36], one of the most widely distributed games books for young girls in the second half of the 19th century. Eighteen editions were published, from the first publication of the work in 1865, until 1900.

Leske firstly recommends to her readers, very sheltered middle-class girls, indoor games and entertainments, among them needlework, cooking and playing with dolls, followed by various Fröbel activities involving paper and card, drawing, painting or working with thread. In the area of classic board games, girls were to busy themselves with dominoes, draughts, backgammon and lotto. Lotto and lotteries had been educational games for children since the late 18th century. The adult equivalent had led to a veritable lotto mania in broad sectors of the population in the

18th century and left many in poverty. All these two versions had in common, however, was the basic, harmless principle that numbers were drawn and called out, which in the case of children encouraged concentration, together with the anticipation of a small win, usually consisting of nuts or apples. Later counting lotto and lotto with many different topics including grammar, world history, geography or natural history were added.

Marie Leske grants the girls a lot of freedom of movement for ball and gymnastics games. Amazingly, even "Preußisches Exerzieren" (Prussian Drill) or a "Chasseur" (Rifleman) war game in the open air were mentioned. One assumes, however, that the young ladies preferred to play other things than war. The female desire for entertainment probably found the numerous conversation games, oracles, proverbs, puzzles, charades and riddles from the girls' games book more congenial. Riddles as literary art form started flourishing in the 18th century and were circulated in popular form above all in the family journals of the 19th century. In spite of all the banalities of the riddle genre, its best examples show glimpses of philosophical insight: "The contented man desires me, the poor man possesses me, the rich man needs me, the miser gives me away, the spendthrift saves me and all take me with them to the grave". The answer is: "Nothing."[37]

The counterpart to the girls' games book had already come onto the market a year previously as the "Illustrated Book of Games for Boys". With 27 editions up to 1922, its author, Hermann Wagner, was even more successful than Marie Leske. As he saw it, the main field of action for a boy lay in outdoor games and entertainments. He was to strengthen his body and overcome any fear by running, hopping, jumping, doing gymnastics, swimming, throwing or archery: "We must be careful to allow [the boy] free time for play and for use as he thinks fit, every day. If he learns a few words of vocabulary less as a result, let him stay at school for an extra year; later on he will be all

*Cover illustration
for Marie Leske,
Illustrated Book of Games
for Girls, Leipzig 1900*

the more healthy, strong, practical and skilful for it."[38] According to the ideals of the time, a boy should be "toughened up", and learn early on to master life.

Pleasure and the achievement of technical-manual skills were also to be part of a son's education. That is why entertaining Fröbel-type activities were also recommended for boys: games with wooden sticks, weaving, paper folding, cutting out figures, painting, working with card, shaping, modelling and others. On long winter evenings they could practice chess or have fun with lotto, dominoes, nine men's morris, backgammon and siege. A boy was sure of a grateful audience when he could master practical entertainments or conjuring tricks. As well as amusement, conjuring also provided new manual and social dexterity. "Furthermore, it is a necessary condition for conjurers large and small that they draw the attention of the audience to themselves through agreeable manners and that they entertain pleasantly."[39]

The proportion of entertaining elements in the games books of the 1860s and 1870s kept on increasing. This coincided with an ever-growing supply of magazines and annuals for children. Among these were the two very enduring and extremely successful periodicals "Töchter-Album" (Young Ladies' Album, 1855 - 1933) and "Herzblättchens Zeitvertreib" (Little Darlings' Pastimes, 1856–1936). Illustrations and picture quality also became more luxurious. Lavish chromolithography and decorated covers characterised children's book layout from the 1870s on and made many a publication for small readers a prestigious Christmas present.

If the Biedermeier period was marked by the self-satisfaction and the idyllic lifestyle of a modest middle class, the late 19th century's leading stratum of society developed an extraordinary need for show. The billions of marks which flooded into the country with the victorious war of 1870/71 led to the founding of large industrial concerns and gave the "Gründerzeit" (time of founding – epoch of rapid industrial expansion, from 1871 on) its name.[40]

As a result of the far-reaching social change which took place in the course of industrialisation, there were also changes to family life and to the bringing up of children. In middle-class families the mother's lack of independence constituted a counterpoint to the father's unchallenged authority. With the growing importance of the army and the construction of the imperial fleet, the ideal of the boy in a sailor suit was born, while the girl, as later mistress of the house, had to learn all the duties entailed by this task. In spite of all criticism of this conservative family ideal, the middle-class home was regarded as the scene of loving relationships between man and wife, and between parents and children, which led to the ideal of the family as a place of privacy and intimacy.

This change in the family ideal found its parallel in games literature. Thus from the 1880s onward, it was noticeable that many sets of instructions aimed at encouraging joint play by adults and children, by parents and brothers and sisters.[41] The reason for this is probably that family relationships were less work-based and rather were idealised under the aspect of leisure and social intercourse. The "Illustrirte Allgemeine Familien-Spielbuch"[42] (Illustrated General Family Games Book) by Dr. Jan Daniel Georgens and Jeanne-Marie von Gayette-Georgens fits into this pattern. Along with the games collections of Elm, Leske and Wagner, the Family Games Book was also published by Otto Spamer in Leipzig, a company which dedicated itself to the publication of games literature and in 1882 published this complete collection of all games and game types of any consequence. The authors had carried out years of research and collected old treasures in the area of games and analysed many foreign books and books of rules from Britain, France and Scandinavia.

"Quoits"
Illustration from: Jan Daniel
Georgens and Jeanne Marie
von Gayette-Georgens,
Illustrated Book of Family
Games, Leipzig/Berlin 1882

The user – whether child or adult – was presented, in over 600 pages, with a great variety of games from different social circles and nations. The "Familien-Spielbuch" aimed at furthering and stimulating interest in games, for all work and no play makes Jack a dull boy: "The proper view of life demands work and relaxation. Constant work weighs down the soul, and constant relaxation is tedious." [43] This philosophical insight with regard to games had already been stated almost 90 years earlier by Gutsmuths, and then had been pressed into a "didactic corset" by Fröbel and towards the end of the 19th century was again recognised as important for keeping the family together.

A contemporary, who had published a relatively modest book on games in the family circle,[44] writes on the value of the family game: "With … work there is always … anxiety regarding success and all too often also the depressing feeling that, in spite of all efforts, nothing perfect can be achieved. With games this cannot happen. To be busy and nevertheless not working, obeying a rule and nevertheless being free, enjoying oneself and nevertheless not being idle, doing something eagerly and nevertheless not having to worry about how it will turn out, enjoying iridescent soap-bubbles and nevertheless seeing them burst without any feeling of grief … that is the essence of games."

gez. v. E. Limmer.   H. B. B. XXXI.

Der Zauberer Honolulu.

"The Magician Honolulu"
Colour lithography
by Emil Linner (1854-1931)
from: Thekla von Gumpert,
Little Darling's Pastime,
31st vol., Glogau, no year
[1886]

Marion Faber

Nuremberg – City of Games

Nuremberg has more than 600 years of tradition as a city of toys. Its name is usually linked, above all, with doll's houses and kitchens, pewter figures and tin toys of all kinds. Far less well known is the fact that the manufacture of, and trade in, games can look back on a long and distinguished history.

The first to produce toys locally were the "Dockenmacher" who made doll figures of clay, and later of wood, alabaster or papier-mâché. The dice-maker's trade is also documented around this time, their "bone dice" and "revolving dice" still being mentioned and praised even around 1800.[1] Nuremberg wood turners also produced many games of skittles, chess figures and games boards from bone and wood. From the 16th to the 18th century, Augsburg and Nuremberg were centres for the turning of elaborate draughts pieces.[2] Even more important for the region's economic history, however, were the makers of card games, who as early as the beginning of the 15th century made the city a leading centre for the production of playing cards. Counters made of brass and copper were usually used for games with dice or cards, and Nuremberg was a well-known place of production for these, too. Important pewterer's workshops, producing painted tin figures for parlour games, were accommodated within its walls and in the neighbouring town of Fürth.

The existence of such diverse trades, which could produce good quality games components from various materials, was fundamental to the birth of games production. A second important prerequisite, which more or less predestined Nuremberg to be a city of games, is its long tradition in paper manufacture, graphic art and printing. Germany's first paper mill was founded here in 1390, forming the starting-point for centuries of production and trade activities. Nuremberg paper mills manufactured everything, from fine writing paper to thick paper in different colours and weights, and sold it at external trade fairs and markets. From Albrecht Dürer's time at the latest, Nuremberg became a stronghold of the woodcut and of the copperplate etching. Following the introduction of letterpress printing to Nuremberg by Johann Sensenschmidt from Eger in 1469 and the roughly simultaneous adoption of this technique by Anton Koberger, probably the most important printer of these early days, the city developed into one of Germany's most important printing locations and has remained so – with interruptions – to the present day. Nuremberg distinguished itself particularly in the area of children's books. Special catechisms, Bibles, ABC books and books of etiquette for children were appearing by the 16th century.[3] Nuremberg then became famous as a result of the printing of the epoch-making "Orbis sensualium pictus" by Johann Amos Comenius, published by Endter in 1658. In this richly illustrated and educationally innovative textbook, learning through the use of pictorial material was propagated for the first time.[4] It thus became the forerunner of the picture book.

The political and economic decline of the Free City of the Holy Roman Empire in the course of the 18th century also affected toy manufacture and printing, but thanks to the efforts of the active merchants, Nuremberg was able to reverse this general development and become the main centre for the distribution and sale of toys.

Nuremberg wholesalers sold, above all, products made in the Thuringian, Saxon and south German centres for wood crafts under the heading "Made in Nuremberg" or "Nürnberger Tand" (Nuremberg knick-knacks) all over the world.[5]

Trade in haberdashery, fancy goods and manufactured goods, to which toys belonged, was in full bloom in 1800, as can be gathered from "Geschichte des Nürnbergischen Handels" (History of Nuremberg's Trade) by Father Johann Ferdinand Roth: "Children's toys of all kinds even go to England, a large proportion remaining there, and a lot of them then being put on the market in America, Africa and Asia by the English. Poland, Russia, European Turkey, even Central Asia and the remote Tartar nations spend large sums of money on all sorts of large and small Nuremberg factory goods every year."[6] Central and South America were mainly supplied via Spain and Portugal. In Germany itself there was hardly a largish city which did not at least have one shop stocking Nuremberg goods. This was the case in Berlin, too: Here businessman Peter Friedrich Catel had kept a "Nuremberg Shop" since 1780 and from 1785 even published a printed toys "directory" which he had on offer in his shop and also sent to clients by post.[7] Nuremberg professor of education, Johann Sigmund Stoy, also referred to Catel when in 1791 he published a list of educational aids and toys which could be ordered from him.[8]

Bestelmeier's Catalogue

Any toy collector who would like to trace a toy or game back to its origins, does not, however, turn to "Catel", but to "Bestelmeier", for this catalogue documents a much larger, representative cross-section of toy production around 1800. Georg Hieronimus Bestelmeier was a Nuremberg wholesaler who from 1793 on brought out regular annual editions, initially in booklet form, of one of the most comprehensive toy catalogues

Portrait of Georg Hieronimus Bestelmeier (1764-1829) Etching, around 1800

available.[9] His "Pädagogisches Magazin"[10] (Educational Gazette), as the work was initially called, contains, on finely printed copperplates, hundreds of detailed illustrations of toys and teaching aids, their descriptions and also their pictures corresponding directly with those of Catel.[11]

The first five editions of Bestelmeier's "Gazette" from 1793 to 1797 and his systematic "directory"[12], of 1798, cover 116 "entertaining and educational games for children and adults". Among them are riddles, forfeits, question and answer games, geography, travel, fortress and conquest games, ABC and mathematical games; further metamorphosis games and various puzzles. Of course, long-standing and well-known games are also to be found: chess, draughts, cards, lotto, lotteries, try-your-luck stalls, skittles, billiards, badminton or compendiums of games. Some very topical games based on political events also appeared, only to disappear again after a few years. Bestelmeier quotes, for example, a "revolution game or new mathematical game of triangles with an accurate depiction of the Bastille in Paris" or a "Game of monarchs, with case". It is not known whether those games with eternal themes, such as "Friendly Alliance", "Game of Hope" or "Game of Lovers" were just passing crazes. "Happiness and Friendship, a new and very entertaining parlour game, with an illustrated game board and several friendship songs" may have contributed to many an amusing evening of song, only later to sink into oblivion.

The strong interest of the time in the arts is reflected in some parlour games with musical and literary themes. Mozart can be found in the drawing room with "Die Zauberflöte" (The Magic Flute) and "Die Entführung aus dem Serail" (Seraglio). The "Freischütz, a completely new parlour game, consisting of 1 game board, 12 cards, 7 balls and 2 dice" is probably based on the folk legend by J.A. Apel and F. Laun, which Weber used for his opera, premiered in 1821.[13]

As Bestelmeier announced in the first issue of his "Gazette" in 1793, he wanted to establish in Nuremberg an entire warehouse of toys made in the city, in order to give non-local people a "general overview of all the toys produced here and already famous abroad". He also had several booklets printed in French, adding a lot of new articles to each new edition. He emphasised that all of these products had been made by Nuremberg artists and craftsmen "with the greatest of accuracy and beauty", although he also sold goods by non-local producers. The wooden toys manufactured in Nuremberg and surroundings by emigrants from the Berchtesgaden and Salzburg regions seem to have played a role here.[14] Since even at that time buyers preferred good and cheap products, Bestelmeier increased his

range to include small and inexpensive articles: "In this supplement some very charming items are to be found; although they cost very little, they are just as finely worked as the more expensive ones and will provide our young people with pleasant entertainment."[15]

Bestelmeier must have been very successful with his shop and mail order company in Königstraße right from the beginning, for the range of toys and fancy goods presents itself as enormously wide and varied, even by today's standards. And he was able to satisfy both the demanding and the simple tastes of his customers. His catalogues, which from 1803 appeared under the new title "Magazin von verschiedenen Kunst- und andern nüzlichen Sachen" (Catalogue of various artistic and other useful objects)[16], now became increasingly more extensive and in the 1808 edition had over 1,200 illustrations.[17] As well as parlour games for children and adults, the catalogues offer all kinds of wooden toys and numerous items of scientific and technical apparatus and teaching materials. The many devices and materials for conjuring tricks or other amusing pastimes reflect the delight in mechanical skills and the fascination of all things magical. Bestelmeier's 1803 "Magazin" contains the first written evidence of "sleight of hand equipment", as conjuring sets were then called.[18]

As a businessman, Bestelmeier proved very forward-looking in that he involved educationalists and teachers in the creation of new games and toys. Right at the beginning of his business venture, he invited them to send in drawings of inventions and suggestions, which he would then have produced. Educational games as a preparation for and complement to school played an important role for him. There were letter and counting lottos, vocabulary games for learning foreign languages, and games introducing players to geography, history and mathematics. Sets of building bricks (one of them for assembling a tower of Nuremberg's city wall) and the now

Tab: VI

Conjuring apparatus and physics teaching material Copperplate from: Georg Hieronimus Bestelmeier, Magazine of Various Artistic and Other Useful Objects, Nuremberg 1803

proverbial puzzle "Nürnberger Tand" or "Zank-eisen" (requiring the player to manoeuvre several rings on a buckle-shaped fork inside one another) aimed in the same educational direction. This wire puzzle, which originated in China, had been known for centuries and was one of the Nuremberg toy dealers' most popular articles, which probably explains its name.[19]

Apart from toys, which took up roughly half of his catalogue, Georg Hieronimus Bestelmeier also dealt in domestic consumer items, jewellery and decorative articles. From 1802 on, he also ran a

furniture store, which the city's carpenters were strongly opposed to, because some of the furniture came from non-local craftsmen. This dispute which flared up regularly for decades, not only led to verbal attacks and court cases, but also to physical violence, which even became a subject of contemporary caricatures.[20] Bestelmeier published his last known catalogue of toys and fancy goods in 1823.[21] Three years later his son, Johann Martin Christoph Bestelmeier joined the manufacture, fancy goods and wholesale business with affiliated wallpaper manufacturing and managed it after his father's death in 1829 until 1854.[22]

27

Games on Illustrated Broadsheets

It emerges from Bestelmeier's catalogues that Nuremberg boasted a considerable games production at the beginning of the 19th century. Unfortunately it is not known, though who supplied Bestelmeier with games. It is certain, however, that, in a city with such a long tradition of printing, there were enough suppliers for games' production, above all those publishers who printed games on broadsheets, such as Johann Trautner, Friedrich Campe, Johann Andreas Endter, Georg Paul Buchner, Johann Raab and Christian Martin Trummer. Bestelmeier and his brother were closely linked by marriage and godparenthood, with publishing families Endter, Lotzbeck und Felsecker.[23]

The mostly coloured broadsheets had their heyday in the first half of the 19th century. The broadsheet publishers were very often also involved in the book and art trade, which enabled them to handle their own sales. The most important among them was bookseller Friedrich Campe who, after taking over Trautner's workshop, developed production of broadsheets for children into a rapidly expanding, independent branch of publishing. Like his uncle, children's author Joachim Heinrich Campe, he was an admirer of Rousseau's and an advocate of the Enlightenment and striving towards new principles in the education of young people.[24]

If at first copperplate engraving and etchings predominated in broadsheet printing, lithography gradually won through in the first decades of the 19th century. The advantages of lithography lay above all in the uncomplicated method of transfer of a drawing onto stone and in the almost unlimited number of prints possible, since, in contrast to copper plate, stone hardly ever wore out. Although the invention and spread of lithography began in Bavaria in 1797 with Alois Senefelder, Nuremberg publishers were slow to adopt it. Friedrich Campe did open a lithographic printing

"New travelling game by railway from Berlin
to Paris in passing Cologne and Brussels"
Illustration for box lid
Coloured lithography,
around 1840
Verlag C. Abel-Klinger, Nuremberg

works in 1807, but made only occasional use of it in his publishing concern.[25] Because of his personal aversion to lithographs, which he disparagingly described as "stone-print daubings", Friedrich Campe continued to give preference to copperplate and etchings with all his broadsheet production.[26]

Four further lithographic printer's were founded by 1815, among them the workshop of artist Georg Paul Buchner.[27] In comparison, there were in Nuremberg at this time 63 copperplate printer's, who fought against lithography tooth and nail. To protect existing businesses from economic competition, the Bavarian government issued a royal decree in 1815, declaring lithography, previously regarded as a free art, to be a trade requiring a licence. This meant that anybody who wanted to become self-employed in this field, could only set up a new concern with proof of training in lithographic drawing and with the consent of established lithographers, copperplate engravers and printers.[28] These regulations proved a strong hindrance to the further spreading of the new printing technique.

In spite of the difficulties in the early stages of lithography in Nuremberg, in the following period more and more art dealers and booksellers succeeded in surmounting the legal obstacles. In 1838 Georg Nicholas Renner, who along with Campe was the most important broadsheet publisher in Nuremberg, applied to the municipal authorities, together with his printer, Rebhahn, for permission to set up a lithographic printer's. Initially Nuremberg's lithographers rejected the application unanimously. Only after the mediation of Karl Alexander von Heideloff, teacher at the municipal Polytechnic, was Renner issued a limited licence, in 1839.[29] His illustrated broadsheets and cut-out sheets show the usual subjects of the time: soldiers and battles, paper theatre decorations, landscapes, natural history and religious pictures. In their decorative layout and price, they met the requirements and tastes

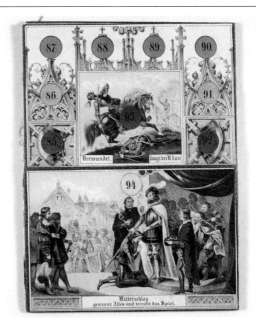

"Latest Game of Knights, Tournaments and Saracens for Young and Old"
Game board with case
Coloured lithography, around 1850 (detail)
Verlag J. L. Lotzbeck, Nuremberg

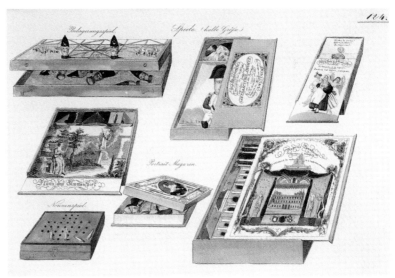

Sample sheet for games:
"Game of Siege", "Characters or Change the Head",
"New Question and Answer Game",
"Flora, the Flower Game", "Game of Nuns", "Portrait Compendium",
"Modern Building Art for Pleasant Entertainment"
Coloured copperplate and etching
Nuremberg, around 1830/40

sr. and Georg Wolfgang Faber jr., both not only lithographers but also mechanical wizards, brought out charming, movable paper toys and dressing-up dolls. G. P. J. Bieling Publishers, resident in Nuremberg since 1630, published children's games in the first half of the 19th century.[30] Decoratively laid out, their game boards and picture cards, with their gilt-edged, illustrated packaging and titles in several languages, give a colourful and varied impression showing the cultivated tastes of the consumer in the convivial and game-loving Biedermeier period. Coloured pictures at that time were, incidentally, still produced by colouring in black and white drawings by hand or with the aid of stencils. Although these games were still to a great extent produced manually, their serial character already heralded the epoch of industrial production of parlour games.

By around 1850 lithography had become established everywhere as a popular method of printing parlour games, children's book illustrations and other popular graphics. Its technical and economic advantages, and improvements to the presses themselves enabled publishers and printers to produce goods more cheaply and efficiently. A lithographic industry could only develop once F.G. Sigi had invented the "high-speed lithographic press" in 1852. Lithography was used wherever changing purchaser tastes had to be quickly reacted to. To this end manufacturers and wholesalers had toy catalogues printed, offering their range to their customers.[31] Although in the Nuremberg sample books from publishers Fr. Scharrer or A. Kolb from around 1840/50, parlour games play only a minor role, this is made up for by the especially colourful presentation. Puzzles, metamorphosis games and games of siege, conjuring tricks and outdoor games are illustrated in this catalogue.

The sale of games depends on the visual appeal the packaging has for the purchaser. And the predominantly small games boxes and boards of the

of many customers. The predominant themes of games on illustrated broadsheets were dressing-up dolls, dice games, picture lotto and depictions of children playing. Following Renner's death in 1854, his brother Johann Christian continued to run the company until 1863. The illustrated broadsheet printing business in Nuremberg died with the Renner brothers: the demand for pictures and entertainment could quite simply be satisfied better and more quickly in the long term by new media such as illustrated young people's and family magazines.

The Beginnings of the Games Industry

In addition to innumerable games variations on inexpensive, simply illustrated broadsheets, art dealers offered many games made of board and paper, in appealing designs. These mostly small-format games from the first half of the 19th century were composed with imaginative skill and great care and often published without details of artists or publishers. Only very few publishers marked their names on games and paper toys, among them Nuremberg companies C. Abel-Klinger and J. L. Lotzbeck. Georg Leonhard Faber

Biedermeier era, with their delicate graphic design and their discreet colouring, could not in the long term, offer this mass appeal. That is why in the second half of the 19th century production of games by craftsmen gave way to industrial manufacture. The change from manual colouring to colour printing is an example of this. The founding of numerous new lithographic printer's strongly reflects this development: While the number of such companies in Nuremberg stood at fifteen in 1851, it rose to approximately fifty in the following thirty years.[32]

Almost all consumer goods began to be mass-produced with advancing industrialisation. Factories which made this possible through the use of machines and low-cost labour, increasingly replaced small businesses. Games, too, were now manufactured inexpensively in greater quantities and were thus affordable for more and more people. The decisive factors that enabled the lithographic trade to develop into a major industry (apart from the introduction of freedom of trade in 1868), were the growth of the transfer industry and the rise of chromolithography, which made time-consuming colouring by hand unnecessary.

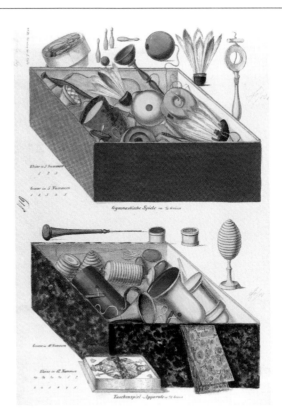

Sample sheet for games "Gymnastics games", "Conjuring apparatus" Coloured lithography, around 1830/40 Verlag A. Kolb, Nuremberg

Chromolithography is a polychromatic picture printing technique for the reproduction of painted pictures which was used from the 1870s on. It led to the setting up of specialised companies and had its heyday in the 1880s and early 1890s.[33] This high-quality reproduction technique for water-colours or oil paintings became the epitome for high standards and very quickly took over the extensive area of luxury paper printing.[34] The process used a key-plate, on which the boundaries of the various coloured parts were carved out using the painted original as a template. Each colour required a separate printing plate. For illustrations in children's books and games usually eight or ten plates were used, for high-quality chromolithographs it could be as many as fourteen to twenty and more.

The range of warm-toned colours used in the initial years of chromolithography resembled the darkly splendid tones of the interiors of the Gründerzeit, of the drawing rooms with their dark fabric wall coverings, heavy velvet curtains and subdued lighting. In this sense the achievement of chromolithographic colour printing ran parallel with the general development in taste.[35] In addition to these elegantly coloured pictures, however, chromolithography, in its less artistic form and random choice of bright colours, also promoted that pretty-pretty taste, which can be seen in children's transfer pictures, album pictures, postcards, children's books and games. Admittedly, though, these colourful creations of the printing industry must have had a strong appeal to children's eyes!

Transfers

Printing of transfers made a considerable contribution to the development of Nuremberg's chromolithographic trade in the last third of the 19th century. Mass production – export-oriented right from the beginning – of the small colourful pictures used as stamps and decorations for consumer goods, for toys or for advertising purposes began with Carl Anton Pocher's company (founded in 1858).[36] Along with Pocher, the following businesses were the most important transfer factories in the city: Carl Mayer, Georg Brunner, Carl Schimpf, as well as Huber, Jordan and Koerner.[37] In the neighbouring town of Fürth, too, Johannes Hesse (founded in 1828) and Gerson Löwensohn (founded in 1844) produced quality transfers. With the introduction of chromolithography, Löwensohn (today Pestalozzi Publishers) had in addition, since the 1870s, built up an internationally significant reputation in the area of picture book publishing.[38]

With the diverse uses and the simplicity of the process it is easy to understand why Nuremberg with its highly developed printing industry became the most important manufacturing location for the trade in Germany up until the First World War. With 243 high-speed printing machines, 282 hand presses, 31 treadle presses and 543 lithographers employed, the lithographic printing establishments reached their peak in 1911.[39] The main export markets for chromolithographic products up until 1914 were Britain and the USA.[40] Transfers also played an increasing role as patterns to be fired onto porcelain and stoneware, and for the printing of picture postcards and picture books[41].

*Lithographic printer's in Nuremberg
(presumably Carl Mayer's Kunstanstalt)
Nuremberg 1889*

Nister and Stroefer, Publishers

One of the largest factories for children's books and transfers for ceramics, Ernst Nister, was founded in 1877. It excelled not only in chromolithography, but also in all other branches of modern graphic printing, such as heliogravure, collotype, autotypy, chromotypy or zinkography.[42] Similar to Jacob Wolf Spear, who started his company in 1879 with oil card goods, Nister was one of those typical entrepreneurs who participated in the economic upswing of the German Reich after the war of 1870/71. Parallels to the economic careers of Nister and Spear can also be seen in the company history of Theodor Stroefer, who set up on his own in Munich in 1877 after having been a partner in a New York art publisher's.[43] Stroefer moved to Nuremberg in 1893 as a result of his flourishing business relations with Nister's art printer's and their shared interest in new colour printing techniques in a photomechanical process. Here he published a wide range of picture books, publications for young people, calendars, postcards, colouring books and a few jigsaws and picture cubes.[44] Both Nister and Spear as well as Stroefer had a British-American "past", with extended stays in England and the USA. All three were self-made men who worked up from small beginnings, turning their businesses into the largest in the Nuremberg paper and card toys industry.

The market-leader in the production of picture books and to some extent also of sawn jigsaw puzzles was Ernst Nister, who, with his publishing house and fine art printing works, was the most strongly committed to Anglo-American exports. He had his own English publishing house, founded in London in 1888, and also a bookbindery equipped to modern standards and an embossing workshop, all of which ensured him a good order book. New York company E. P. Dutton, too, published many children's books which were printed in Nuremberg by Nister. London and New York became his doors to the English-speaking world: His printed products found their way into the furthest corners of the world. In addition to illustrated children's books and jigsaws, his range comprised greetings cards, wall mottoes, calendars, posters and advertising articles.

"Happy Times Puzzle Pictures"
Box containing five puzzles
Chromolithography, around 1890
E. Nister Publishers, London/E. P. Dutton & Co., New York

Der Kinder Freude"
(Children's Joy)
Box containing five puzzles
(Motif: A merry donkey ride)
Chromolithography, around 1894
Verlag Th. Stroefer, Nuremberg

Nister would never have attained such great international prestige with his lithographic art printer's, had he not built up close relations with England and the USA. German goods did not have the best of reputation abroad prior to 1900. International opinion held that things of elegance and good taste must be bought in France, and sturdy things in Britain, but the cheap "trash" in Germany, as one correspondent reported, in 1891, on the occasion of a German trade exhibition in London.[45] This assessment was certainly not completely unfounded. Often enough German manufacturers oriented themselves on the "lowest common denominator" of their clientele: Toys had to be large, colourful and cheap. As a rule, most customers did not bother whether products were solidly finished and aesthetically pleasing. It could hardly concern them either, since high-quality toys were beyond their financial means anyway.[46]

Nister also became famous particularly because of his games and books with flaps, turn and pull mechanisms, which he was always bringing out in new and surprising variations.[47] The books for the English-speaking market were designed in London, but printed in Nuremberg.[48] For his German-speaking children's book range, which followed the English in text and illustrations, Nister could rely on the co-operation of Theodor Stroefer Publisher's in the 1890s. When, in 1904, that was no longer sufficient he started up a new publishing house, in Nuremberg and Leipzig, for which well-known authors and illustrators such as Adolf Holst and Ernst Kutzer created artistically superior children's books.

Games Production around 1900

Games are to a high degree subject to the vagaries of quickly changing public taste. Between the turn of the century and the outbreak of the First World War such manifestations of change were to be found above all in the area of graphic layout and its technical transfer into print as well as in the preference for new types of games. Thus illustration style changed with the emergence of artistically produced children's books and games around 1900. The quaint character and bright colours of chromolithography were increasingly regarded as aesthetically unsatisfying. Instead graphically oriented colour lithography and chromotypy were increasingly used. The attempt to imitate paintings in illustrations was completely abandoned. Instead, the artistic effect of printing with simplified colour effects came to the fore. The bold, simply designed children's book illustrations by Gertrud Caspari and the artistically laid out parlour games of the Joseph Scholz company in Mainz were perfect examples. Colour lithography, chromotypy and other colour printing processes were now used to a greater extent for game boards, but chromolithography still remained in use for a considerable time, gradually being superseded by colour offset printing.

Also, around the turn of the century the playing public got more and more weary of the ubiquitous dice games and was ready for a change. Mechanical games which still contained dice elements, but also brought elements of movement or chance into play were much in demand.[49] Another new trend to be observed around 1909 was the tendency towards outdoor ball games of all kinds.[50] These games of movement were modelled on the example of England, the classical country of sports, where horse-racing, rowing, lawn tennis and ball games of all kinds had enjoyed a long tradition. The German public above all rated games of skill, such as "Diabolo", very highly. Since buyers had been inundated with parlour games, especially board games,[51] new and interesting games had to be brought out all the time. Although old tried and tested board games were still in demand, mysterious titles such as "Salta" (1899), "Lasca" (1911) or oriental games names such as "Allah" (1902) or "Ti Tu China Schach" (1909) greatly promoted product sales.

J. W. Spear & Söhne were extremely successful in taking up these fashion trends in their first years of games production and thus managed to influence the style of their time to some extent, as can be seen from their table football game "Snipkick" and the table tennis sets they offered in various editions, as well as in the board game variation "Cetro" or the game "Sahap", a version of snakes and ladders, which all came onto the market shortly after the turn of the century. Reasonable pricing also contributed to the wide circulation of such new games, of course. At the same time, amazingly, even before the First World War department stores were influencing prices to a great extent by way of price-squeezing and special discounts. The best deal could obviously be made with one-Mark games articles, as the "Guide" announced in one of its reports: "The great majority of department stores turn down new board games if these are not brought out for one Mark."[52] Here, too, Spear were one step ahead. In their earliest known price list, of 1904, they offered 55 games at one Mark. In addition all titles could be had in a cheaper version for 50 Pfennigs. There were only 20 games in better editions, though, priced at two or even three Marks.

Against this background, an amazingly large number of Nuremberg businesses courted favour with the public in the years leading up to the First World War. Thus the city company directory of 1909 lists among the total of around 250 (!) toy companies no less than 56 games manufacturers. Of these, 27 entrepreneurs were producing games made of paper and board, and the rest were producing billiards equipment, dominoes, dice, cards, chess boards, counters, conjuring apparatus or sport and activity games made of wood. Thus around one fifth of all Nuremberg toy companies were involved in the production of parlour and sport games. Nuremberg was undoubtedly the place for games in Germany at this time. In 1910, the "Guide", the central organ of the German toy industry, confirmed: "In parlour games for outdoors and indoors Nurem-

berg's achievement has always been outstanding, from chess and dominoes to dice games of all types."[53] The city's nation-wide importance in games production, however, also had an international dimension, for just as with almost all other Nuremberg toys, most games were manufactured for export: as well as going to Britain and the United States, they were also sent to Spain, Portugal and Central and South America.

Nuremberg's games industry could only be so successful prior to 1914 because it was competitive and continuously brought new products on to the market which appealed to the tastes of customers at home and abroad. Marketing possibilities were thoroughly researched and the goods geared exactly to the price levels demanded. Only the larger concerns had the resources at their disposal to be able to react to the demands of an international public to such an extent, of course. Thus a good dozen Nuremberg companies dominated the games market before the First World War. Apart from Spear these were primarily C. Abel-Klinger with educational aids and parlour games, C. Baudenbacher with conjuring articles and G. Neiff with Fröbel games. Also of great importance were: J. W. Arold for compendiums of games and construction kits, J. Breitenbach for chess figures, J. A. Kithil for picture cubes, Chr. Lauer for toy money, A. Marsching for roulette, G. J. Pabst for activity games, C. Quehl for conjuring articles and games of all kinds, J. G. Schrödel for "Ideal" sport and parlour games and J. Stief for movable wooden construction kits. Publishers E. Nister and Th. Stroefer pointed the way in the area of chromolithographic printing, transfers and games picture books. Further, Fürth companies G. Löwensohn and L. Kleefeld & Co. were in close contact with the Nuremberg games industry. New, important names came along in the 1920s, and some older companies achieved greater importance, above all: Bing Spiele & Verlag, Nürnberger Spielkarten-Verlag, G. Reulein (Noris), F. Schmidt, Schwager & Steinlein, Tietz & Pinthus (ABC-Verlag) and Vauen.

Julius Stief

„Ideal" J. G. Schrödel

Gustav Neiff

Abraham Marsching

Nuremberg Games Manufacturers

Many of the companies mentioned are hardly known even to games historians, since their history has been badly documented and only in the rarest of cases continues up to present times. Some merged with larger companies, while others ceased their activities in the 1930s. Others lost their archives as a result of bomb damage during the Second World War, or the company papers were thrown out thoughtlessly by new owners. As a result, in many cases, trying to gather even the most basic information on the history of these companies is like a piece of real detective work. To finish with, an overview of some of these concerns in the order of their dates of founding attempts to snatch at least some facets of their existence from the mists of oblivion.

One of the most well-known Nuremberg educational aids and games publishers was, since its founding in 1785, **C. Abel-Klinger**.[54] Above all, globes of all kinds and sizes were among their export specialities for a long time. Excellently designed parlour and activity games formed a second main stay. The company attached great importance to artistic product design, even before 1900, around which time children's books, games and toys had to face increasingly strict educational and aesthetic judgement as a result of reformed educational theory. Thus in 1890 C. Abel-Klinger published a "Nuremberg Shadow Theatre" based on designs by artist Theodor von Kramer, Director of the Bavarian Museum of Trade and Industry. Additional scenes and figures were brought out each year.

The quality of Abel-Klinger games exceeded that of the usual merchandise of the 1890s, although many articles were offered for fifty Pfennigs or a Mark. From 1897 the products bore the trademark Heimchen-Spiele (Homely Games), which can certainly be taken as an expression of the trend of the time towards playing games at home within the family circle. Around the turn of the century a department with wooden toys was added which included particularly open-air games, such as badminton, spinning tops, sand toy sets, and also picture cubes, doll's tea sets and easter eggs. In 1904 Abel-Klinger joined up with the old-established Nuremberg company G. J. Pabst (founded in 1835), leading to an extension of the range in the area of activity games and educational aids.

In 1907 Abel-Klinger appeared on the market with Heimchen-Zauber-Apparate (Home Conjuring Apparatus). Another of the company's main articles was horses' reins, which were very popular with young people at the time and were recommended by educationalists because of their educational and health value. For the horse game there were one- or two-horse reins, with little bells and arm loops, so that children could quite nicely imitate coach and horse and cart trips. According to the company's advertisements, increased demands by the young people spurred them on to make even more efforts to bring out original and inexpensive new games every year. This endeavour led to such games as "Lumpaci-vagabundus" (Wandering Rogue), "Durch die Luft mit Zeppelin" (Through the Air in a Zeppelin), "Kegelbahn" (Skittle Alley), "Die Schule" (School) or "Jugendwehr und Pfadfinder" (Boys' Brigade and Scouts) in addition to the popular jockey, post office and ticket collector's outfits.

The great variety of the range and the wealth of materials used can be established from a list published in the Guide of 1919, when Abel-Klinger had their new trademark (skittle-shaped play piece with the initials CAKN) registered at the Reichspatentamt (Imperial Patents Office). The registered trademark referred to "goods made of wood, bone, cork, horn, tortoise-shell, whalebone, ivory, meerschaum, celluloid and similar materials. Turned, carved and woven goods, picture frames, figures for tailoring and hairdressing purposes, paper, card, paper and card goods, raw

Game board for
"Nansen's Nordpolfahrt"
(Nansen's Expedition to
the North Pole)
Chromolithography,
around 1900
Verlag C. Abel-Klinger,
Nuremberg

◁ Advertisement for
C. Abel-Klinger in "Guide to
the Toy Industry", 1898

Advertisement for Julius Stief in "Guide to the Toy Industry", July 1895

Advertisement for Abraham Marsching in "German Toy Gazette", February 1931

uncertain business situation, Abel-Klinger succeeded in raising sales considerably by way of suitable pricing and product presentation. With the purchase of wooden goods company Paul Kraus & Co. and the improvement of mechanical equipment, all articles could be brought out in better quality and in colourful designs. In spite of all these improvements prices could still be kept relatively low.

Drastic changes took place when, at the end of 1936, former shareholder Ludwig Senkeisen became the sole owner. After the Second World War, Vereinigte Kunstanstalten L. Senkeisen and C. Abel-Klinger, with company headquarters in Fürth, brought out picture and drawing books, games of Old Maid and happy families, transfers and parlour and activity games. In 1971 Abel-Klinger was sold to the Altenburg-Stralsunder Spielkartenfabriken in Leinfelden (ASS). With the exception of around fifty games, mainly from the 1930s to the 1960s, which are now in the possession of the German Playing Cards Museum in Leinfelden, the company archives have not been preserved.

Founded in Nuremberg in 1840, **Julius Stief** was regarded as a specialist producer of teaching aids and activity games. This company became well-known from 1895 for its wooden construction kits with moveable parts, whose pieces could be put together without nails or any other accessories, to create aeroplanes, motor-cars, train sets, bridges, mills or ships.[55] Further, the company also produced parlour games and shadow theatres. In 1895 the game "Nordostsee-Kanal" (Kiel Canal), with a large game board and war ships, came out. The 1907 range included "Rheinreise" (Rhine Journey), "Wettrennspiel" (Racing Game), "humorous" shadow theatres and a "Polyorama" with changing pictures.

and partly finished materials for paper manufacturing, wallpaper, saddler's, harness and bag maker's and other leather goods, writing, drawing, painting and modelling implements, billiard and marking chalk, office and accountancy equipment (excluding furniture), teaching aids, toys, gymnastics and sports equipment."

The concern's productivity must have been enormous in the 1920s. In spite of the generally

The founder of Nuremberg company Johann **Georg Schrödel** started as an independent bookbinder in 1846, after his apprenticeship and a term as journeyman.[56] His son expanded the bookbindery to include production of cardboard packaging, and from 1870 on supplied boxes on a large scale to the A.W. Faber [pencil] factory in nearby Stein. Around the turn of the century the founder's grandson started the production of parlour and sport games under the brand name "Ideal". In one of the company's first advertisements, in the Guide of 1903, table football, Circus-Tivoli, table tennis and open-air games such as toy parachutes and shooting games with suction arrows were advertised. By way of many patent applications in the sport games sector and by extending the factory grounds, the third generation laid the foundation for the company's international importance. Their main buyer at this time was F.W. Woolworth's chain of department stores, in the USA. Up until the present day sport, shooting and throwing games form the core of the family concern's range. In the 1980s pewter moulds were added as an important new product group.

The **Abraham Marsching** roulette and games factory of Nuremberg was founded in 1858, as the first of its kind in Germany.[57] At the Bavarian State Exhibition in Nuremberg in 1906 their games of roulette were acclaimed as a Nuremberg speciality.[58] They were offered in all sizes, from children's toys up to casino roulette, with the appropriate equipment such as rakes and chips. A new type of folding games table which along with roulette included boards for chess and for nine men's morris, was also mentioned. Because of old age, Abraham Marsching sold his business to major Nuremberg trader Julius Cäsar Fuchs in 1911. Fuchs succeeded in selling his products all over the world. In the 1930s, along with roulette, games tables, compendiums of games, chess and dominoes were regarded as Marsching specialities. After the destruction of the company's premises in the Second World War Fuchs succeeded in reconstructing the business on a smaller scale. Marsching was taken over by J.W. Spear & Söhne in 1967.

TIETZ & PINTHUS · ABC-VERLAG G.M.
B.H.
NÜRNBERG   Fabrik für Spiele und Ankleide-Puppen
Neue Meßadresse: LEIPZIG, Stentzlershof III 368-70

around 1910

around 1925

Children could get considerably more out of these articles than from just putting cubes together to make six matching pictures.

Nuremberg company **J.W. Arold** (proprietors: Drittler & Erlanger) became well known in the 1890s with their Patent-Universal-Holzbaukasten (Patented Universal Wooden Building Bricks), whose parts were joined together using firmly fixed brass rods. The system is comparable to the Lego building brick system developed decades later. Around 1900 J.W. Arold manufactured large wooden games boxes with games of chess, draughts, dice and dominoes, from the cheapest to the finest quality.[60] The concern labelled its games with the initials J.W.A.

J. Breitenbach was founded by S. Federlein in Nuremberg in 1897 as a bone and horn goods manufacturer's.[61] From the start, chess figures and boards of wood, bone, horn and ivory were the main articles produced. Breitenbach was also the specialist company in the Nuremberg area for dice, counters, draughts pieces, games of pick-a-stick, dominoes and complete compendiums of games. In the mid 1920s Hans Hempfling took over the company which then traded under the name Spiele-Hempfling, vorm. J. Breitenbach Nachf.. After the destruction of the factory in the Second World War, Hans Hempfling succeeded in building up his company again and in distributing chess figures all over the world, from the simplest, machine-manufactured ones up to the hand-worked luxury editions. In addition, right up to its closure in 1977 (the last two years in Zirndorf), the company also included tiddlywinks and roulette in its range.

J.A. Kithil, founded in 1865, specialised in picture cubes and building bricks of all kinds.[59] They set great store by high quality, artistically produced chromos, printed in their own works, while they obtained wooden parts from their own sawmill in Lam in the Bavarian Forest region. A new development launched in 1913 was travel picture cubes in wooden boxes for playing away from home. The company also brought pyramid cube, mosaic and domino games onto the market. In 1921/22 Kithil was for a time part of the Bing Spiele & Verlag company. Their 1931 range offered imaginative and varied possibilities for playing and building, which considerably exceeded the bounds of normal cube games. Thus a clock and arithmetic cube, a fairy tale cube theatre, an illuminated cube or a church pyramid were offered.

In 1863 Ignaz and Adolf Bing founded a trading company in Nuremberg which from 1879 also produced metal household goods and toys.[62] Around 1910 **Gebrüder Bing A.G.**, with roughly 3,700 employees and a total turnover of around 12 million Reichsmarks, was quoted as Germany's most important and the world's largest toy factory.[63] At this time it was certainly one of the most modern of its kind, with various specialised departments for electrical toys, soft toys, toy cookers and doll's kitchen equipment.

The Bing group extended its activities to include publishing when it became sole distributor of young people's magazines and picture and drawing books produced by Ernst Nister & Co., at the beginning of 1919.[64] Since they would only have been able to produce their own children's books by setting up a lithographic printer's they decided to take over completely the sales of an already existing company. Bing also published a special price list for the new department, which included children's books with illustrations by E. Kutzer, A. Jöhnssen, P. Hey, W. Planck and C. Röger.

Nister-Verlag's production and Bing's games department range were merged in the newly founded **Bing Spiele & Verlag GmbH Nürnberg** in 1921.[65] The new publishing house brought books produced by Nister and games manufactured in their own production facilities onto the market. Two further departments were established as a result of the merging with two additional smaller companies, J.A. Kithil (picture cubes) and G. Neiff (activity games). The overall production of the independent publisher's thus encompassed books, picture cubes, conjuring sets, doll's equipment, stone building sets and parlour games such as halma, happy families, dice, board and silhouette games.

The J.A. Kithil department was closed down in 1922 and appeared once again as an independent company from this time on. The reason for this separation was that, with its own sawmill in the Bavarian Forest, Kithil's production had grown dramatically and the company could cultivate the market much more intensively on its own. Neiff merged with J. W. Spear & Söhne in 1927. The subsidiary's publishing activities ended in 1932 at the latest, when Bing stopped its toy production completely.

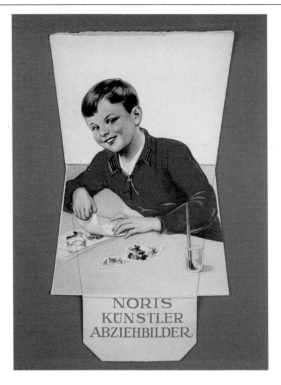

"Noris Künstler Abzieh-bilder" (Artists' Transfers) Design: Richard Borrmeister for Nuremberg company Georg Reulein, around 1935

Tietz & Pinthus, publishers of parlour and activity games[66], was founded in Magdeburg and moved its headquarters to Nuremberg between 1922 and 1925. From this time the company carried the additional name of "ABC-Verlag". Artistically designed games by picture book illustrator Astra Drucker received a lot of attention. In the 1920s and 1930s Tietz & Pinthus also employed the versatile artist and designer Richard Borrmeister (signature: RB or Ribo) from Berlin who had made a name for himself in advertising art. The publisher's remained loyal to their artistic direction, bringing out the new Serie Extra (Special Series) in 1931, with twelve different activity games made of first-rate materials and based on ideas provided by nursery-school teachers and designs by craftswomen. In 1938 the ABC Verlag was taken over by well-known Fürth manufacturer of children's printing sets, Georg Reulein (founded in 1907 in Nuremberg), which today still produces a wide range of "Noris" games.

Bing Spiele & Verlag GmbH

Tietz & Pinthus ABC-Verlag GmbH

„Noris" Georg Reulein

Company founder Jacob Wolf Spear, around 1875

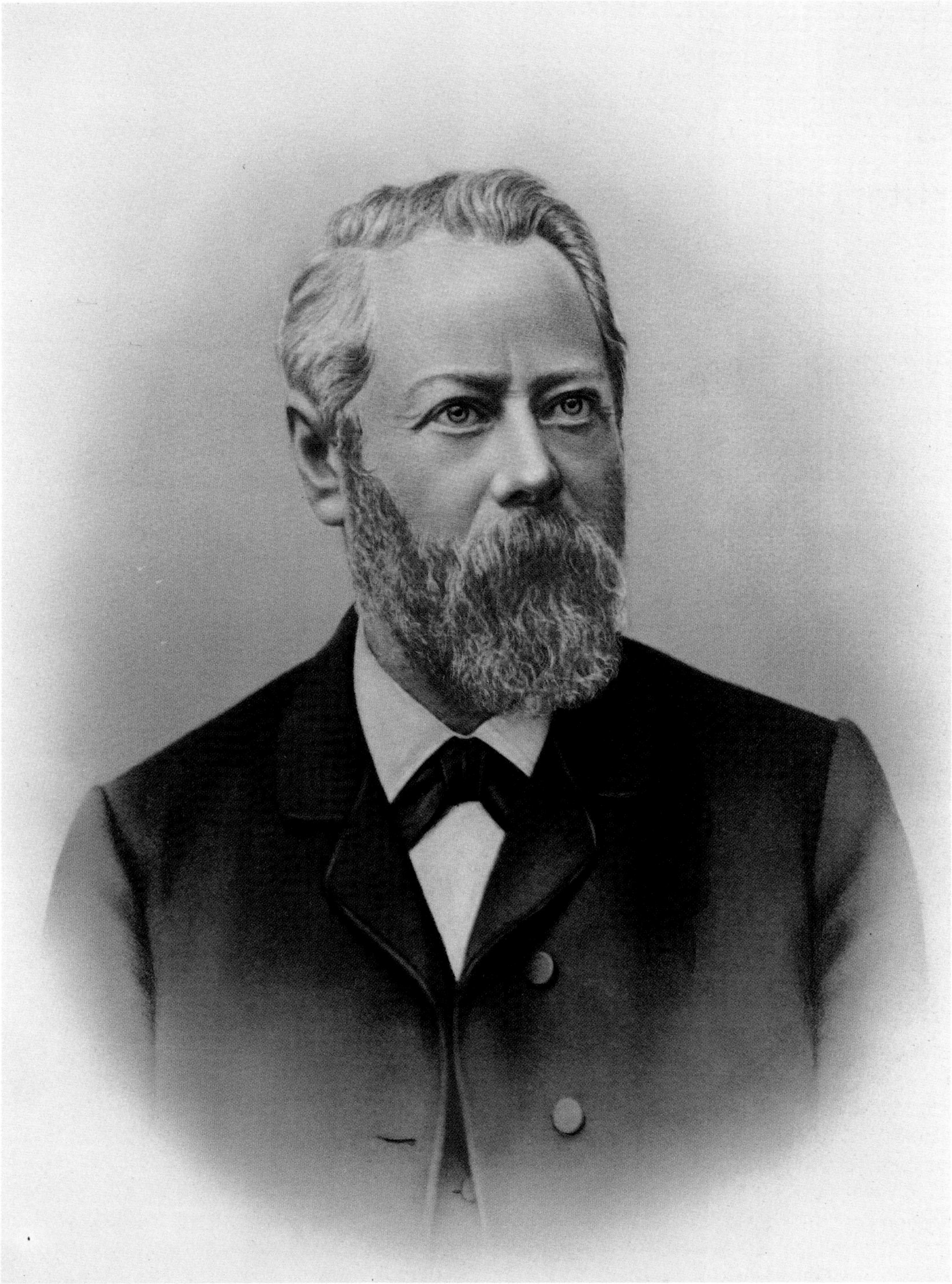

Helmut Schwarz

Games We Play

History of J. W. Spear & Sons

The beginning of the family and company history takes us to Merzhausen, in the Electorate of Hesse, in the administrative district of Ziegenhain. Jacob Wolf Spier was born in this little town in the Schwalm region on 23rd April, 1832 as the youngest child of Jewish soap maker and later dealer Wolf Joseph Spier and his wife Gidel Spier. As can be seen in the register of the Merzhausen Jewish congregation, the marriage produced three children. Jacob Wolf Spier had two older sisters: Sprinz (born 1817) and Beyer (born 1825). His mother died when she was just 44 years old, only four years after the birth of her son.[1]

Nothing other than these bare details is known about the Spier family background. It can be assumed, however, that it became even more difficult for the head of the family to support his children after the death of his spouse. The trade of soap maker was, after all, in the lowest group on the social scale, and could only provide for the bare necessities – especially in the notoriously poor Schwalm region. Jacob Wolf Spier started elementary school in his home town in May, 1838. Nothing is known about his career after he finished school. In particular, it is not clear whether he followed in his father's footsteps or perhaps took up an apprenticeship in commerce or as a tradesman, something which would have involved great obstacles, considering the restrictive conditions applying to Jews at the time. Economic need, the repression during the period of reaction following the failed revolution of 1848/49 and hope of a better life resulted in emigration swelling to massive proportions around

the middle of last century. Well over a million Germans left their native country in the 1850s, the favourite destination being the United States of America. Jacob Wolf Spier, too, was one of these mainly young, enterprising people who no longer saw any future in their native land and who wanted to build themselves a new and better existence on the other side of the Atlantic. In June, 1852, with fifty Thalers in his pocket – money saved for a rainy day rather than starting capital – he acquired a "discharge from allegiance to the Electorate of Hesse" from the authorities allowing him to emigrate to the USA. His profession is not stated in the register entry. This could indicate that a normal training had not been possible.[2]

Jacob Wolf Spier remained in the USA for ten years. How he got on in that decade, whether his hopes were fulfilled, and how he earned his living, is all lost in the mists of history. At any rate we know that he settled on the East coast in Hartford, Connecticut and that he obtained American citizenship there in October, 1860 after a five year wait. Three years prior to this he married twenty-year-old German-born Sophie Rindskopf (born in Großlangheim near Kitzingen in Lower Franconia) in New York. The marriage produced two children in the USA: Ralph (born 19.7.1858 in Hartford) and Joseph (born 6.10.1860, also in Hartford).[3] By this time, the family already bore the name "Spear" since, in accordance with quite normal practice in the USA, the German name had been anglicized in keeping with the pronunciation, "a spelling which I then kept," as Jacob Wolf Spear was later to say for the record.[4]

The Spear family returned to Germany in November, 1861, counting thus among the roughly ten per cent of German emigrants to the USA who — for whatever reasons — turned their back on the land of their (disappointed) dreams in order to settle in the Old World again. Economic reasons did not necessarily play the most important role in this difficult decision: in many cases overwhelming homesickness drove the emigrants back.[5] According to stories handed down through the family, it appears that Sophie Spear in particular had considerable problems in getting used to the American way of life.[6] Perhaps indeed her wish to return was decisive; but perhaps it was also the fear of the effects of the American Civil War, which had broken out shortly before, in the spring of 1861. After all, there was a real danger that Jacob Wolf Spear as a 30 year-old new American citizen could be called up sooner or later for military service for the Northern Union. These considerations belong in the realm of speculation, however; the real reasons for the return to Germany will probably never be established.

The up-and-coming Bavarian trading and industrial town of Fürth constituted the first stop on the way to the building up of a new existence. After just nine months, however, in September, 1862, J.W. Spear moved to the small upper Franconian town of Reckendorf near Bamberg, where he worked for four years as manager of Reiß & Co., a factory producing wooden goods.[7] It is not known which products this company manufactured, or whether toys were among them. It can be assumed, however, that Jacob Wolf Spear would hardly have attained this position without relevant knowledge of wood processing. In any case the four years in Reckendorf certainly represented an important step on his road towards commercial independence and to later entry into toy production.

The next stop in Jacob Wolf Spear's journey through life was Sonneberg in the duchy of Saxonia-Meiningen. In August, 1868, the family settled in this centre of the extensive Thuringian toy industry, with its world-wide export market, and was to remain here for a decade. By now the Spears had to look after five children, as three further children had been born since their return to Germany: Lina (born 4.11.1862 in Fürth), Carl and Jenny (born in Reckendorf on 1.8.1864 and 2.8.1866 respectively). Four more children were to follow in Sonneberg: Wilhelm (22.8.1867), Minna (23.8.1869), Sigmund (5.8.1870) and Isidor (15.2.1872, whose name was later changed by deed poll to "Erich").[8] This was the family background – a tenth child (Hedwig), a late baby, was born in Fürth in 1880 – for the Spears' well documented entry into the toy trade.

On 23rd June, 1869, Jacob Wolf Spear joined Sonneberg firm C. Hartwig & Son as a partner.[9] The concern had been founded around 1825, at first purely as a trading firm, by businessman Julius Carl Hartwig.[10] In the beginning the main goods were slate pencils, nails, and boxes of all descriptions. By the time the firm's founder died in 1865 the range of goods already boasted paintboxes, dominoes, money boxes, cribbage boards and race games. His son, Robert Hartwig, took over the firm, which was deeply in debt, and tried to put it back on its feet – from 1869 onwards with the additional help of the new partner. When Sonneberg businessman Fritz Bergmann joined as a third partner, the old firm was wound up, on 22nd June, 1872, only to be entered in the register of companies under the new name of "Hartwig, Spear and Bergmann" on the same day. A business partnership of this kind, between a Protestant (Hartwig), a Jew (Spear) and a Catholic (Bergmann) was so unusual at this time that a derisive phrase was soon coined in the Sonneberg vernacular in regard to the missing third major monotheistic religion: "Hartwig, Spear and Bergmann are looking for a Moslem."[11]

The new concern was no longer purely a trading firm; it now also employed homeworkers and

produced its own goods, especially paintboxes, money boxes and games. The main sales markets other than Germany were England and France. While Robert Hartwig dealt mainly with exports and foreign clients, production and the German market belonged to Jacob Spear's domain.

In 1876 Hartwig left the firm and set up on his own what later became a very successful wooden goods and toy factory. The company chronicle allotted Fritz Bergmann sole blame for the break-up, as he was "no great businessman and only had an eye to his own interests": it even accused him of fraud against Hartwig. Unperturbed by this, Jacob Wolf Spear continued working with Bergmann whose brother Joseph now joined the firm as a partner. Just two years later, Jacob Spear also left the firm which continued under the same name but with changing partnership, until its bankruptcy in August, 1893.[12]

The time had now definitely come for such a restless creature as Jacob Spear to take the leap into independence. Sonneberg no longer seemed the right place for it, though. That is why in August, 1878, he emigrated a second time from Germany, taking his entire family. This time, however, England was his destination; his previous firm had enjoyed the best trading connections with this country. In London, in September, 1878, he founded "J.W. Spear", an import company dealing in fancy goods. But this was hardly established when the family were already packing their cases again. While the three oldest sons, Raphael (Ralph), Joseph and Carl, were to take care of the company in London, the rest of the Spear family moved to Fürth where they settled in July, 1879. Not long after, on 6th November, 1879, Jacob Wolf Spear registered a "fancy goods import and export business" in the Fürth register of companies, with himself as sole proprietor. This date is

An industrial background:
Fürth, around 1890,
Jacob Wolf Spear's home
and factory were situated
close to the railway station,
near the Ludwigsbahn line
(r., above station building)

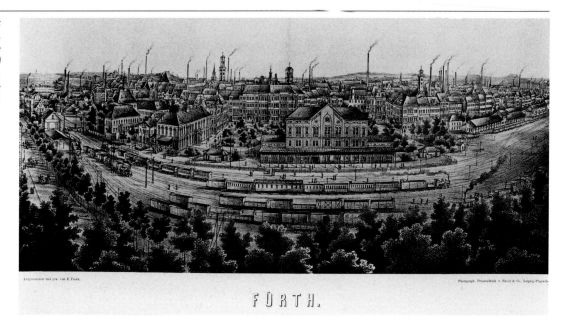

FÜRTH.

to be seen as the actual founding date of the J.W. Spear & Sons games factory, for out of this, initially a trading business, their own toy manufacture gradually developed.

In contrast with his first stay in Fürth in 1861/62, Jacob Wolf Spear now also possessed the capital for such a venture. Quite obviously he had made a considerable fortune in his Reckendorf and Sonneberg years which he now proposed investing in the construction of a factory. Spear was initially only the subtenant in a mirror factory at 'Dambacher Weg 26, but in 1883 he purchased a prestigious villa at Königswarterstraße 26 for 55,000 Reichsmarks and in the same year had a factory building erected at the rear of this property. According to Fürth's municipal authorities, Spear was at that time already running a "largish toys and fancy goods export business" which employed on average sixty workers and exported mainly to England. The town council added: "Spear is generally regarded as a very good businessman and nothing has become known against him during his stay here, with regard either to his business or his political dealings".[13]

Jacob Spear himself informs us about initial production: "Our business, which has been operating in the factory facilities at Königswarter Straße 26 since 1883 consisted of the processing of printed, painted and other kinds of paper and cardboard into games, embroidery patterns, picture albums, small picture books and some small articles for everyday use such as place mats etc. Printed material, coloured papers and card were bought in. We had no printing at all in the factory other than a hand-press which produced only overprints. Some things, such as games and place mats were varnished with spirit lacquer and dried on racks."[14]

The first advertisement for the company appeared in the "Toy Industry Guide" in April, 1887. A wide spectrum of fancy goods, toys and stationery were offered for sale under the first Spear trademark, an English pillar box with the inscription "VR" for Victoria Regina, including "pens, patented pencils, automatic pencils, erasers, painting and drawing sheets, embroidery patterns, transfers, chromo and religious albums, Chinese shades, writing cases, folding waste paper baskets, lamp mats as well as dominoes, chess and draughts boards, race games, bell and hammer games, lotto, and various other games, compendiums of games, greeting cards." The "Victoria Book Bag, elegant, practical, light, durable and cheap, in calico, leather and oilcloth" is highly praised as a special new article; "an eminently saleable item", as the trade journal presumes in its editorial section.[15] From further company advertisements of the same year it can be seen that even at this time it had showrooms in Berlin and Hamburg and was represented at Leipzig's spring and autumn trade fairs.

In 1889 the factory was considerably expanded and modernized as a result of the change-over to steam power. New machines were added and according to the proprietor now included the following: "Steam-driven machines used by us were a paper cutter, a card cutter, and a cutting and scoring machine. Machines not driven by steam were the embossing presses, cutting presses, wire stitching machines and other small auxiliary machines."[16] At the same time the production programme for "oil-card goods" such as small dishes, boxes and cases was extended. In 1892 a Fürth police officer described the production process in detail: "After the objects in question are cut, pressed or formed in some other way from card they are soaked in raw or boiled linseed oil. This is done simply by dipping the relevant objects in oil and removing them again immediately. When an appropriate number of objects has been prepared in this way, they are taken for baking in the drying oven and placed on iron racks or wire netting. Heating pipes run through the drying room; the furnace is to be found outside the building and is similar to that of a small boiler firing system. According to the foreman a heat of at least 80° Réaumur (100 °C) is necessary for baking the card in the drying room. As soon as the treated goods have reached the relevant degree of dryness, they are removed, painted with black base coat and subjected to a second drying process as above. After this they

The old Spear villa at Königswarter Straße 26, around 1950. Parts of the old factory building are still visible in the background. The late classicist building, built in 1860, is now listed.

are varnished and dried in a special drying oven... Neither hot oils nor hot varnishes are used and the preparation of the goods and the varnishing are carried out at room temperature. The varnishes are bought in ready mixed."[17] Obviously the inclusion of the new oil-card goods – described as "exceptionally popular, and quickly introduced mass-produced articles"[18] – made for a considerable expansion of the product range. Thus, in the year 1892, according to Spear, the company was already employing 130 to 140 workers.[19]

The expansion of the 1880s also had its effect on the management of the family concern. In 1884 and 1885 respectively the two oldest sons, Ralph and Joseph Spear, became partners in the firm and thus the name of the business was given the form it would keep for decades: J. W. Spear & Söhne (J.W. Spear &Sons). The head office was in Fürth and the London branch was still kept going, initially. Both sons, however, left the management again in 1886 in unknown circumstances. Three years later the London branch was closed. Directly after leaving their father's firm Ralph and

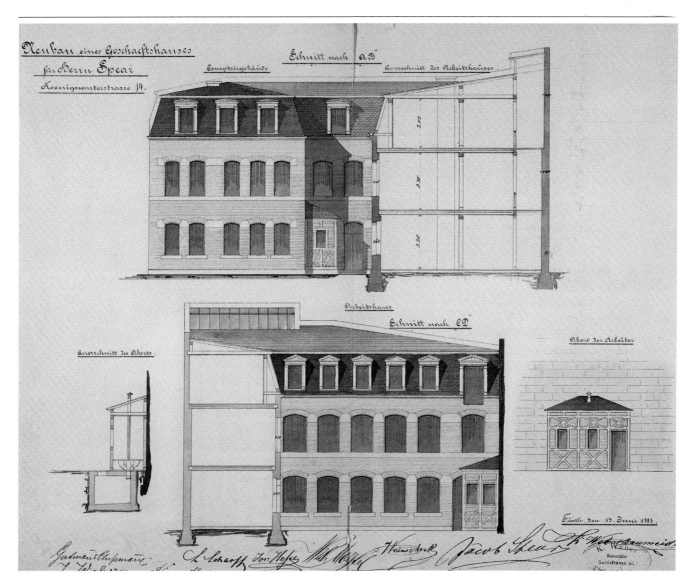

Building plans for the Spear factory
at the rear of Königswarter Straße 14 (new numbering: 26).
The factory was planned and built in 1883.

Joseph Spear set up a games and fancy goods business in Fürth under the name of "Gebrüder Spear" (Spear Brothers). Joseph Spear left in 1890, however, and moved to Nuremberg.[20] Ralph Spear continued with the firm and in the period following manufactured "picture cubes and fancy goods" (Fürth Address Book, 1896). It is not certain whether the two oldest sons had a business relationship with their father's firm.

Jacob Wolf Spear continued as sole proprietor of his concern for five years until he finally took his next youngest sons Carl and Wilhelm into the business as partners. After his business training Carl Spear had followed in his father's footsteps, spending several years in the USA. There he had tried, among other things, to sell fountain pens for London company, Thomas de la Rue. Carl Spear was summoned to Fürth by his father, who wanted him at his side in the management of the expanding concern. His help was desperately needed, especially in these years, for the firm was heading for troubled times.

On 26th May, 1892, an unusually hot day, a major fire broke out shortly after work, its cause unknown and resulting in extensive damage. A large part of the stock was burned, the factory building and the top floor of the office building fell victim to the flames. With much trouble the fire brigade succeeded in stopping the fire from spreading to the neighbouring properties. Seven firemen had to be taken to hospital with heat-stroke.[21]

The financial loss to the Spear firm was even more painful when it quickly transpired that "some things were not sufficiently insured and others not insured at all", as Jacob Spear said in a statement: "But we'll suffer most damage from the interruption to what was a quick and efficient operation, which in the most favourable circumstances will last ... about six months according to our calculations. We estimate a loss of at least 100,000 Marks this year as a result of the fire tragedy …" Under these conditions, and in view of the some 140 now unemployed workers, Jacob Spear pushed the authorities for early permission to rebuild.[22] The submitted plans were indeed authorized quickly, and shortly before Christmas, 1892, the factory was able to take up production again, in a modified and slightly larger form.

As well as the financial loss, the fire also had further far-reaching consequences for the firm. Bordering directly on the factory were not only residential buildings but also several buildings used for commercial purposes, and the owners were understandably alarmed by the extensive blaze.

They were afraid that such a fire disaster could occur again at any time due to the nature of the games and paper goods production. The day-to-day use of highly inflammable materials (paper, card, wood, varnishes, spirit) in their neighbourhood represented a danger to them which had to be eradicated once and for all. For this reason additional fire protection measures were implemented when the factory was rebuilt, and Jacob Spear also undertook to shut down the notoriously critical drying plant within 18 months. His neighbours kept a very close watch on the plant from then on, however.[23]

In May, 1893, in this atmosphere of worry and suspicion, a second fire broke out in the drying plant. It was extinguished quickly, but it prompted a police enquiry in the course of which the neighbours – on the whole business people and other rich citizens – demanded the closure of the business. They collected signatures and complained in the local newspapers not only about the danger of fire but now also about the nuisance of a strong smell emanating from the factory, especially during the summer months.

Jacob Spear stood more and more with his back to the wall as the dispute escalated by the minute. Sarcastic letters aggravated the conflict further. Fürth's medical officer confirmed in a report that the waste gases from the factory were not poisonous, and that there was thus no reason for official intervention, but he also noted quite a nuisance resulting from the emissions. In the end, and partly because of this report, the municipal authorities refused in August, 1893, to close the business. They did, however, recommend that the complainants consider civil action.

On top of all this, accusations were now being made that Spear himself had set fire to his factory complex the previous year. Jacob Spear was taken into custody pending trial, but was remanded on bail of 25,000 Marks shortly after.[24] The accusations affected the entrepreneur all the more since they must have reminded him of a violent and in part publicly fought conflict which had happened years ago.[25]

A Nuremberg pharmacist, Baron von Engelbrecht had expressed doubt as to Jacob Wolf Spear's identity and integrity in 1881 in the course of a business disagreement regarding the exploitation rights for an invention allegedly made by him: a "transfer album". He associated Spear with a low criminal by the name of Abraham Spier, Speyer or Spear (the Baron did not know the proper spelling) who had become known for his misdemeanours in the USA between 1858 and 1861. This man had – according to Engelbrecht – "cheated German emigrants with false land titles, started fires in his offices, and lured whole shiploads of unfortunate girls from Hesse and elsewhere and of all social classes with temptingly high wages and free passage to America, and then sold or hired these hundreds of poor girls to brothels in the larger cities".[26]

These accusations, which in 1882 had pushed Jacob Spear almost to having the reputation of a notorious criminal, were never followed up. Fürth's municipal authorities refused at that time to look at these rumours in detail. But as always in such cases: something sticks. The memory of these age-old defamatory accusations, the financial losses from the fire, the quarrel with the neighbours, the detention under suspicion of arson and the possibly imminent closure of the business: Jacob Wolf Spear could no longer cope with these heavy burdens at the end of his eventful and busy life. "According to a reliable source", the Fürther Tagblatt wrote, "Mr. Spear had been deeply worried since the time when the suspicion of a punishable charge against him flourished, and with a sense of the injustice he had been done, he had shown symptoms of deep melancholy and mental disturbance, the latter making him commit suicide while in a state of unsound mind."[27] Jacob Wolf Spear hanged himself in his factory on 3rd September, 1893.

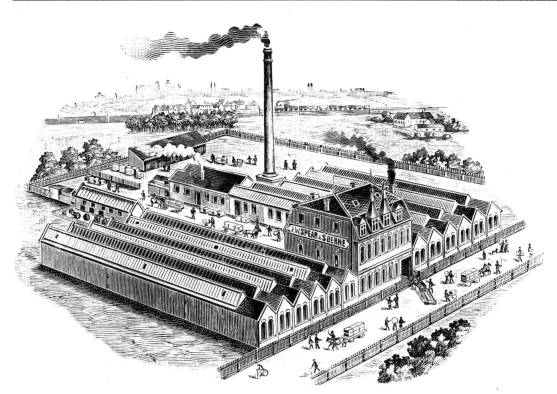

*Outside the city walls:
View of Spear's factory at
Höfener Straße, 1904.
Using artistic licence, the
graphic artist shifted the
silhouette of Nuremberg's
Old Town into the back-
ground. In reality, there
were only fields, ponds
and woods.*

The Move to Nuremberg

Carl and Wilhelm Spear initially carried on the business in Fürth after the death of the company's founder. Their mother, Sophie, became a partner in spring, 1894.[28] After everything that had happened it must already have been clear at this time that the factory location in Königswarterstraße was no longer tenable. Quite apart from the hostile atmosphere, there were no more opportunities whatsoever for expansion in the highly built-up neighbourhood. So the two young entrepreneurs set out to find a suitable new location. They struck it lucky right on the other side of the boundary with the neighbouring city of Nuremberg. In March, 1898, they purchased a 3.5 acres piece of land – surrounded by fish ponds and woodland – on the road connecting Doos and Höfen.

The new factory location was chosen with care, even if some of Carl's friends probably shook their heads at first, in view of its situation on the periphery of both cities, three kilometres from the centre of Fürth and six kilometres from Nuremberg's Old Town. The factory was connected to the national rail network by the nearby Nuremberg-Doos railway station and linked to the Ludwigsbahn, the first ever section of German railway, which had linked Nuremberg and Fürth since 1835. At this time there were scarcely any residential buildings in the area; rather it was a distinctly industrial area which was just being developed at the time. The Sirius Bicycle Works had been established on the opposite, west side of the street, and to the north a large soda factory was being built. Fields, fish ponds and woodland extended to the east and the south: there were, therefore, potentially enough areas for

expansion for the games factory, and indeed in the course of time, by buying more land, the area owned by the firm was expanded to 25,000 m^2 (6.2 acres).[29] Thus J. W. Spear & Söhne never had to deal with the problem of lack of expansion opportunities, right up until the closing of the factory in 1984. Undoubtedly this indicates an entrepreneurial far-sightedness, which had surely been sharpened by the extremely difficult experiences of the time in Fürth.

The Spears' property in Fürth was sold, but remained within the trade since the new owner, Fürth toy wholesaler Emil Bierer, set up his warehouse in the factory buildings. Production was, however, no longer carried out here.

The fact that the Spear brothers could acquire a new partner was extremely important for the new beginnings on Nuremberg soil. Eugen Mayer, owner of a large printing works in Nuremberg, joined the concern in June, 1898. The business was converted to a limited partnership

when he joined, his investment amounting to 50,000 Reichsmarks.[30] As Carl Spear's son, Richard Spear, recalled, the purchase of the land and the construction of the factory was made possible only by Eugen Mayer's capital. Mayer obviously had great trust in Carl Spear's business acumen: "He gave him 200,000 Marks. That was a lot of money back then ... and he didn't put it down in the contract. He probably assumed that my father would let him do his printing. He always said 'I'll do your printing, if you like, and if my prices are competitive, but there's no obligation', and in that way he got every contract."[31]

Through its new partner the firm had direct access to an old-established and efficient printer's whose chromolithographs were of a high standard. This became exceptionally important for further development, since the printing quality of the game boards and lids was and remains an important selling point. As Swiss toy wholesaler Franz Carl Weber remarked, Spear was the first German company which could produce excellently designed games in large runs and, as a result, inexpensively.[32]

Production began in the newly built factory at Höfener Straße No. 46 in May, 1899. Their letterhead read: "Lacquered Card Goods and Games Factory. Steam Embossing and Gilding Establishment."[33] Two long one-storey brick buildings dominated the length of the street frontage and were arranged symmetrically around a central, two-storey office and residential building. Having ground level production shops, workshops and storerooms meant, the production could be much more efficiently organized than in the old factory premises in Fürth. The machines in the production shops were powered by a steam engine via line shafting. And the drying oven for lacquered card goods was also heated by steam, in a separate building.

When production began in the new factory the company's extremely diverse range of goods was restructured and divided into two sections. The manufacture of toys (Section I) came more to the fore, although the diverse card fancy goods (Section II) – religious wall mottoes, flower pot covers, photograph frames, small wall brackets, etagères and pipe holders – still played a major role. Unlike earlier times Spear now simply traded under "games factory" in advertisements in the "Guide". The oldest known catalogue, from 1904, also uses this description. In this carefully illustrated and beautifully designed price list the firm displays its wide range of games with the trademark it had been using – a couchant lance with shield and the inscription "J.W.S.& S."[34]

The catalogue lists over 130 articles from A for "Angel-Spiel" (Fishpond) to Z for "Zitter- oder

Picture lotto at the photographer's studio: Hermann, Emilie and Richard (left to right), Carl Spear's three children, around 1905

53

*Title page of the first
Spear's Games catalogue,
1904*

Häkchen-Spiel" (Spellicans), parlour games for children and adults dominating. Race games such as Snakes and Ladders, The Game of Goose and Steeplechase are to be found alongside classic board games such as Nine Men's Morris, Draughts and Chinese Chequers. Picture Lotto and card games such as Old Maid, Poch or Snap were included in the range, as were several games of skill (Tiddlywinks, Darts, ball and quoit games). But also activity games based on the principles of educationalist Friedrich Fröbel were offered for sale: perforated card patterns for embroidering, sewing and tracing, patterns for learning to draw step-by-step on chequered paper and paper-plaiting for creating patterns from coloured strips of paper. Scaffold-like constructions could be fitted together from small wooden rods and discs of punched cork, following printed instruction sheets, in a kind of building game, and a bead mosaic had a tray with indentations for organizing little coloured balls into figures and geometric patterns. In contrast, the delightful soap-bubble game seemed to be really just for fun. A bar of soap in the shape of a fish, straws, clay pipes and a little soap dish were enclosed in the box. A pewter "jolly jumper" could be fixed to the clay pipe with a wire so that a soap-bubble could form around it.

Many of these games had already been in the Spear range for some time. A hand-written new product directory,[35] begun in 1893, which lists the company´s German and English range under running article numbers, reveals for October of that year, for example, parlour games such as "The Ocean Race" and "Bicycle Race" alongside standard games such as Nine Men's Morris, Draughts, Dominoes, Chinese Chequers or Chess. "Parcheesi", "Steeple Chase", "Yacht Race", "Stop Thief", "Football Match", "Curling Game" and "The Game of Authors" were added in 1894. Some of these games still appeared in the 1904 catalogue, others had been discontinued by then. Perhaps, however, they were carried on in new forms and with different names.

Undoubtedly table tennis was a product of the 20th century, and it took an important and special position in Spear's games range. As a fashionable parlour game, it was aimed predominantly at an adult, middle-class public. The sports movement coming from England and the high regard for physical activity as a means of keeping healthy, found its socially acceptable entertainment form for ladies and gentlemen in this game. As early as April, 1901, Spear, quite with this in mind, produced exclusively designed table tennis sets with wooden bats, celluloid balls and net. The 1904 catalogue sang ping-pong's praises as the indoor version of lawn tennis. "No other game is as entertaining and, as a result of the physical activity required, as healthy as table tennis, for one's attention is fixed constantly on the game, and not only eye and hand but the whole body moves lightly and gracefully, providing lively and healthy stimulation, for the entire person."

As the firm's advertising had it, table tennis was an absolute "hit" for Spear in that first decade of the new century. No other article was produced in such great variety. All in all, 24 variations were offered in 1904, in three different price groups. Thus the fashionable home sportsman could choose from various net clamps, buy bats with or without polished handles, and try out his playing skills with bats with a shiny wooden surface or with coverings of imitation parchment, sheepskin, calfskin or calico. The wholesale price ranged from four to 96 Marks per dozen, according to model.

While table tennis games were also offered for sale by other companies, especially by English producers of sports articles, the second "hit" from the early Nuremberg years was a new creation from the House of Spear, and one of a quite different nature. On 8th May, 1899, while construction work on the factory was still in full swing, Carl Spear registered a new trademark for his latest development which bore the title "Die fliegenden Hüte" ("Flying Hats").[36] This enter-

Good quality for little money:
Parlour games from the
1904 Spear catalogue

"What You Will" - The Twenties

The German toy industry was faced with a whole host of problems after the end of the First World War. In addition to the losses to the workforce, raw materials continued to be rationed, with long-lasting effects. The uncertain political situation and social struggles which followed the collapse of the old order created an atmosphere of uncertainty further aggravated by inflation. In addition to this, foreign competition – shielded from German imports during the war years – had increased considerably in significance. In the next years, many states – among them above all the USA, which had gained enormous strength as an economic power – sought to protect their young toy industries by means of high import duties, too. Germany's traditionally very export-orientated toy production had great difficulties in overcoming these trade barriers throughout the 1920s. Thus German toy producers, reacting to strong competition, sought to develop new markets at home and abroad. The result was a major rationalization and concentration process, and the overall winners were clearly the large concerns.[47]

Against this backdrop J. W. Spear & Söhne withstood the challenges of the 1920s with style. This was due to its smart management, which was rejuvenated and received new impetus by the recruiting of Carl Spear's two sons: Jakob Richard (born 22.11.1897) and Hermann (born 9.9.1899). A further essential fact was that Great Britain, traditionally Spear's main export market, luckily did not cut itself off from German imports until the end of the 1920s: while at the beginning of the decade German world-wide toy exports had dropped by roughly one third compared to the pre-war period, exports of German toys to Great Britain in 1925 were even higher than in 1913.[48] Plainly Spear counted among the beneficiaries of liberal British economic policy. In addition, the concern apparently had sufficient capital to survive the difficult post-war years well, thus possessing a considerable advantage over its competitors.

By expanding production in its main lines, by taking on new product lines and by taking over other companies, Spear grew considerably towards the end of the 1920s. At the same time, the company was given a new structure, so that ultimately it embraced four separate business areas: parlour games and games of skill, activity games and sports games formed Section I. By 1919 picture book publishing was added, becoming Section II. In the same year Spear bought the well-established Nuremberg wooden toy company C. Baudenbacher; production was carried on in the new Section III. In 1927 the G. Neiff toy factory, likewise an old established Nuremberg producer of activity games and doll´s clothes and accessories, was added as Section IV. Takeover of children's and family card games produced by the major Frankfurt company, B. Dondorf, rounded off Spear's expansion in 1929, adding to the range of Section I.

In this way the range of goods and volume of business grew considerably during the 1920s, without the need of buying in products. Basically it was a growth in areas which had been represented since before the First World War, but which now reached a new level, in both quantity and quality. This shows a very goal oriented business policy avoiding the typical error other toy factories had made by "taking up the manufacture of new product groups which in no way fitted in with their product line". This concentration on the traditional market segment was completely in keeping with the recommendations of the Verband der Deutschen Spielwarenindustrie (German toy industry association), which was advising its members to specialize in particular types of toys. At the same time it was also promoting the slogan "idea, good taste, quality" as the motto for those industrialists who wanted to keep their hold on the world market.[49] It appears as though Spear's management felt themselves to be com-

1932

Spear-Spiele

DIE MARKE, DIE VON IHRER KUNDSCHAFT VERLANGT WIRD

ABTEILUNG I SPIELEFABRIK u. VERLAG

Gesellschaftsspiele
Beschäftigungsspiele
Geschicklichkeitsspiele
Sportspiele, Quartettspiele

ABTEILUNG II BILDERBÜCHER - VERLAG

Unzerreißbare Bilderbücher
Aufstellbilderbücher
Papierbilderbücher
Malbücher

ABTEILUNG III (BAUDENBACHER)

Fabrik feiner Holzspielwaren

Sommerspielwaren
Kegelspiele
Zauberkasten

ABTEILUNG IV (NEIFF)

Fabrik feiner Stickkasten

Strick- und Webgeräte
Beschäftigungsmittel
für Mädchen
Puppenausstattungen

UNERREICHTE GÜTE UND AUSWAHL · MEHR NEUHEITEN ALS JE ZUVOR
LEIPZIGER MESSE: MARKT 13 STIEGLITZENSHOF, 2. OBERGESCHOSS.

J. W. SPEAR & SÖHNE NÜRNBERG-DOOS

MUSTERLAGER IN BERLIN S. 42, RITTERSTRASSE 35

mitted to exactly these central ideas. At least, the great success of the 1920s confirms that they had recognized the demands of the times.

The concern gained a strong position not only on the German but also on the international market. A large part of the range was issued in German, English, French, Spanish and Dutch and could thus be sold practically all over the world. As a purely marketing company, subsidiary concern J. W. Spear & Sons Inc. of New York looked after sales of Spear's games in the USA and Canada from 1927 on. The most important market was and remained Great Britain, with its colonies worldwide. In June, 1931 the company's accounts revealed gross turnover of 3.5 million Reichsmarks. No less than 38 per cent originated from the British section of the business, Germany taking second place with just 25 per cent. At this time the company employed 598 people: four senior managers, 61 white-collar workers, 493 blue-collar workers and 40 homeworkers.[50]

This figure is all the more remarkable since eighteen concerns in Germany which fell under the description of games factory at the time, employed only about 1500 people in all.[51] Thus Spear had risen to become by far the largest games factory in Germany and at the same time counted among the very few large companies of the toy industry as a whole.[52] The company´s importance to the trade is also manifested in the fact that Richard Spear was appointed as representative of the company's management to a committee of experts which between 1927 and 1929 had to provide the German Reichstag with information regarding the economic circumstances of the toy industry and trade in a major survey. The young businessman found himself in the best of company, for the representatives of the "aristocracy" of the German world of toys were on the committee: Bing, Bub, Märklin, Steiff, Dressel and Heubach on the industrial side, and Karstadt, Tietz, Woolworth, John Heß and Vedes for the trade.[53] Carl and Richard Spear were also heavily involved in the founding of the Vereinigung deutscher Spielefabriken, with its headquarters in Nuremberg. This association of Germany's famous games manufacturers – among them C. Abel-Klinger (Nuremberg), L. Kleefeld (Fürth), J. Scholz (Mainz), A. Sala (Berlin) and Otto Maier (Ravensburg) – was constituted at the end of December, 1926. The basic intention was to promote common business interests. Among the Association's tasks were the "support and advice for members, in all branch and customer matters" as well as the "fixing of minimum prices and minimum sales conditions". Carl or respectively Richard Spear were on the board of this syndicate up until 1933.[54]

The rapid growth of the Spear Toy Factory in the 1920s was closely linked with the success of the "What You Will" picture book and game range. "Twelfth Night; or what you will" is the title of Shakespeare's last comedy, which was first performed in London in 1601 or 1602 and in time became his most widely played comedy in Germany.[55] In taking up picture book production in great style under the trademark "What You Will", Spear wanted to take up the renown of author and work (and maybe also allude to their name being contained in "Shakespeare").

"With the 'What You Will' picture book collection we take particular care that the subject matter is suitable for children, and that ... the books are both entertaining and educational. The illustrations have been done by first-rate artists", promised the special catalogue for the picture and drawing books.[56] Of course, this high standard could not always be kept up. Graphically some things appear just as clumsy as the company's 1920 advertisement for the new series. A bearded grandfather in spats and stand-up collar obviously suffers considerably because his stiff body is made up of the unwieldy letters of the word Spear, but he still bends down to his grandchildren, a picture book in his hand, and seems to be saying "I can give you what you will".[57]

C. Baudenbacher – Toy Factory

In taking over the C. Baudenbacher company in 1919, J. W. Spear & Söhne purchased a well-known concern with decades of experience in the production of high-quality wooden toys. A look back at the company's origins shows what difficulties young, enterprising craftsmen had to cope with before the introduction of freedom of trade in 1869, if they wanted to become self-employed in Nuremberg.[1]

Company founder Caspar Baudenbacher, born in 1803, came from a poor family of wood turners which had been resident in Nuremberg from as early as the beginning of the 18th century. Caspar Baudenbacher served his wood turner's apprenticeship in his father's workshop and concluded it with the examination to become a journeyman. Bad thyroid and lung complaints prevented the eager-to-learn young man from going on his travels, though. Instead he did courses in mathematics, projective geometry, technical and freehand drawing, physics and chemistry at Nuremberg's Polytechnic for five years. In his own words, it was poverty which gave him the incentive "to be able to meet all possible kinds of demands" later on as a well-educated professional.

As headmaster Johannes Scharrer, one of Nuremberg´s great modernizers, certified, in these years Baudenbacher indeed developed into an "excellently skilful and efficient worker, not only in his own trade, but also as professional sculptor. Commissioned by the school, and involving work which took years, he made illustrative models of Classic columns, finely worked in wood, the quality of which was estimated by competent visitors from near and far as ranking even higher than corresponding works in the educational collections of the famous technical colleges of Vienna and Paris. At the same time he made wooden models for the moulds of a wide variety of artists and iron founders. His clients numbered, among others, the Royal Bavarian Iron Foundry in Bodenwöhr and his

Ball game from hand-drawn sample book produced by C. Baudenbacher around 1850

teacher at the Polytechnic, famous architect and protector of historical monuments Carl Alexander von Heideloff. In spite of his untiring work, these honourable commissions only brought in just enough money during his student days to pay for the high costs of treatment for his illnesses. In order to keep his head above water financially, he produced simple wooden knick-knacks – including toys – commissioned by merchants.

In January, 1838, Caspar Baudenbacher passed his examination for master craftsman's diploma as wood turner. In spite of his lack of means – he possessed nothing apart from a lathe, tools, materials, clothes and some modest furniture – he now wanted to set up on his own as model maker and get married. He was engaged to the daughter of a precision instrument maker who also came from a very modest background. In accordance with the trading regulations ruling at the time he needed a licence from the city of Nuremberg's municipal authorities, who in turn as a rule followed the vote of the craftsmen already resident in the town: in spite of the best of references – as a result of his studies Baudenbacher was far better trained than the great majority of his professional colleagues – the municipal authorities did not issue the desired licence.

The heads of the wood turner's guild argued that the bad economic situation would not allow for the settling of further wood turners in the city. Baudenbacher and his bride, they said, were so poor that they would soon have to depend on charity. What was more, he was "mostly ill" and, after all, there were already twenty applicants before Baudenbacher on the waiting list for a wood turner's licence to become available. Furthermore, they played down his qualifications and expressed the view that there were too few contracts for model makers to ensure the young man's livelihood and that of the family he wanted to raise.

Baudenbacher was not discouraged, however. He objected, once again mobilized his advocates among the professors of the Polytechnic, and turned to the central Franconian government for help. But at first this, too, was in vain. His application was once again turned down since "poverty among the trader class is rising daily, leaving many honest fathers without food because no orders are being placed by the shops". At any rate he succeeded in setting some of the city fathers thinking and considering how to "keep such a skilful worker in our city". When, finally, in August, 1838, a master wood turner died, his licence – in spite of the long waiting list and against the will of the trade representatives – was awarded, "in view of his excellent skill", to Baudenbacher. In January, 1839, Caspar Baudenbacher was at last able to start his business as an independent master craftsman.

We have almost no knowledge regarding the early products from Baudenbacher's workshop. He sometimes produced small wooden pencils and cases, and in 1866 it is mentioned that he was manufacturing wooden toys and all kinds of utensils in large quantities. The quality of his products was said to have been excellent. As late as 1894, one reference book praised him as follows: "The ornamentation and the way in which his products were decorated were so diverse that they are still in frequent use in the wood turning trade today."[2]

Baudenbacher's products were not only appreciated in his home town: they were even given awards at the World Exhibitions in London in 1862 and in Philadelphia in 1876. In Philadelphia Baudenbacher presented exclusively "physical, mechanical and clockwork driven conjuring apparatus".[3] For several decades it was just these specialities which formed an important part of the range. It was no coincidence, incidentally, that the Baudenbacher company took part in these two World Exhibitions: England and the USA were their main export markets.

Caspar Baudenbacher's son Carl managed the company from 1870 on. Under his direction the workshop developed into a factory, the "Erste Nürnberger Holzspielwaarenfabrik" (First Nuremberg Wooden Toy Factory), as the business called itself in the last decade of the 19th century. At this time its production included a wealth of the most varied articles: "summer games, croquet, lawn tennis and cricket games, racquets, quoits, skipping ropes, spinning tops, cup-and-ball games, swings and gymnastic apparatus, conjuring sets and magic games, games of skittles and various parlour games". There were also "finely lacquered wooden goods such as Easter eggs, chocolate boxes and powder compacts in roughly 90 of the most diverse and fine patterns".[4]

A large format sample book issued by the company, probably dating from the 1850s, gives an excellent impression of the extent and variety of the range. An extremely vivid image of Baudenbacher's goods unfolds in 65 pages of splendid colour sketches. The product illustrations shown in the book are a great credit not only to the company but also to the artist (perhaps Caspar Baudenbacher himself?): the richness of detail, the tasteful choice of colours and above all the charmingly designed Vignettes featuring play scenes, combine to make the pattern book one of the finest of its kind.[5]

Hardly any information is available regarding the further history of C. Baudenbacher up to the takeover by Spear. It is not known how many employees the company had, and above all it is completely unclear why it was sold. At any rate we know from advertisements in specialist publications that the company's range of goods hardly changed over the years. From around the turn of the century, when a certain Mr. F. W. Conradi-Forster joined the management, the conjuring apparatus and sets certainly gained in significance. Conradi-Forster succeeded in "remodelling a considerable number of magic tricks for the family circle and, in fact, especially for the drawing room, which were otherwise only seen performed by professional artistes. In doing so, particular care was taken to ensure that operation of the apparatus was easy and could thus be carried out by the amateur, young or old".[6] The reputation of Baudenbacher's magic gadgets' even reached a middle-aged, aristocratic amateur – Emperor Wilhelm II. His Majesty had quite a large number of Baudenbacher's "little showpieces" ordered for the entertainment of his fellow travellers during the Hohenzollern trip to Scandinavia in 1901. Thus after dinner, to the amazement of all present, semi-concealed sailors would disappear from wooden boxes, skulls would move by themselves and magic wands dance through the air. Being purveyor of magic to the court was certainly good publicity for the Nuremberg magic masters and just as certainly an excellent recommendation for J. W. Spear & Söhne, who purchased Baudenbacher in 1919 and carried on the business as Section III of their concern.

1 The following account according to City of Nuremberg Archives, C7/II, No. 8392; C7/I, no. 18400; C22/IV, no. 13, p.53.
2 Hans Lotter (ed.), Großindustrie und Großhandel von Nürnberg, Fürth und Umgebung, Nuremberg 1894, p. 133
3 World Exhibition in Philadelphia, 1876: German Section, Official Catalogue, Berlin 1876, p. 66
4 Lotter, p. 133
5 The pattern sample book is part of the Spear Archives.
6 Wegweiser für die Spielwarenindustrie, No. 339 (1901), p. 7421

Ganze Größe.
die vordere Figur.

Ring=
Wurf=
Spiel. № 519

Some books from the range itself, which concentrated exclusively on one to six year-olds, seem — from today's point of view — just as old-fashioned as the Spear "letter grandpa". Animal books, such as "Wau Wau" ("Woof Woof"), "Glucke Glucke Henne" ("Cluck Cluck Hen") or "Muh! macht die Kuh" ("The Cow Says Moo"), dominate among the almost 100 titles which made up the picture and drawing book collection of 1925. "Little Red Riding Hood", "Snow White and the Seven Dwarfs", "Hansel and Gretel" and other illustrated editions of Grimms' classic fairy tales played just as important a role as books with children's games motifs such as "My Favourite Toys", "What Children Enjoy" or "Holiday Pleasures". Rhyme, song and ABC books were also to be found. Not to be forgotten are, finally, some stories whose object it is to warn or deter.[58]

In the 1920s, J. P. Werth and Josef Frank (speciality: illustrations of children and animals), Walter Heubach and Willy Tiedjen (animal illustrations), Otto Kubel (fairy tales), Bruno Grimmer (toys) and "Aunt Irma" alias Irma Graeff (illustrations of children) numbered among the busiest illustrators of Spear's children's books. Adolf Holst, Olga Pöhlmann, Karola Kellermann, Marie Sauer, Ferdinand Paumgarten and other authors made up the rhymes to go with the pictures.

Attempts were made to integrate the very heterogeneous aesthetic sense of these artists into a common design for the series, such as those purely involved in book publishing (Insel or Reclam) were doing. But these efforts rarely went beyond the fitting in of series names and of the publisher names on the books´ title pages. In particular they failed to develop a standardized typographical layout. Thus, all different kinds of typeface were used; indeed it could not even be decided whether preference should be given to script or printing, in their Latin or German versions. This did not exactly result in a very cohesive series. Furthermore, the book collection included several series with the most varying formats, from 16 x 11 cm up to 29 x 22 cm, without any sensible grading. Quite obviously there was no-one qualified at Spear who was in a position to give the book programme its own distinctive style. In Höfener Straße, Nuremberg there was never anyone like graphic artist Albertine Dependorf. She, as the wife of one of the owners of the Otto Maier Verlag in Ravensburg, successfully kept watch over visual presentation there from 1927 on and provided the company's programme with more consistent and more modern features.[59]

With respect to both content and layout the book programme of the 1920s thus offered more an impression of respectable mediocrity. Without any excursions into the style of the new functionalism, this line aimed to cater to the tastes of the broad public, which was not exactly keen on new ideas. In this respect the name of the collection, "What You Will" — with stress on the word "You" — , had been very aptly chosen. And there was one thing that the adult purchasing public certainly wanted for their little ones: the good-value, well produced and well printed books that Spear could easily offer. Starting with cheap books for 20 Pfennigs (eight illustrated paper pages, board cover with title picture in colour, 16 x 11 cm), the range extended across a large selection of medium price-category picture books (retail price one to two Marks) right up to the de-luxe editions for five Marks (20 polychrome plates on untearable board, 27 x 20 cm): there was something to suit every pocket in this programme.[60]

From at least 1924 on, the success of the picture book collection prompted the company's management to bring out quite a few of their parlour and activity games from Section I under the same name, some of them in a new form. In the main these were the well established dice games such as "Steeplechase", "The Game of Goose", "Snakes and Ladders" and "Ludo", and travel games such as "Die Schweizer Reise" (Swiss Jour-

B. Dondorf - Playing Card Factory

Over several decades the B. Dondorf playing card factory was one of the outstanding producers of de-luxe playing cards.[1] It was established in Frankfurt in 1833 by Bernhard Dondorf (1809 - 1902) as a Lithographic Printing Works. Dondorf was a lithographer by trade and he distinguished himself throughout his life by his technical inventiveness and excellent relations with leading artists and lithographers from his home town.

As in most such businesses, printing orders of all kinds were taken initially, but by 1840 Dondorf was already offering "printer's implements", such as chalks, Indian inks and litho stones, as well as copperplate or lithographic printing presses. It was at this time that playing cards first appeared in his extensive range, but at first they seem hardly to have found much circulation. Playing card production expanded more and more from the end of the 1850s on. Whereas steel engraving was still preferred at the beginning, chromolithography won through as the predominant printing technique. The construction of a new factory in 1871 was an important prerequisite for the manufacture of luxury paper articles, which was now starting up on a large scale. After the move Bernhard Dondorf could retire and pass on management to his sons Carl and Paul and to his son-in-law, Jacob Fries. In the following period, the concern expanded its activities with great success and managed to acquire an excellent reputation world-wide in the area of high quality playing cards. Particularly the Nordic states, the Netherlands and southern Europe ranked among the main sales areas for Dondorf's decks.

Happy Families by Dondorf, around 1932

Original designs, best graphic rendering of these and excellent printing all commended the de-luxe card games to a discriminating middle-class public. But even the standard pictures produced in large numbers for the less well-off purchaser, still maintained the House of Dondorf's high quality standards. Production reached its peak during the First World War as a result of the enormous demand from the armed forces. In the financial year 1916/17 no less than 8.2 million decks, each of up to 36 cards, were manufactured. The figures dropped considerably in the 1920s. Now a process of concentration also began in the area of playing card production, and the market-leader Vereinigte Altenburger und Stralsunder Spielkartenfabriken (ASS) was to profit particularly. In the meantime headed by the third generation, Dondorf GmbH also fell victim to this economic development: the whole concern had to be sold in 1929. The company management cited the reasons as being the „excessive diversity of the business operations" and "losses resulting from the war and the period of inflation".[2] Dondorf's six departements (playing cards, lithographic printing, paper coating, games publishing, paper requisites and labels) were taken over by six different concerns. The games were purchased by J. W. Spear & Söhne.

With Dondorf, Spear took over a big name – just as with Baudenbacher and Neiff – and was once again able to increase the value of its own range. Although Dondorf's card and parlour games had in fact been overshadowed by their de-luxe playing cards, the company had been offering quality in the former area for some time. Presumably Dondorf had been bringing out all sorts of Happy Families, Old Maid, Question and Answer games, Snap, Picture Dominoes and even some dice games such as "Rennsport" (At the Races) or "Die Ernte" (The Harvest) as early as the 1870s (the exact date when production began is not known). A list cites 40 articles altogether, some of which were brought out in several languages.[3] In the opinion of one authoritative collector: in buying this range of games from Dondorf, Spear secured themselves "litho stones and the rights to the most beautifully made Happy Families and Old Maid games Germany had had up until that time".[4]

1 The following account is based on Franz Braun, Die Spielkartenfabrik B. Dondorf, Cologne 1991 and Detleff Hoffmann/Margot Dietrich, Die Dondorf'schen Luxus-Spielkarten, Dortmund 1981.
2 "Werdegang der Firma B. Dondorf, Frankfurt a/M", Typescript in Deutsches Spielkarten Museum (Playing Cards Museum), Leinfelden-Echterdingen (post 1933, anonymous). Quotation from Hoffmann/Dietrich, p. 43.
3 Braun, p. 128 f.
4 Ernst Krumbein, "Spier oder Spear? Zur Geschichte eines Spielkartenverlags", in fachdienst spiel, issue 5+6 (1995), p.6

ney) and "Durchs Bayernland" (Across Bavaria), but Spear classic "The Piggeries" and some activity games such as "Möbel-Flechten" (plaiting furniture) and sewing pictures were also represented. Apparently the "What You Will" games collection formed the old core of the company's range, and was intended as the trademark for tried and tested games of high entertainment and activity value.

Some of the illustrators who were involved in the picture book collection also worked on the redesigning of the games collection. Mentioned by name in the catalogues and to some extent also on the games themselves are J. P. Werth ("Auf und Ab" ladder game, "Gluck Gluck" chicken game) and Otto Kubel ("Der Wolf und die 7 Geißlein" and "Die Bremer Stadtmusikanten" fairy tale games). "Aunt Irma" (Graeff), too, contributed to a modernization of these popular articles for smaller children with her redesigning of numerous puzzles. Her modernly dressed and colourful little heroes were now allowed to experience adventures in the style and at the speed of the new era: Now one could go "Im Auto über Land" (Through the Country by Car), and "Die glückliche Reise" (The Happy Journey) showed scenes from a train journey. "Butzi", Aunt Irma's comic dog, which accompanied the children as playmate in many pictures, was right in the fashion of the 1920s.[61]

With Section III, formerly C. Baudenbacher, J.W. Spear & Söhne could offer a high quality range of sports and summer toys such as badminton, skipping ropes, quoits, garden croquet and diabolos. Skittles, spinning tops or table croquet were more for indoors. The skittles games, especially, were distinguished by fine lacquering, bright colours and some also by a novel figured decoration. In 1930, for example, the English public could choose from three sizes and ten different figures, such as clown, farmer, policeman, sailor or rabbit.[62] In addition to these, mixed skittles games (for instance: three clowns, three "little Negroes",

three policemen) and "Tom Thumb Skittles" taken from motifs from the "Winzli-Wusch" picture book people, likewise published by Spear, were available exclusively in Germany.[63]

The flagship among the products from the former Baudenbacher company had been the conjurer's set. Spear of course continued this tradition all the more gladly since the company could profit particularly well from this speciality's good reputation. Spear registered the "Hokus-Pokus" trademark for their new conjurer's sets in April, 1919, just shortly after taking over the company. A wide range of magic articles was offered under this name from then on. Thus in 1924, for example, there was a choice, all in all, of 24 different versions. Prices ranged from cheap sets at 50 Pfennigs, with just five gadgets, to the luxury edition for 11.85 Marks which, with its 28 different tricks, almost allowed for a whole evening's magic entertainment.[64]

As was the case with C. Baudenbacher, Spear carried on the tradition of another company they had taken over, incorporating it into Section IV, set up in 1927. It was headed by Mr. and Mrs. Neiff, who also brought some of their experienced personnel into the concern. A large number of Neiff articles were kept on, but the lavish doll's furniture was soon discontinued. Without doubt the Spear range of handicrafts and doll's clothes and accessories experienced considerable expansion and qualitative improvement as a result of the Neiff takeover. Decades later members of the Spear family still spoke extremely highly of the imagination and the great craftsmanship of the Neiff family and their staff.[65]

From 1928 on, the most essential innovations in the Neiff-Spear range to come onto the market were various handwork gadgets for knitting, weaving and knotting; these, in all their variations, were directed at girls of kindergarten and school age as well as at grown up women. A forerunner, from 1926, was the well-known "Knitting Nancy",

G. Neiff - Toy Factory

As was the case with the Caspar Baudenbacher company, the G. Neiff Toy Factory also developed from a crafts concern.[1] Company founder Friedrich Wilhelm Gustav Neiff was born in Berlin in 1817. He trained as a bookbinder, and after his examination to become a journeyman, went off on his travels. He worked in Nuremberg for three years and it was there he met Barbara, daughter of a Nuremberg precision instrument maker, who was later to become his wife. Gustav Neiff attained the title of "Master" in 1843, after returning to his home city of Berlin. In the same year he set up as a self-employed bookbinder and married his Nuremberg bride. The marriage began under tragic circumstances: Barbara Neiff bore three children within a short space of time, but all of them died shortly after birth. As a result the sorely afflicted young woman felt drawn back to her home town. Her husband gave in to her yearnings and in 1848, the year of revolution, they moved back to Nuremberg.

Doll's trousseau from Neiff's catalogue, 1908

Unlike Caspar Baudenbacher, Gustav Neiff was not without means when he began to build himself a new existence in Nuremberg. He purchased a house for 5,600 florins and with it the right to run a public house. He did have to take on a considerable amount of debt for this purpose, but Neiff was confident he could "feed himself as publican, and acquire a clientele", confidence which was also shared by an official observer after a sort of probationary period: "Neiff goes to a lot of trouble to make a living and already has a steady clientele, and so I believe that he will be able to continue as landlord of this establishment". That is why as early as August, 1848, he was granted definitive permission to set up as "citizen and publican" in Nuremberg.

In view of the well-known rigid stance of his fellow bookbinders with regard to new competitors, Neiff did not even try to get a licence as a bookbinder, though he secured himself a permit for the "production of modest cardboard articles". He wanted to obtain additional income with these cheap articles for everyday use, toys certainly being among them. This secondary activity, however, gained in importance, so that in 1853 Gustav Neiff gave up his public house and from then on worked solely as manufacturer of card toys.[2]

Nuremberg address books show that Neiff's small business moved several times within the Old Town before his son, Georg took over and set up a "toy factory" at Brunnengasse 15, around 1875. In the same year, in the trade register for Nuremberg-Fürth, the following entry can be found: "G. Neiff, Fine Toys, Activity Games".[3] It follows from this that his range had already extended further than those original card toys. First evidence of a Neiff game was presented in the 1886 volume of the "Guide to the Toy Industry". It was the game of skill "Es geht" (Labyrinth): the aim of the game was to roll different coloured balls into the correspondingly marked holes in the base of a little wooden box by means of skilful balancing. In the "Guide's" view this original game of skill offered an "inexhaustible source of the merriest humour and entertainment".[4]

In 1896 the company was already describing itself confidently in an advertisement as the "oldest, most efficient factory for Fröbel and activity games". The reference to Friedrich Fröbel established a connection with a wealth of activities such as picture making, weaving, folding, sewing, pinning etc., whose aim it was to foster children's manual dexterity and aesthetic feeling by way of guided, playful use of materials such as paper, raffia, wood, cloth and thread. Clearly activity games of this kind now formed the main focus of the range. A series of advertisements, however, also appeared in the "Guide" in the same year, for parlour games, lotto games, doll's dressmaking kits, trousseaus, picture books and new puzzles in the style of "Labyrinth". In the following years such varied articles as an "Elementary Ready-Reckoner" for adding, subtracting, multiplying and dividing (1902), a "work doll", whose clothes had to be sewn and embroidered (1902) or "Debit and Credit" (1904), a book-keeping game for the "young businessman" were added to the list.

The scope of the product range in the first decade of the 20th century can be seen in an attractively designed G. Neiff Toy Factory catalogue.[5] The fact that the catalogue is presented in five languages indicates that the company was by this time already working for a broad international market. In 48 pages a varied range unfolds, organized into three sections: the first and most extensive section contains "Fröbel and activity games for boys and girls. Puzzles. Conjuring sets". Apart from the classic Fröbel games, which were also produced in the same period and in similar form by Spear, the range encompasses fretwork sets, wood and cork construction sets, plasticine pictures, lovely bead sets and puzzles.

"Doll's clothes and accessories" formed the second section. Along with doll's trousseaus and suitcases in every size and price range, theme sets with groups of dolls, arranged in pretty ensembles, with such eloquent titles as "The First Step", "Come and Play With Me", "I Want to Be a Soldier" or "Mummy Doll's Wash-Day" are to be found. Well appointed bath-houses, beach sets or baby's changing units with or without dolls left hardly any girl's dreams unfulfilled. Generously equipped doll's dressmaking kits allowed for the creation of doll's clothes; some of these even had a fully functional children's sewing machine. The teddy craze of the time might have been what prompted Neiff also to include "The Little Soft Toy Maker" in its range. Along with instructions and pattern sheets this fine set included the materials necessary for the production of soft toys "which can be used as toys or as practical articles, such as pin cushions and the like". Margarete Steiff was undoubtedly the inspiration for this kit: recalling the little pin cushion elephant that started her soft toy success story, in the Swabian town of Giengen, in 1880, a little elephant, of all things, is enclosed as a completed sample.

Finally, Section III incorporates an extraordinarily diverse range of embroidery and crochet kits. Children could embroider, using wood and raffia, and following printed outlines, on white or grey linen, evenweave, felt, Javanese fabrics, ribbons or napkins. All these articles were offered in many sizes and price ranges. G. Neiff undoubtedly catered to the great respect shown in all social classes for handwork as an important part of a girl's education.

Hardly any clues are available as to Neiff's further development, though an undated catalogue from the mid 1920s does provide some information regarding the development of the range.[6] Overall, the product range was reduced; puzzles and games of skill, with the exception of conjuring sets, are no longer to be found. The well-known articles dominate within both main sections, doll's clothes and accessories, and activity games. An assortment of white lacquered wooden doll's furniture, such as wardrobes, chests of drawers, baby's changing tables, cradles, playpens and little beds with an extensive range of linen and clothing accessories. A little knitting device and bead weaving loom were introduced as new articles. This area was the subject of a thorough technical development following the takeover by Spear. For decades, weaving looms and knitting devices were to remain popular articles in the crafts area.

J. W. Spear & Söhne bought the Neiff toy factory in 1927. The old factory in Nuremberg's city centre was given up and production transferred to a new building at the factory site in Höfener Straße. From then on Neiff Toys constituted Section IV at Spear. It was headed by Mr. and Mrs. Neiff, who also brought some of their experienced personnel into the new concern. A large number of Neiff articles were kept on, but the lavish doll's furniture was soon discontinued. Without doubt the Spear range was considerably expanded and improved as a result of the Neiff takeover. Decades later members of the Spear family spoke exceedingly highly of the imagination and the great craftsmanship of the Neiff family and their staff.[7]

1 Account from the City of Nuremberg Archives, C/7II, No. 5267

2 Entry in trade register occurred on 18th November, 1852 (City of Nuremberg Archives, C 22/V,7, page 734), but actual opening of business seems not to have occurred until 1853. In any case the company itself always stated 1853 as year of foundation.

3 This entry also mentioned "Wunderknäuel". Theses were the forerunners of the lucky bag. Strictly in accordance with the educational motto "no sweet without sweat", a large ball of wool with a toy or other small item hidden at its centre only surrendered its "marvel" when the wool was all knitted up.

4 Wegweiser, No. 4 (1886), p. 38

5 "G. Neiff. Spielwaren-Fabrik Nürnberg." The catalogue is undated, but a comparison with the company's advertisements reveals that 1908 was very probably the year of publication. A copy is to be found in the Toy Museum´s archives.

6 "G. Neiff. Spielwaren-Fabrik Nürnberg". A Copy is to be found in the Toy Museum's archives.

7 Spear Archives: Record of conversation regarding company history, of 3.2.1974, p. 29 f.

a simple knitting gadget in the form of a nicely painted figure wearing a crown of curved metal loops. With the aid of a steel knitting needle, even little girls could knit brightly coloured woollen cords, which then, with help from older sisters or their mothers, could be sewn up to make covers, little bags or items of doll's clothing. The "Knitting Ring" followed in 1928, a circular knitting gadget the aim of which was to show girls how to produce nice little items such as napkin rings, coat hanger covers, egg cosies or wristlets. The introduction of the "Kwiknit" in 1929 meant that children and adults could learn to knit woollen goods of all kinds. Spear praised the merits of this gadget in the 1933 catalogue as follows: " Operation and learning are uniquely simple. No stitches can be dropped. Produces wonderfully evenly-knitted rows. One can produce well-knitted, fine and extremely elegant knitting: cushions, scarves, cardigans and pullovers, dresses and whatever else one needs… The new "Kwiknit" pays for itself with the first hand-knitted garment."[66]

Against the background of high unemployment resulting from the world economic crisis, this cost-saving aspect was, of course, particularly important. At the same time it marks the (perfectly fluid) transition from child's activity game to useful adult enterprise. With the motto "handwoven is very fashionable", Spear's advertising for the newly developed "Luise", "Irene" and "Annemarie" looms was now directed above all at the fashion- and cost-conscious housewife. "Cut down your spending on dresses with the 'Annemarie' loom!", a brochure appealed to the customer, calculating that with "Annemarie" a "charming light ladies' waistcoat and matching skirt" could be made for just 9.65 Marks, the cost of materials. Admittedly, the purchase price of 14 Marks for the largest loom had to be added to this.[67] But presumably for a woman with skill this purchase would indeed pay for itself by the second homewoven item of clothing, as was suggested in the company's own customer magazine "Kwiknit News".[68]

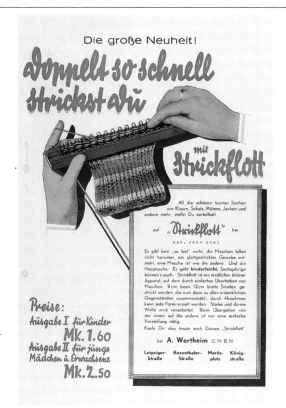

Advertising flyer for „Strickflott" (Kwiknit), 1932

So "weave and save" was the handy phrase with which new areas of customers were to be reached in the 1930s. There is no doubt the company wanted to create a further base. And this was not only necessitated by the generally bad economic situation: with the seizure of power by the National Socialists in January, 1933, the way was paved for difficult times for Spear, as it was for all Jewish concerns and families in Germany. In this situation a decision bearing serious consequences taken three years previously proved particularly far-sighted: 41 years after closing their first London branch, Spears had once again formed a British subsidiary. The leap across the Channel ensured not only the company's continued existence for the next decades; England was also to become a safe haven for most members of the entrepreneurial Spear family.

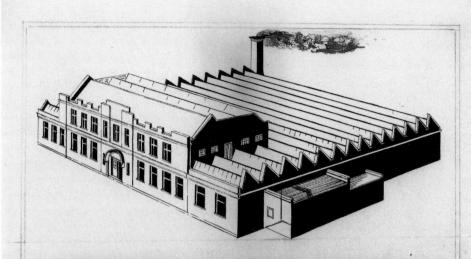

SPEAR'S GAMES

We have pleasure in informing you that we have now

Established a factory in this country

for the manufacture of:-

GAMES & KINDERGARTEN PASTIMES.

ENCLOSURE Nº702

J W SPEAR & SONS LTD

London Showrooms and registered offices

10-12 MILTON STREET LONDON E.C.2.

WORKS GREEN STREET BRIMSDOWN ENFIELD MIDDX.

FULL RANGE OF SAMPLES INCLUDING NEW LINES FOR 1932
ON SHOW AT

MANCHESTER	GLASGOW	NEWCASTLE	BIRMINGHAM	BRISTOL
DEANSGATE HOTEL	CENTRAL STOCKRODING 82 UNION STREET	CENTRAL EXCHANGE HOTEL	THE GRAND HOTEL	THE GRAND HOTEL
23RD MAY-2ND JUNE	15TH MAY-18TH MAY	9TH MAY-12TH MAY	MAY 9TH-MAY 12TH	MAY 16TH-MAY 20TH

Spear's of Enfield

Essentially the company management had two reasons for founding a British subsidiary, in December, 1930. In the wake of the world economic crisis the British government had resorted to imposing high import duties on foreign finished products. Secondly, the government had withdrawn its national currency from the gold standard, leading to a drastic devaluation of the British pound in relation to the Reichsmark. As Richard Spear outlined the situation at the time: "Taken together, both these facts made us uncompetitive. We had to choose between giving up the English business, which was the largest, or starting up over there."[69] Basically they had no other choice, if the company was to survive: Thus Richard Spear was given the task of building up the J. W. Spear & Sons Ltd. subsidiary in London, while his brother Hermann remained responsible for the Nuremberg factory.

Initially the activities of the English company were restricted to ordering goods from Nuremberg and selling them with the help of former Spear importers, G. Greiner & Co. It soon became clear, however, that in the long term the only promising solution was to set up their own production in the British Isles. In looking for suitable factory premises, Richard Spear struck it lucky in Enfield, a highly industrialized suburb in the north of London. A sign factory had erected a large new building in Green Street (in the Brimsdown district) but because of the poor economic situation this was now partly empty. Richard Spear rented 1400 square metres (15.000 square feet) of space there, and with a team of four technical and commercial staff from Nuremberg, prepared to start up production. Among these were foreman Leonhard Bachner, who was responsible for production, and young businessman Fritz Kahn, who had been working for Spear since 1928 and who was to become a director and head of sales. Raw materials, tools, toy components and part of the necessary machinery were transported from Nuremberg, but it soon became clear that the latter were not completely suitable for English conditions. In Enfield, machines for certain production operations – such as covering games boxes – were being used, which were not yet

J. W. Spear & Sons factory in Green Street, Enfield, 1932. Production began in premises rented in this new, partly vacant factory complex belonging to a sign maker's.

used in Germany because the work could be done cheaper by hand there. Recruiting workers was no problem. On the contrary: In times of mass unemployment each newly created job could have been filled several times over. Spear's of Enfield took up production on 1st April, 1932, with around 20 workers and capital of £8,000.[70]

It was agreed from the beginning that Enfield was principally to be responsible for the production and sale of all products for English-speaking countries. Thus the British colonies and North America were to be supplied from England, too. Products in all other languages continued to be produced in Nuremberg and sold from there. The respective ranges hardly differed from each other in the 1930s. This is not surprising, for traditionally Spear's had oriented themselves very strongly on the needs of the British market.

"Spear Works Bavaria, boxed in England": As these imprints on games boxes reveal, at the beginning game boards and game components often still came from Nuremberg, only being boxed in Enfield. This changed relatively soon, however, for as National Socialist policies drove Germany into isolation, the possibilities for international trade and communication worsened.

The spacious Nuremberg site provided an ideal chicken run, the chicken being bred by chauffeur Franz Krucker and his family. The picture shows his daughter Betty. The bosses were, of course, among her customers.

Inevitably the British subsidiary gained in independence, and from around the mid 1930s produced complete games in the factory in Green Street. Richard Spear commuted regularly between England and Germany during the first years. Fürth remained his main place of residence, however; his wife Gertraud and both his sons, Ralph (born 1929) and Francis Alfred (born 1931) lived there. But increasing National Socialist repression of the Jewish population gradually brought about the decision to emigrate to England. Richard Spear applied for permission for his family to leave the country and was finally granted permission to emigrate, taking with him furniture and other personal belongings. The Spear family arrived in England on 15th March, 1935, building up a new home in Enfield thereafter. This involved both emotional burdens and financial difficulties. Since the German authorities had forbidden Richard Spear to take more than a small amount of money with him, most of his wealth remained tied up in German bank accounts. After lengthy negotiations, however, he at least managed to have half of large delivery from the Nuremberg Spear factory to Enfield paid from the blocked private accounts. Thus he succeeded in transferring at least part of the blocked capital to England, where it was urgently needed not only for the family but also for the further building up of the company.

World-class company for free

In Germany the J. W. Spear & Söhne parent company and its owners had to suffer increasingly under the Nazi regime. The boycott of German goods by some foreign countries, above all by England and the USA, as a reaction to the aggressive, anti-democratic and anti-Semitic politics of the National Socialists, hit a mainly exporting company like Spear particularly badly. At home some customers were influenced by the National Socialist boycott of Jewish businesses and the slander campaigns which went along with this, and broke off business connections with Spear for fear of possible reprisals. As a result of these developments turnover fell drastically: While in business year 1931/32 it still stood at over 2.6 million Reichsmarks, it sank to 1.2 million by 1936/37. The large drops in turnover had consequences for the profits, of course. The concern, so used to success – in 1926/27, a record year, the profit realized was 340,700 Reichsmarks – had to record a continual drop. From business year 1934/35 onward the company was no longer operating profitably and in the three years following, it was in the red. No-one was made redundant at Spear, however; the number of employees even increased slightly – from 294 in 1932/33 to 324 in 1937/38.[71]

According to a testimony by former members of staff, there was a good relationship between employees and management at Spear prior to 1933. This certainly was not only due to the fact that wages at Spear were above the going rate.[72] A remark by former foreman, Leonhard Bachner, to his daughter is characteristic: "They're always talking so badly of the Jews, but there's no Christian who can compete with the Spears!"[73] Or in the words of the chauffeur's daughter: "The Spears, they did everything for their workers".[74] After 1933, however, the National Socialist ideology increasingly made itself felt within the company, too: Nazi activists were rude to former members of staff visiting from England, who also discovered a poster in the factory: "Beware! There are traitors among you!"[75] Party members from the "Deutsche Arbeitsfront" (DAF – German Workers' Front), under the leadership of the not yet 20 year-old Party member Friedrich Burr, had a decisive influence on the company's works council and pressurized management with all kinds of demands. The motto was "to harm the Jews whenever possible".[76] Thus in April, 1938 Hermann Spear was forced to agree to the dissolving of the company's own pension and welfare fund. The money was to be used for the construction of a clubhouse and canteen. Hermann

Spear was to contribute the remaining funds required to reach the estimated total sum of 40,000 Reichsmarks.[77] When he refused, in view of the company's precarious financial situation, the workers' council issued the DAF an ultimatum just a few weeks before the November pogrom "to appoint an Aryan manager immediately".[78] At the same time rabble-rousing letters

Hermann Spear (second from right) with members of the sales staff in the company's sample room, around 1930.

from a "German businessman" were published in the Nazi newspaper "Der Stürmer" against the "Jewish company of Spear & Söhne", which were to pillory the company. The offence: five years after the Nazi's coming to power they were still signing their letters "with best regards" and not with "Heil Hitler"![79]

The enormous pressure Hermann Spear saw himself exposed to at work was accompanied by the daily anti-Semitism in his private life. His only son, Herbert (born 1924) was made painfully aware of the exclusion of the Jews from the "national community" which was implemented everywhere after the Nazi's came to power. At school he was suddenly sworn at, called "bloody Jew", whereas he had never been exposed before to any anti-Semitic bad language whatsoever. In view of the fact that his mother, Else, came from a respected, Protestant Fürth family the only thing he could think of in his child's naïvety was to answer "I'm not a bloody Jew, I'm a half-Jew". He certainly had to learn that it did not make any difference whether you came from an orthodox home, or from a liberal home in which the Jewish religion – just as with almost all members of the Spear families – only played a subordinate role. The racism of his Christian fellow citizens affected even him, the baptized and confirmed Protestant. In 1935, like many other families, Hermann and Else Spear were also forced to sack their young "Aryan" maid and take on an older woman. The time of the Nazi Party Rallies, at the beginning of September each year, always led to particularly drastic hostility and rioting against Jews in Nuremberg and Fürth. Not least for this reason did the parents ensure that their son spent the summer in far-off children's holiday camps or later went to summer schools abroad, while they themselves left the city during this time.[80]

The life of suffering experienced by German Jews at the time of National Socialism is reflected in the fate of Hermann Spear's family. The years of exclusion, deprivation of rights and intimidation culminated in the organized pogrom of 9th/10th November, 1938. During this night the family was turned out of bed by SA men at five o'clock in the morning and driven from their flat at Bahnhofsplatz to Fürther Freiheit Square, where numerous other victims were already waiting. Under guard, the assembled Jews had to march to the Berholzheimerianum [an adult education centre established by the Jewish businessman Berholzheimer] and there undergo extensive interrogation. On the same day, Hermann Spear was deported to the concentration camp at Dachau. Else Spear and her son were permitted to return home.

Just a few days later the machinery of Aryanization was already in full swing. Else Spear was forced to sell her private car, just two years old, to the Fürth SA, for a ridiculous 100 Marks (list price: 4,975 Marks).[81] At the factory, notorious Party representative, Friedrich Burr was appointed as new temporary works manager. At the beginning of December, 1938 the company premises were "aryanized" in favour of deputy Gauleiter Karl Holz, at ten per cent of the estimated current market value of roughly 260,000 Reichsmarks. At this time the Aryanization authorities found an entrepreneur who was interested in buying the games factory, one who was no stranger across the country: Hanns Porst, owner of the highly successful photographic company of the same name. Porst was a real self-made man who had left his job as a clerk with the City of Nuremberg in order to open up a small photographic shop. Against the backdrop of the great enthusiasm for photography in the 1920s, he managed to rise to owning the largest photographic company in the world in an amazingly short period of time, thanks to his distinct entrepreneurial talent. He was a model entrepreneur, whose business during the "Third Reich" even found its way into a sort of "hall of fame" of the German economy which presented in book form businesses run in an exemplary manner.[82]

SA troops marching past the Spear factory in Höfener Straße.
This impressive photograph by Fürth photographer Ferdinand Vizethum was presumably taken
during the NSDAP Party Rally in September, 1938.

Hanns Porst, around 1960

Reichsmarks.[85] Else Spear, who was having to fear the worst for her husband in custody in Dachau, heard rumours of all this and asked Porst at least to do what he could for her imprisoned husband in return: "Listen, Mr. Porst, I've heard stories. Can you help me get my husband out of Dachau?" – "Yes, I need him, he has to sign for things", Porst was said to have answered. Indeed he did then succeed in getting Hermann Spear released from the concentration camp.[86]

Hanns Porst was appointed new temporary manager by the Aryanization Office on 13.12.1938, after making a preliminary contract with Hermann Spear regarding the sale of the company. Porst really showed his appreciation: At the "suggestion" of the Aryanization officer, he handed over a cheque in the sum of 20,000 Reichsmarks to the "Deutsche Arbeitsfront" – against the Spear business account! A large proportion of the money was immediately used to finance a Christmas party for the employees of the DAF.[87] Thus the Jewish dispossessed also had to sweeten Christmas for those Christians who had dispossessed them.

While Porst began reorganizing the company with great zeal in accordance with his own ideas, the actual sales contract was drawn up in negotiations which lasted for months. Since two of the part owners, Richard Spear and his sister Emilie, lived abroad, Hermann Spear and the fourth partner, his uncle Wilhelm, who still lived in Fürth, were forced to obtain an unlimited power of attorney from them. Fearing for the safety of their relatives they granted the powers of attorney, while at the same time Richard Spear endeavoured to obtain an immigration permit for Hermann and Else from the British authorities. He succeeded in this, but the German authorities made the exit dependent on the completion of the Aryanization procedures.

Since Porst tried everything to get the price down, the negotiations regarding the final

Although Porst was completely unfamiliar with the trade, the Chamber of Industry and Commerce had already asked him at the end of 1937 whether he would be interested in taking over J. W. Spear & Söhne. The company would suit his capabilities and "above all demand a lot of taste and good organizational talent", as the photo businessman later wrote. "As a result I had a look at the Spear company from the outside and regarded it as really workable."[83] Since he did not want to go into the factory, he unwound a ball of string along the front of the building in Höfener Straße, which he later measured at home in order to get at least an impression of the concern's dimensions.[84] This initial contact had no consequences at first; Porst was not (yet) interested in purchase negotiations. He acted fast when, following the pogrom night, the Aryanization Office suggested he should take over Spear's for the ridiculously small sum of 100,000

"Aryanization" in Nuremberg and Fürth [1]

Since the mid 19th century Jewish merchants and industrialists had played a considerable part in Nuremberg's rise to becoming the industrial heart of Bavaria. Their entrepreneurial drive, especially in retailing and wholesaling, in the building of world-wide exports, in banking and in important areas of industrial production contributed to Nuremberg's becoming an important economic location with international connections during the time of the Weimar Republic. One only has to remember, for example, that it was mainly due to the activities of numerous Jewish hops trading companies that Nuremberg had long been the world's leading exchange for the "green gold". Nuremberg's ranking as city of toys of international standing, would also have been unthinkable without Jewish merchants and industrialists. On a purely numerical basis, according to a survey of 1930 only 29 of the 273 Nuremberg toy trading and production companies were owned wholly or in part by Jewish citizens, but among those were such eminent companies as the Bing-Werke (largest toy factory in the world), Schreyer & Co., Trix, Tipp & Co., Josef Krauss & Co., Georg Kellermann & Co., Johann Distler, Josef Falk, Gebr. Einfalt, Bechmann & Ullmann, Cuno and Otto Dressel, C. Abel-Klinger and, of course, also J. W. Spear & Söhne. The situation was similar in Fürth, where numerous export companies dealing in fancy goods and toys, such as L. Bierer, M. Apfelbaum, Eisenmann & Co., Moses Kohnstamm, Hans Rindskopf, S. D. Zimmer and toy producers such as L. Kleefeld & Co., Menki Zimmer or G. Löwensohn were resident.

According to the afore-mentioned survey by the secretary of the Jewish Religious Community, Bernhard Kolb, in 1930 there was a total of 865 businesses with Jewish owners or partners in Nuremberg. By the end of 1935 the number had already dropped to 728; at the same time in Fürth the number was barely 500 out of a total of around 5,700 companies listed in the Nuremberg-Fürth trade register. A further four years later all remaining Jewish companies were in the hands of "Aryan" owners or had been wound up. This was the sad result of the National Socialist policy which from 1933 onwards used all possible means to drive the Jews out of economic, cultural and social life in Germany.

The Nazi regime used brute force as well as a wealth of pseudo legal measures to this end, gradually depriving the Jews of their civil rights and their wealth, and thus at the same time paving the way for the Holocaust. Between 1933 and 1945 over 400 laws, decrees, edicts and orders appeared, creating "special legislation" for Jews. Within the framework of this policy, the elimination of Jewish business people from trade, crafts and industry had a special

status for the Nazis. With it, they met on the one hand the wishes of sections of the non-Jewish business world who hoped to rid themselves of unwanted competition, while on the other hand the Nazi regime wanted to get hold of Jewish assets.

The "lawful", nationwide "elimination of the Jews from Germany's economic life" did not begin until 1938. Franconian Gauleiter and fanatical anti-Semite Julius Streicher and his clique, however, had already generated a latent pogrom atmosphere in the previous years in Nuremberg and Fürth by means of slander, boycotting measures and physical violence; this led earlier than elsewhere to numerous Jewish business people having to sell their concerns and emigrate. Complaints about the Nazi terror, which at this time was not covered by any legal regulations whatsoever, were pointless; the local administration and judicial authorities declared their helplessness against the all-pervading power of the self-appointed "Frankenführer" (Franconian Leader).

In 1934, for example, in a completely unauthorized interpretation of a relevant imperial law, Streicher succeeded in ordering that every Jewish employer had to have a National Socialist representative, with independent decision-making powers, in his concern. This special Nuremberg provision was unique in the country and vividly illustrates the criminal energy with which, under the motto "Franconia first", Streicher and his retinue wanted to remove the Jews from his realm of power. As one of Adolf Hitler's few close friends, Streicher could be sure of the "Führer's" approval in this. Thus even the Minister of Trade and Commerce, Hjalmar Schacht, could do nothing but advise his old friends in Nuremberg's Jewish business world "to rescue what can be rescued and emigrate", after the Nuremberg Racial Laws were decreed in September, 1935. Although these unholy laws initially had no economic implications he suspected, not without good reason, that Streicher would push ahead with the dispossession of Jewish companies entirely on his own authority.

When, in April, 1938, the phase of state-legitimized "Aryanization" began with numerous new government decrees, the Nuremberg and Fürth National Socialists felt encouraged finally to realize their great aim of removing the Jews completely from the regional economy by their own methods. According to the state regulations, Aryanization contracts required approval by the municipal departments or regional administration. The Gauleitung and the Chambers of Industry and Commerce were to be involved in the Aryanization proceedings. Only in exceptional cases, which required special consent, were officials of the National Socialist Party and of its subdivisions to be considered as potential new owners of Jewish companies. Moreover they were forbidden to accept any financial contributions or "donations" from prospective buyers. The object of these regulations was to have the Aryanization of businesses carried out by state organisations in order to ensure that the large profits expected from Aryanization flowed into the state's coffers and not into the pockets of corrupt party members. All these legal precautions missed their target completely within the Franconian Gauleiter's sphere of influence. Here the Aryanizations became purely the concern of the Party, the authorities functioning as mere enforcers of the will of the "Frankenführer" and his retinue, who shamelessly made their fortunes, especially when the very last scruples were forgotten following the November Pogrom of 1938. The extraordinary brutality shown towards the Jewish population in Nuremberg and Fürth during the night of 9th/10th November – of 91 pogrom victims nationwide, 26 died in these two cities alone – continued in the weeks which followed, during the period of compulsory expropriation of Jewish property.

The procedure for this followed a basic pattern: "A company spokesman acceptable to the Party was appointed to a Jewish company. The Jewish owner made out to him an irrevocable power of attorney on a form provided. Then Strobl[2] and/or the representative of the appropriate branch of industry negotiated with the person interested in taking over the business. The role of the Jewish owners was taken on by the appointed company spokesman. He and the prospective buyer could together choose a valuer. The valuers were experts; they determined the value of the business. This was then agreed as the purchase price. The contracts were drafted according to a particular plan. According to the contracts, the buyer had to pay either nothing or a disproportionately low price for fittings and machinery. He only paid for stock and business premises. The value of the stock was set very low. Government authorization was merely a formality. After the authorization was effected, the agreed purchase price was not paid to the Jews but credited to a blocked account ... Shares owned by Jews, too, were deposited in a blocked account. In addition, the debts and liabilities of the Jewish sellers were debited to the appropriate account for the respective branch of industry. These were not taken on by the purchaser of the business. The Jews were also granted a cost of living allowance from the blocked account, according to their need (which had mostly just been created). Only the representatives for the Aryanization of the relevant branch of industry were authorised to draw on these accounts."[3] Any resistance on the part of the dispossessed to this Aryanization machinery, which included estate agents, land registry officials and notaries public, was broken by threats, arrests and physical violence.

The present state of the records makes it impossible to determine the exact extent of dispossession carried out in Nuremberg and Fürth in the way described. It is probable, however, that the great majority of the more than 700 Nuremberg companies still Jewish-owned at the end of 1935 were not "Aryanized" or liquidated until 1938/39. The profit realized can no longer be estimated accurately either, but according to an enquiry commissioned by the NSDAP, 33 large companies "Aryanized" after 9.11.1938 alone accounted for over 14.3 million Reichsmarks. In addition over 600 properties in Jewish ownership worth over 20 million Reichsmarks were expropriated. All Jewish owned vehicles, too – more than 300 in both cities – were forcibly transferred to new owners after the November pogrom.

In the course of the Aryanization measures in Nuremberg and Fürth there were numerous cases of private moneymaking on the part of the party officials involved. At the same time the coffers of all sorts of Party subdivisions were filled from these stolen fortunes and from the more or less voluntary "donations" of "Aryan" buyers. The scale of corruption and of infringements of procedures laid down by the German government led to Field Marshal Hermann Göring appointing an investigating committee in 1939, which ultimately uncovered the machinations of the Streicher clique. The results of the investigation led in the end to the Gauleiter's losing his power within the Party and to a diversion of the Aryanization profits to state accounts. Not one of the victims of Aryanization was, however, given back what had been stolen from them.

1 The account is based on: Robert Speichler, Arisierungen. Am Beispiel Nürnbergs. Magisterarbeit in der Philosophischen Fakultät I/II der Friedrich-Alexander-Universität Erlangen-Nürnberg, Erlangen 1989. This paper is based on intensive studies of available archive materials and on the published hearings of the International Military Tribunal in Nuremberg in 1945/46.
2 Strobl, as president of the Chamber of Industry and Commerce and as the Gau's economic adviser, was appointed as Aryanization representative for trade. District representative of the Deutsche Arbeitsfront, Emmert, was responsible for the "Aryanization" of industrial concerns.
3 Speichler, 1989, p. 50

arrangements for the enforced sale dragged on and on. In an evaluation which was calculated far too low as it was, Dr. Drottboom, director of Vedes (German toy traders' association), came up with a total value of 286,376 Reichmarks. The properties and the large debts outstanding were not included in this sum.[88] By the time the final sales contract was concluded on 6th April, 1939, Porst had nevertheless managed to reduce the purchase price for the concern, including all production plant, stocks of raw materials and goods, investments and patents, to the 100,000 Reichsmarks originally agreed on. Porst only took over the company's assets; all liabilities were to be borne by the sellers. Further, he obtained the right to take 20 per cent "commission" for the collection of outstanding debts amounting to almost 500,000 Marks. Thus Porst could have paid almost the whole purchase price for the factory from the company's assets, a financial trick which – according to his calculation, at least – would give him a world-class company for free.

Hermann Spear, around 1935

Under pressure of the circumstances Hermann and Wilhelm Spear could do nothing but sign this oppressive contract. After all, the emigration permit was directly dependent on the completion of the Aryanization process. At the same time there was the hope that through this contract at least part of the stolen assets could be retrieved. This hope was not fulfilled, however. Contrary to the written agreements, no payments whatsoever were made to the rightful owners up to the collapse of the German Reich.[89]

For Hanns Porst, however, the contract brought no satisfaction in the desired manner, either. The reason for this, above all, was that the regional administration – contrary to all expectation – did not grant its approval without an audit. In the meantime, the "special" Nuremberg-Fürth Aryanization practices, which had bypassed all state offices, had been abandoned as a result of investigations by the so-called "Göring Commission". Instead the authorities actually checked in detail whether Party member Hanns Porst – member of the NSDAP (National Socialist Party) since 1933 – had withheld large sums from the Nazi state, because he had bought Spear at far below its value. After a lot of comings and goings the purchase contract was sanctioned in March, 1940, on the condition that Porst pay "compensation" of 181,944 Reichsmarks to the Reich, being 70 per cent of the now newly calculated "Aryanization profit". Reluctantly he agreed, "in view of the Reich's current great need of money".[90] Shortly after, Porst purchased the company's premises, too, for 263,000 Reichsmarks. The money was transferred to a special Gestapo account, the Spear family receiving not a penny.

Thus in summer, 1940, in accordance with the law then in force, Porst owned J. W. Spear. That by no means meant that the disputes with the various Party and state authorities were over, though. Indeed they escalated, when in November, 1940, warrants were issued for Porst's arrest and that of his company secretary, Karl Rühle, and buyer, Edgar Stockhausen. They were accused, in the main, of keeping an illegal coal store at the factory. In addition there were various accusations against Porst in connection with the Aryanization of the Sigmund Spear printing establishment in Nuremberg, which for many years had worked mainly for the J. W. Spear & Söhne concern, there being a family connection between them. Porst had bought the whole company in December, 1938, for the ridiculously low price of 2,612 Reichsmarks, within the framework of the Aryanization operations, and had had all usable machines and stocks of goods transported to the Spear games factory or sold them to other interested parties, some at exorbitant prices. Since he had had the company files destroyed, it was no longer possible to check the course of events or to assess the value of the company on which the amount of compensation was based.[91]

In January, 1941, after six weeks in custody, the warrant was lifted. There was no preferring of charges. Just a few days later, however, Nuremberg's criminal investigation department once again instituted legal proceedings against Porst, "on suspicion of embezzlement". The main accusation now was that Porst had "made a considerable profit" from the Aryanization of both Spear companies and attempted "to deprive the Reich of the compensation moneys".[92] It is not known what consequences these renewed accusations had. Porst was arrested for the second time and released shortly after. The same thing happened again in 1943. One Porst biographer writes: "It was really serious – but Porst knew the right people. Both times he got away with just a black eye."[93] Even as late as April, 1944, however, Porst had to justify various financial transactions to the Franconian Chamber of Commerce in connection with the "Aryanization of J. W. Spear & Söhne".[94] Irritated at this, he complained to the chairman of the association of German games manufacturers that "strangely the Spear Arya-

nization file of all things has been taken up again, although other far 'more interesting' cases have been discarded for reasons of administrative simplification". He then lists a dubious array of figures according to which he had apparently paid over 800,000 Reichsmarks for Spear: "You can see from these figures that the remark sometimes made that Photo-Porst paid nothing or not much 'for Spear' does not fit the facts."[95]

The complete, historical truth can no longer be established in detail, especially since there are no more authentic documents whatsoever from the Porst family.[96] It can still be emphasized, however, that the owners of J. W. Spear & Söhne lost all their possessions in respect of buildings, land, stocks, receivables and shareholdings within the framework of Aryanization, without receiving even a penny's compensation. In this sense the largest German games factory was indeed disposed of at no charge. Apparently Hanns Porst had to learn the hard way that even a model entrepreneur could not escape the demands of the totalitarian state. At any rate, his intention of purchasing a world-class company at a give-away price with the help of the local Party clique was not fulfilled.

While the dispute regarding the allocation of Aryanization spoils was in full swing, the situation of the members of the Spear family living in Nuremberg and Fürth steadily worsened. Robbed to a great extent of their assets, Hermann and Else Spear had to rely on selling their private possessions and on family help to secure their livelihood. Hermann Spear was prohibited from taking up work. As already mentioned, he had an immigration permit for England, but he could not emigrate until the Aryanization was finally completed. Only his son, Herbert Spear, was able to leave Germany – on completion of the contract – in April, 1939; he was taken in by his Uncle Richard in Enfield. Perhaps there could have been another opportunity to emigrate at this time, in spite of the official ban. It emerges from letters to

Richard Spear, who had been urging them to leave Germany as quickly as possible, that preparations for this were already underway, and that some of their furniture had already been sold. But apparently in spite of all the injustice he had suffered Hermann Spear was still hesitant about pushing ahead and seriously getting on with his emigration. One reason for this might have been, as Herbert Spear suspects, his concern about his already quite frail parents-in-law.[97] He and his wife appear to have feared acts of revenge against them, if they emigrated. Perhaps Hermann Spear hoped, too, that after the Aryanizations were over the persecutions of the Jews would finally die down, and they might no longer affect him as husband of a Christian woman. Whatever the reasons for his hesitation, it had fatal results, for after the war began in September, 1939 it was almost impossible to leave the country legally.

Wilhelm Spear died in early 1940. His death spared him the last stages of that life of suffering which his remaining relatives in Nuremberg and Fürth, like millions of other European Jews, now had to lead. A renewed attempt by Hermann Spear's brother and sister to get him out of the country through Switzerland failed in spring, 1940. He was arrested several times and his home searched by the Gestapo. Valuables were confiscated. In a last despairing move he converted to Christianity in 1942, when the deportations to the extermination camps had already begun. Five members of the family of Fritz Spear, owner of the Kunstanstalt Sigmund Spear, were among the 426 Franconian Jews who were abducted in March, 1942, to Izbica, in the district of Lublin, in occupied Poland. These were, in addition to the head of the family, his mother, Clärchen, his wife, Else and both daughters, Inge and Liselotte, aged 14 and 15 years. All five were murdered. Hermann Spear suffered the same fate: He was arrested by the Gestapo in March, 1943, and spent some weeks in Nuremberg's police gaol before being deported to Birkenau on 1st April. He was killed in Auschwitz on 10th July, 1943.[98]

Bombs on England

When Hanns Porst took over the Spear company as temporary manager in December, 1938, he was venturing onto completely foreign ground. The successful entrepreneur, whose photo mail order company achieved a turnover of 7.5 million Reichsmarks in the financial year 1938/39 and who employed a staff of over 400,[99] quite understood this as a challenge, testing his business talent on a new subject. To him the plant seemed completely antiquated, the organization of the stores too complicated, the administration completely over-staffed, the wages too high and the range far too extensive. This criticism, uttered

Porst games from 1939/40: Whereas "In Flight Across Großdeutschland" was the politically topical version of a previously harmless geography game, the new game "Bombs on England" consciously fanned the flames of hatred against England.

in the course of the Aryanization negotiations, coincided to a certain extent with the view of the Vedes director who in his valuation of February, 1939 had pointed out several weak points in the company organization: "The various work stations and stores are very far apart, and thus a very large amount of time and labour was wasted. The machines could not and still today cannot be fully utilized, since for present turnover a third at the most, and at peak times only half of the machines are used. In the offices, too, very much was overorganized, while more important things were not catered for. The individual departments mostly did not work hand in hand; rather, each formed its own isolated body." [100]

Against this background, Porst developed a modernization programme to lead the company back into the profit zone after several loss-making years. This goal was to be served by, among others, the following measures: "clearer cut areas of responsibility, reduction in the range of finished products, new numbering of games, simplification of organization, standardization (raw materials, unfinished/finished products etc.), improved quality, reworking of out of date games, better design and punctual production of new articles" and the "improvement of sales organisation (advertising etc; customer service)". [101]

Many of the measures suggested were necessary and useful, as even the Spear family realized in retrospect. [102] Some were indeed also put into practice. Thus the organizational division of the four sections which had existed up to now was done away with and the production of new picture books discontinued altogether. The complete range was reduced in size; the over 700 different box sizes in use up until then were drastically reduced by means of standardization. By the time the 1940 catalogue came out all products had been given five-figure article numbers, a system which was retained even after the war. The finished products warehouse was reorganised, resulting in a considerable improvement in the processing of orders. New office machines were purchased and numerous repairs and improvements carried out in the workshops and offices.

In this way Porst attempted to apply the management principles which had allowed his mail order company to become a model concern also to the "Spear-Spiele-Fabrik Hanns Porst", as the games concern was now temporarily called. With this in mind he also had a "workforce clubhouse", with canteen, built and promoted leisure activities which, quite in the spirit of the DAF "The Beauty of Work" programme, were to strengthen the sense of community and ultimately with it also the workforce's productivity. Thus he supported Spear's harmonica and singing groups, its sports group and rambling and table tennis association. He also tried to promote a better acquaintance between the workforces of his two companies.

Above all Porst demanded that his workers, of course, follow the dictate of the Nazi work ethos: "The convictions of every National Socialist are first proven in his willingness, in his diligence and ability to perform the work entrusted to him by the national community." [103] The company's "super Nazi", Friedrich Burr, of all people, fitted this requirement least of all: After just a few weeks Porst dismissed the agitator, who was feared by many employees, a move which surely created enemies for him within the local National Socialist Party and perhaps also contributed to the disputes with state offices and Party sections.

Whether Porst's modernization measures really would have made the company profitable again, can only be speculated upon, for the situation changed fundamentally with the start of the Second World War in September, 1939. When the 1939/40 new products catalogue appeared, Porst had to add the rider: "Index of numbers which are **expected** to be produced in 1940". [104] The adjustment to war conditions, with central raw materials rationing and the loss of labour resulting from the conscription of men fit for military service naturally made production planning considerably more difficult. At the same time, however, Porst also sensed sales possibilities for new articles which were "in keeping with the times". With its slogan "Spear's Games. This brand guarantees quality", the traditionally peaceful Spear's range acquired exceedingly militaristic and chauvinistic characteristics. Now one could go playfully "In Flight Across Greater Germany", and with "Do You Know Nuremberg?" each Party member was to think back "fondly on the uplifting hours spent in Nuremberg, the city of the Party Rallies". "Bang!" was the concise name for a new attack and defence game in which "gunners, machine-gunners and guns" attacked each other on a chess-like board. "Fretwork, up until now so harmless, also embraced the cause of military training. The little modellers on the home front could now saw "anti-tank defence troops and mortars, marching and attacking infantry" or an "infantry music band" in plywood, "painted in true to life colours".[105]

What was especially horrid was the fact that Porst brought out two games which were firmly directed at the country in which many members of the Spear family had found refuge. "U-Boats Attack England" was the name of one game, which was even "judged as desirable" by the Wehrmacht's Supreme Command. And the Luftwaffe may well have been pleased about "Bombs on England!". In a variation of the old Spear's hit "Flying Hats", the aim of this game was to hurl little tiles ("bombs") at the United Kingdom's industrial cities and ports with the aid of a pivoted cardboard plane. In the instructions, signed "Yours, Uncle Hanns" as were all games of the Porst era, Porst stirred up the belligerent instincts of his "dear playmates": "Wouldn't you like to be there when our brave airmen fly to England to bomb that country's naval ports, munitions factories and other similar installations important for the war effort, as punishment for attacking Germany, and for its treachery and hypocrisy?

Perhaps you won't have the opportunity in the near future, but with this game you can try to emulate our untiring German airmen."

These Porst games had absolutely nothing in common with the old Spear games any more. Porst, himself, too, seems to have been aware of this, for gradually he now eliminated the established name of "Spear" from his concern. In May, 1940 he began with a quite ridiculous redefining of the brand name: following the Porst advertising slogan "Knipse, aber richtig!" ("Snap right!"), "Spear" was now to be understood as the abbreviation of the newly-created slogan "**Sp**iele, **a**ber **r**ichtig!" ("Play right!"). Porst's hope: "After just a few years no-one will remember that Spear was once a name. Everyone will see it as a compound word, just like Agfa (Aktiengesellschaft für Anilin-

"Uncle Hanns" and his games, 1939/41: the games range became drastically militarised under Hanns Porst's management. Bombs and tanks brought war to the nursery.

fabriken).[106] But perhaps Porst did not quite believe in his own prophecy, for a year later he had the new "Porst Spiele" trade mark registered and at the same time renamed the company "Porst-Spiele-Fabrik Hanns Porst".

While Porst was still able to produce games, right up to spring, 1943, Spear's of Enfield had to be switched over to armaments shortly after the beginning of the war. New machines were installed for the production of a multitude of products important for the war effort. Rifle cases were produced for a local arms factory, for instance. Steel helmets were given their lining here and detonating caps for incendiary bombs were moulded in heavy presses. The "Bombs on England" game soon became terrible reality with the Luftwaffe's attacks, and in a way also affected the

Spear factory in Enfield, which was included in the local air-raid warning system. A large drum installed on the factory roof warned the population about the approach of German bomber units. Fortunately, however, the factory escaped serious bomb damage throughout the war.

Nuremberg, the city of the Nazi Party Rallies, suffered quite a different fate. In the course of the war begun by the criminal Nazi regime, 44 Allied bomb attacks reduced the former "treasure chest of the German Reich" to rubble. In 1943, the Spear factory, on whose spacious grounds other businesses had also been established in the meantime received severe hits. The damage was temporarily repaired, but in February, 1945 a bomb attack destroyed a large section of the factory complex for good.

Bombs on Nuremberg: Allied air raids reduced a considerable part of the factory compound in Höfener Straße to rubble. The photograph was taken in summer, 1945.

Phoenix from the Ashes

Post-war circumstances for reconstruction were quite different in Enfield and Nuremberg. J. W. Spear & Sons had a factory in Brimsdown which had not been destroyed, and they could start games production again relatively quickly. The factory certainly benefited from the acquisition of heavy metal processing machines which had been necessary for the war effort. In addition to wood and cardboard processing, metal components for games production could now be manufactured in their own workshops. Thus now – in a fine analogy to the biblical peace prophecy "Swords into ploughshares" – even machines once used to produce bomb components were now used for producing humming-tops! With years of production stoppage in Nuremberg, the factory in Enfield, managed by Richard Spear, became much more independent, and from this time on all necessary games components were produced there or were obtained from outside suppliers. Thus in the first years after the war the foundation was laid for further development – what was once the British subsidiary was to outstrip by far the former German parent company in terms of economic importance.

In Höfener Straße initially reconstruction of the games factory was hardly even to be considered, in view of the scene of destruction there. The main building was completely destroyed, stocks mostly burnt, many of the machines were no longer functional and numerous stores and outbuildings were in a terrible state of repair. Else Spear, widow of murdered director Hermann Spear, had avoided even so much as a glance at the stolen games factory during the war years. After the war was over, former manager Edgar Stockhausen, who had worked for Spear before the Porst era, talked her into visiting the badly damaged factory site: "When I had seen it I went home along the Höfener Straße. I didn't care what people thought: in plain German, I cried my eyes out when I saw it …".[107]

In addition to the destruction caused by the war, there was the damage caused by chaotic post-war conditions. The company property had been requisitioned by the American military government. A US Army HGV squad were billeted in those buildings which were halfway useable. Else Spear: "But they got no heating fuel. So they burned the inner frames from all the double windows and they burned the fence. And then, when they had to move out, the man in charge was ashamed to give it back in the state it was in. He employed some Poles to clear up. They then cleared up so well that neither a toilet bowl was left nor a handle on a window, nor a water tap. They took everything with them."[108]

Everything was lacking: money, building materials, coal, raw materials, means of transport, personnel, business connections. And: who would, or could, think about games, in view of the universal poverty and despondency? The unclear legal situation following Nazi Germany's total defeat also had a crippling effect. Hanns Porst, whose Nuremberg company headquarters were in ruins, too, was in prison in Bayreuth. The American military government had sentenced him to three years' imprisonment at the beginning of 1946.[109] His assets were seized and now administered by a trust. Edgar Stockhausen had been appointed as trustee of the games factory. With great personal commitment Stockhausen tried to prevent further losses and to begin a modest reconstruction. It was clear that with the collapse of the Nazi regime the laws of terror, basis for the "Aryanizations", had lost their legal force. But how and to what extent the victims of Aryanization were to be compensated for their financial losses was not clear until the restitution law of 10.11.1947 was decreed by the military government. Hanns Porst, released early for "good conduct" after 20 months' imprisonment, sought an amicable agreement with the Spear family. Richard Spear remembers the notable meeting: "It was really easy. Porst said to me: 'Well, Mr. Spear, let me keep the business. I'll pay you com-

pensation.' That was the worst thing I could have done, for the compensation was really pathetic. So I said: 'No, Mr. Porst, I won't do that.' Then he said: 'In that case we'll do it together, fifty fifty.' Then I said: 'No, I won't do that either. I want my factory back, for the family.'"[110]

The restitution process which was then initiated at the regional administration took months and months. Balance sheets had to be drawn up and audited and a mass of information submitted before a contract could be agreed between the Spear family and Hanns Porst with the involvement of the authorities. This was signed on 22nd October, 1948. Porst, by now "denazified" by means of a Spruchkammer (special court) trial, had to return the games factory to Spear, including all buildings, factory plant, land, cash, stock in hand and intellectual property, and along with a compensation payment of 225,000 Reichsmarks. Spear took over the business, complete with all assets and liabilities with a balance sheet value of 785,000 Reichsmarks, as of 20th June, 1948. The contract was backdated to 21st June, 1948, the date of the currency reform in the Western Zones. The compensation was therefore converted at the decreed rate of 10:1 – to 22,500 DM, payable in four monthly instalments. With this, all Spear's claims on Porst were satisfied. The only other thing Porst had to do was to undertake "at no time to become involved, directly or indirectly, in the founding, or setting-up or running of a concern in the same or similar area of business within Germany."[111] With the renaming of the company back to "J. W. Spear & Söhne", the Porst era, which had lasted almost ten years, was considered over.

Richard Spear wanted to start up volume production in Nuremberg again, but it was doubtful whether the Nuremberg concern would ever again be able to achieve its previous outstanding position in Germany. For Spear, who had been a British citizen since 1939, the English concern was decidedly more important. He did not intend to return to Germany on any permanent basis. In his opinion, Spear of Nuremberg ought to work its way back up again, under a largely independent management, preferably using its own resources. Following this premise, the reconstruction of the German concern encountered considerable difficulties. Production did begin again, shortly before Christmas, 1948, on an extremely modest scale. But manager Edgar Stockhausen and later also Else Spear, who joined the management in 1950, were faced with great problems: "Mr. Spear is planning to start up volume production. This will mainly be a question of finance, but the raw material situation will also have to improve", Stockhausen wrote in January, 1949.[112] Indeed the necessary investments in the following years could only be made by taking on expensive bank loans, creating a heavy burden on the business.

Things only got better slowly at Höfener Straße. Repairs to damaged buildings dragged on, and the destroyed main factory building was not reconstructed. Tenants which had established themselves on the site, including a coffin-maker, only left gradually. A letter to the staff on the occasion of the 1954 jubilee year is indicative of the company's financial situation: "This year our company can look back on 75 years of business. Unfortunately various circumstances, such as Aryanization and the destruction of the factory during the war, have set us back so much that in 1948 we had to begin again almost from scratch and on a very small scale. Much has been reconstructed and improved upon in the meantime, but we cannot yet afford to have any large celebration for the jubilee, for since the start of rebuilding we have had to work with loan capital and will have to do so for many years to come …Even if, for the reasons stated, we cannot do much, we would at least like to allocate a small sum of money to our workforce, and so we have decided on the occasion of the jubilee to give each member of staff a present of DM 5,– …We hope that you will all continue to enjoy working with us, in helping to build up the company again

and gradually getting it back to the same importance it enjoyed up to 1938."[113]

A communication to business associates in the same year on the occasion of the jubilee displayed at least some cautious optimism: "Thanks to our loyal clientele and to the support of our long-standing raw materials suppliers, it has been possible to bring back our business to a certain level, and the upward trend of the last few years gives us the hope that we will recover from our setbacks."[114] By 1956 the number of staff had already increased to around 150. In subsequent years, this figure was not exceeded by much, but by the beginning of the 1960s at the latest, Spear's games from Nuremberg were once again well established on the German market.

Richard Spear was so busy running his English company that he only came to Germany occasionally. He allowed the Nuremberg Spear factory extensive freedom of policy, which included development of new products. There was only a framework agreement to the effect that no English language games would be manufactured in Nuremberg, and no German language games

Nuremberg Spear staff outing to Egloffstein in the Fränkische Schweiz, 1960

lished parlour and activity games, but at a very much reduced level. Picture book production, discontinued by Hanns Porst, was not taken up again. The 1950s catalogues contain only a few genuinely new articles; many games were offered with new designs, or were given playing pieces made of plastic. There is always an exception to the rule. Thus, in 1954, the educational and amazing quiz game "Magihara" came out, in which – by means of a magnetic mechanism – a figure in the form of an oriental wise man gave the correct answer to every question. Games of badminton took up a brief, but important role in the Spear range from 1956 on, being produced in the company's own woodwork department in four different qualities, from leisure to de-luxe edition.

Enfield, too, continued with its main pre-war product lines. The English range did indeed surpass the German one, but on the whole it contained only further developments and new layouts of tried and tested articles. One of the important exceptions was "Spellmaster", a patented letter learning game for pre-school children which remained part of Spear's programme for several decades, as well as "Contact Quiz", a very successful quiz game which was launched in 1954. With the aid of a metal pin which was connected to a battery, players could touch contact points on a questionnaire. If a second sensor was placed on the correct answer, a lamp lit up. Unlike other electric knowledge games whose fairly simple wiring was easy to see through after only a short time, the Spear's game had much more sophisticated circuitry. Thus "Contact Quiz" which was also brought out in Germany, under the name of "Pfiffikus" continued to be exciting, even after prolonged playing.

Another game became of major importance for the new Spear range: "Brickplayer", a construction game which had been offered shortly before the Second World War, but which could not begin its success story until after 1945. It was a modern product: its clay bricks could be joined

in Enfield. Every product developed in-house in either company tended, however, to be available to both partners. This agreement worked well right up until production ceased in Nuremberg, in 1984. The level of independence can be seen, for example, in the fact that out of several hundred articles offered by the Spear group in the mid 1970s, only around 40 games were sold by both the English parent company and the German associate.[115]

In the 1950s, the range of Spear of Nuremberg took up the tried and tested mixture of estab-

J. W. Spear & Sons's stand at the British Industries Fair in London, 1949. The stand radiates modern elegance with its gently curved design, tubular furniture and globe display.

Spear's stand at the British Industries Fair in London, 1950: "Brickplayer" is at the centre of their display, which shows a marked difference to that of the previous year.

"Brickplayer" window at Selfridges, London, 1955. Size and design of the display give some indication of the importance attributed to this product in the 1950s.

Spear's stand at the Needlecraft Fair in London, 1959. Senior schoolgirls and adult women were the target group for Spear's most popular looms, which could produce useful textiles at low cost.

together with special cement, following original building plans, to make realistic reproductions of buildings. While German reconstruction was reflected in the play-world by a wealth of new metal construction kits, British parents obviously preferred – apart from the well-known Meccano punched metal strips – to see bricks as the building material of the new age in their sons' hands. Copying tried and tested Meccano marketing strategies, Spear also regularly announced building competitions, offering fairly high money prizes, and then published the plans of the winning models as examples for little home architects. Undoubtedly the pretty brick houses owed a considerable part of their attraction to the fact that they could be used for the realistic decorating of model railways, thus accommodating the wishes of mostly adult model railway buffs. Up until its gradual ousting by "Lego" and other construction systems made of plastics in the early 1960s, "Brickplayer" at any rate remained one of the most popular items in the very varied range of English Spear's games.

The one product which proved to be of outstanding importance to Spear's further development, however, was "Scrabble". A new, extraordinarily successful era in the company's history began in 1954 with this crossword game.

Scrabble – Birth of a Classic

Word-building games had existed long before Scrabble. Around 1900 Spear already offered a game called "Word Builder" in its range, for example, but the structural element of the crossword puzzle was still missing, as it was in other word games. Games which came very close to the Scrabble idea were the "Pulok" games from Stuttgart publishing company J. F. Steinkopf, and above all "Typ-Dom" (abbreviation of "Typen-Domino"), developed by Viennese radio dealer Franz Weigel and his friend, Norbert Bornatowicz. This interesting word game consisted of

toothed letter tiles, without a game board, which could be linked to form combinations of words, similar to a crossword. The aim of the game was to put down all the letter tiles drawn from a pool as quickly as possible. The game was patented in Austria in 1936, and met with great response in Europe. Leading American manufacturers also predicted a great future for the game at the

Lord of the letters:
Scrabble inventor
Alfred M. Butts (1900-1993)
in 1985.

World Exhibition in New York in 1939. But the outbreak of war in the same year brought production to a standstill and prevented further popularising of this quite original game.[116]

Independently of these European games ideas, in the USA, Alfred M. Butts, an architect from New York, had been working since the beginning of the 1930s on the development of a word game which would combine luck, strategy and knowledge in a new way.[117] Crossword puzzles, anagrams and other word games had always fascinated Butts, and when he was made redundant in 1931, at the height of the world economic crisis, he decided to cash in on his hobby by inventing a game. He studied the US games market of the time and ascertained that no really interesting word games were available. In 1933 he had completed a first, still very vague game prototype: the simple basic idea consisted of drawing seven letters from a pool and then forming a word from them. If this could not be managed, the unused letters could be exchanged for new ones from the pool. The game was finished when the first player managed to form a suitable word containing all letters.

James Brunot (centre) and
Hans Schowanek (right)
inspecting stored wood in
front of the sawmill

In a further stage of development Butts introduced letter values for the whole alphabet. When a player had completed the game by putting down a word with seven letters, the other players were allowed to form shorter words; the total number of points from these determined the further placings. The overall number of letter tiles was set at 100, a number which Butts himself was prepared to cut out using his electric band-saw. The little racks for the letters were also new. Butts took the idea from Mah-Jongg, a game which was very popular in the USA at the time, and bought long skirting boards at a do-it-yourself store which he then cut to the right length for racks. He approached various manufacturers with this game, which he tested extensively on friends, under the name of "Lexiko". Nobody wanted to give the game a chance, however.

James Brunot and Hans
Schowanek examining the
quality of wood blocks

The game which was to become Scrabble certainly benefited from this failure, for after long trials Butts introduced a game board with various bonus squares, as a decisive new development. The players now had to take turns in trying to put down words on the game board, joining each other in the manner of a crossword puzzle. The aim now was to gain the highest number of points by skilled combination of the letter values and bonus squares. Butts also foundered with this new version, which was very like the later Scrabble: no manufacturer showed any interest in "It", as the game was now rather unimaginatively called – "too elitist", "too serious" or "too complicated" were the reasons given for refusal.

Handy-sized boards leaving the gang saw

As a result, Alfred Butts scrapped the idea of a commercial exploitation of his game for the time being and once again took up his former occupation as architect. About 50 handmade copies of "It" were in circulation and for years these served only as entertainment among family and friends. James Brunot, a high ranking state official in welfare, numbered among the enthusiastic players of "Criss-Crosswords", as the game was now known after yet another change of name. Butts had given him a copy as a present, and when Brunot was looking for a lucrative sideline after the war, he thought of a commercial exploitation of the crossword game. In 1948 the time had finally come: Brunot and Butts agreed to attempt the manufacture and sale of Butts' game by a company they founded especially for this purpose – the "Production and Marketing Company". Butts was to receive royalties (five per cent of the wholesale price) on every game sold, the game now having been given a more pithy name: From a long list of suggestions, Brunot chose "Scrabble". Name, game board and game rules were registered at the US Copyright Office in the same year.

In the factory the boards are ripped into square sections.

Scrabble production began in 1949 in Brunot's house in Newtown, a small town in the state of Connecticut. Boxes and components were

Crosscutting machines cut tiles of 5 mm thickness from the square sections.

Unfinished tiles are smoothed off in large drums, using a polishing compound.

Having a critical glance at some barrel-polished tiles

A further tumble gives the tiles their silk-smooth surface.

bought in from outside companies, and the games were completed as homework, as it were, in Brunot's living room, and then later in a former school building. Newspaper advertisements, mail shots and mouth-to-mouth propaganda at first only helped the new game to modest sales figures: Exactly 2,251 copies were sold in 1949. In 1950 it was almost 4,800 and another year later all of 8,500, but costs still exceeded income. By mid 1952 the sales figures were still small, and Brunot was already considering stopping production when a coincidence changed things overnight: Jack Strauss, head of the world-famous New York department store, Macy's, had come to know and love Scrabble while he was on holiday. On his return he discovered to his surprise that his toy department did not stock the game. Strauss immediately ordered from Brunot and, using all his concern's advertising power, launched Scrabble in New York. Within a very short time the Big Apple was seized by a veritable Scrabble fever, which soon spread right across America.

Brunot's capacity was completely overtaxed by the sudden success. Work went on right round the clock, but the little concern got further and further behind with production. Since Brunot did not want to get into production and sales on such a large scale, he awarded the American licence for the standard edition to the well-established New York company Selchow & Righter, but continued producing the de luxe edition in this own company. Over 800,000 Scrabble games left the Selchow & Righter factory between May and December, 1953. The craze reached Europe by the end of the same year. Brunot's "Production & Marketing Company" now had to look around for competent licensees there.

The J. Schowanek company of Piding in Bavaria was chosen for Germany. This company was already delivering high quality letter tiles to Selchow & Righter.[118] The concern had originally been founded in 1896 by wood turner Johann Schowanek in Dessendorf near Gablonz, in

Bohemia. The wood processing business developed from humble beginnings into a respected concern which in 1914 employed over 500 workers and manufactured wooden goods of all kinds, above all high quality wooden beads which were exported in great quantities throughout the world. Hans Schowanek, son of the company founder, took up toy production as a new branch of manufacture in 1927. Within a short period of time, construction kits, games pieces, counting frames, mosaic games and parlour games were being produced and earned great respect from experts. Hans Schowanek was a man well-versed in technical things. The special machines, gadgets and production processes which he developed himself were patented in many countries all over the world. After the end of the war the concern was expropriated by the new Communist rulers. Hans Schowanek had to flee to Austria. The State of Bavaria approached him in 1949 with the request that he build up a concern in Piding, where there was a large transit camp for ex-pellees. Schowanek took up this offer and set up a new factory. The new beginning was a success, and orders and number of staff rose steadily: from 150 in 1951 to 250 in 1953.

The Schowanek company's proven competence made it an obvious choice for the production of Scrabble tiles. That is why at the end of 1953 Brunot assigned them the Scrabble licence for Germany, Italy and several other European states. Hans Schowanek's inventive mind also expressed itself in the development of special machines which cut precisely formed Scrabble tiles from strips of beech wood, polished them off in large drums and printed them automatically in a stamping machine. Even when Schowanek lost the Scrabble licence in 1958, he still remained the supplier of parts for Selchow & Righter. The new licensee, J. W. Spear & Söhne, also bought Schowanek games components for a time, before the Lorenz company, also resident in Upper Bavaria, was awarded the contract for this technically demanding work of producing the letter tiles.

Workers sorting the flood of printed letters

Letters for America: New York company Selchow & Righter received the bulk of the letters produced in Bavaria.

At the height of Scrabble-mania, Schowanek's tractors had to transport tons of letter tiles to the railway station every week.

The Big Winner

Scrabble appeared on the British market just in time for Christmas, 1954. The success was fantastic and above all lasting: Scrabble turned out to be a best-seller which was still going strong even decades later. By means of clever sales and advertising campaigns the sales figures for the most successful word game of all time, did not reach their peak until the mid 1970s. At this time over 700,000 games a year were sold in Britain alone! And by the time of the company's centenary in 1979 over 40 million games had already crossed the counter worldwide.[119] In Britain, the birth of a Scrabble Club movement and the running of national competitions from 1971 onwards ensured extensive publicity and certainly contributed to the game's great popularity at all social levels. There is now a Scrabble game in more than half of all British households, and along with innumerable unknown fans of the game, prominent figures have confessed to their passion for Scrabble, among them advertising tycoon Charles Saatchi, actress Joan Collins, Roger Taylor of the rock group Queen and the Queen Mother.[120]

This "jewel" was carefully looked after at Spear's of Enfield and in the 1980s it still quite steadily brought in around 40 per cent of the company's turnover. The company was gradually awarded the Scrabble rights for more and more countries by Brunot's "Production and Marketing Company". At the end of 1968, when the childless James Brunot retired from business life, he finally sold the world rights – with the exception of those for the USA, Canada and Australia – to the Spear Group. The previous licensees, Selchow & Righter (USA, Canada) and Tibor R. Urban (Australia) purchased the rights for their respective countries.

More important for potential Scrabble friends around the globe than this division of the Scrabble world was the fact that wherever possible, in time, versions in their native tongue were

Schowanek's automatic embossing machine for Scrabble letters, around 1955: the blank tiles glide from a container to the revolving stamping mechanism, where they are automatically embossed with the letters and letter values for a complete Scrabble set. The embossing dies could be exchanged for the different languages.

Several games manufacturers tried to get the Scrabble licence for Britain. Brunot did not simply choose the highest bidder, however. Richard Spear did appear to be very interested when asked; but at the same time he entered the contract negotiations quite warily. After all, the new and highly promising word game "Key Word" from Parker Brothers had just been brought onto the market by a competitor, and even James Brunot himself was still not quite sure whether the Scrabble craze would indeed last. The fact that Spear, in spite of these reservations, finally got the licence for Great Britain and Ireland in November, 1954, can mainly be put down to the fact that the company was regarded in the trade as an exceptionally solid concern. For Brunot this counted more than extravagant promises.

Championship Scrabble

The year 1971 was pre-destined to be the year in which Scrabble was to have its first Scrabble Championship. Two important things happened. The first was that during the January Toy Fairs in the UK, Mr. Richard Spear commissioned those involved in sales and marketing to carry out a feasibility study into holding a National Scrabble Championship. This had to explore the playing rules, format and forecast any possible problems that could arise. The study had to be held involving ordinary members of the public and in a location where it would not attract unwelcome media attention and be close enough to Enfield and Central London for the Spear personnel involved to be able to control the exercise without undue travel and expenses.

The playing rules and format having been decided, the location was selected. It was to be High Wycombe in Buckinghamshire, about 40 minutes drive from central London. This town had a number of factories on several industrial estates which had a highly-organised interchange of sporting and social activities. The first sessions were arranged.

At this stage, the second important event happened. J. W. Spear and Sons Ltd. observed some unauthorised advertisements in *The Times* advertising a proposed National Scrabble Championship. There is an important story behind these advertisements when it comes to the start of the National Scrabble Championships. A young graduate from Oxford University, Gyles Brandreth, was visiting Bristol Prison doing research for a book when he observed a couple of prisoners playing his favourite board game – Scrabble. He knew that Scrabble was his family's favourite board game and that of Her Majesty Queen Elizabeth, but had not thought of it as having a universal appeal. His brain started working and he thought that if other games like chess could have their championships, why not Scrabble.

Returning to London, he gave the matter some more thought and

British Scrabble Championship, 1972: Richard Spear and organiser Gyles Brandreth during the finals in London restaurant "Quaglino's"

a few days later drafted an advertisement which he inserted in the Personal Columns of *The Times*. It was this advertisment that was seen by Spear's Games and by thousands of Times readers. Three thousand of these had written to Gyles to say that they were interested in taking part in a Championship. They ranged from schoolteachers, schoolchildren, builders and engineers, to housewives and nurses. The oldest was a lady globetrotter who was in her eighties and who never travelled anywhere without her Scrabble set.

Having seen the advertisment, Spear set up a meeting with Gyles Brandreth (important trademark issues were involved). Following that meeting, it was decided that the two courses of action - Spear's and Gyles' - should get together. Spear had the resources and manpower; Gyles had already started a Championship train in motion and had several thousand potential entrants. Rapidly, wheels were set in motion, entry forms printed, a venue booked and all the 101 things involved in such an event organised. The first National Scrabble Championship was on its way with Gyles at the helm of the ship provided by Spear's Games.

The first National Scrabble Championship was held in June 1971 and it was won by Stephen Haskell, an unemployed schoolteacher. The event with 100 finalists attracted considerable media attention. The youngest finalist was an 11-year-old schoolgirl. One hard-nosed editor thought that it must be a publicity ploy to have her in the finals and sent one of his writers to play a game of Scrabble with her. To his amazement, she beat him by a large margin. Thinking this must be a chance result, he challenged her to a second game - the result was the same. To give him his due, he wrote a long complimentary article praising the girl's word skills.

The Championship proved so popular that in order to select the 100 finalists (Grand Finalists) Regional Finals (with Regional Champions) were instituted to select the top players in the country.

The next major change was in 1989. By this time, there was an elite of Scrabble players and it was decided to divide the Championship into two sections. The 'expert' section would provide the National Champion. They played against overall time limits using chess clocks with the champion being the player who did not lose a single game in the event. Substantial prizes were also introduced for this division. The other division was the British Amateur Championship which comprised players who had not won any major tournament.

Over the years seventeen of the National Scrabble champions were men. The youngest Champion was 15-year-old Alan Saldanha (who has also qualified for the World Championship). The eldest is certainly one of the six women to have won the event, but politeness forbids us to enquire the age of a grey-haired lady. A brother and sister, Russell and Esther Byers, have both won the event. And, Philip Nelkon was National Scrabble Champion four times – 1979, 1981, 1990 and 1992. Three other players have won the event twice thus proving that the chance element in Scrabble can be overcome with skill and tactics.

Margaret Rogers, British Scrabble Champion of 1988

Within a matter of months of the first National Scrabble Championship being held players started to get together to play their favourite word game. The London Scrabble League and the Leicester Scrabble Club were the first two clubs to be formed. Soon there was a nation-wide movement and in 1978 the National Scrabble Club Tournament was launched and sponsored by Spear. This was like a football championship. It was played by teams on a knockout basis, first in regions and then the winners of each region playing off for the title.

While this was happening in England, the French-speaking nations had started their own competitive events but unlike the English-speaking countries, they played Duplicate Scrabble which like Duplicate Bridge, means that every player holds the same letter tiles. It does not involve strategy or tactics but relies more on word power and anagram skills. They had their own Francophone National and World Scrabble Championship.

In the USA and Canada a thriving Scrabble Club movement had developed with its own championship but playing to an American Dictionary with American words and spellings. The remainder of the English-speaking world were playing to an English dictionary and Official Scrabble Words published by W & R Chambers Ltd.

During the late 1980s the Scrabble Club Co-ordinators of Britain and the USA worked to devise a way in which the "two English languages" and the US and UK rules could be combined to create a World Scrabble Championship. A small international group were consulted and draft rules were devised. J. W. Spear & Sons plc hosted the first World Scrabble Championship (in English) in London in 1991 which was won by an American, Peter Morris. The next Championship held in New York in 1993 was won by an Englishman, Mark Nyman. Back in London in 1995, the event was won by Canadian David Boys.

Scrabble is being played internationally on the Internet and since the game's popularity seems to know no bounds, it is probably inevitable that sooner or later a world-wide net Scrabble championship will be devised. Because of time differences it will probably be run along the lines of Postal Scrabble with a gamemaster controlling the games and telling the players which letter tiles they have drawn and maintaining the master playing board which will be communicated via the Internet to the contestants. This could be Competitive Scrabble of the Millennium!

Leonard D Hodge

also brought out. Spear's were pleased to oblige, and gradually game sets were developed in numerous languages. By 1993, the year of Alfred M. Butts' death, there were 23 different language versions in existence. Among these were – in addition to the world languages of English, French and Spanish – also those in Afrikaans, Arabic, Greek, Hebrew, Turkish and Icelandic. Today a Braille version enables blind people to play the stimulating game of words and points.

In Germany, Scrabble was presented as "America's greatest best-seller" at the Nuremberg Toy Fair of 1955.[121] The sales figures did not reach the expected high level at first, however. Obviously licensee Schowanek was indeed a technically well-versed production partner, but he lacked marketing competence. Not until the end of 1958, when Spear's obtained the licence for the

German-speaking countries as well as for Belgium and Luxembourg, was Germany also permanently established on the world map of Scrabble's success. The Nuremberg Spear's concern brought Scrabble onto the German market in 1959, with a new box design and in two versions – adult and junior. The crossword game was now advertised extensively, with large print runs of leaflets, window displays for retailers, sales training and "Scrabble parties" in the larger cities in the country. At these parties "leading personalities from administration, industry and commerce, education, youth organisations and the press were introduced to the game".[122]

The opinion of experts and prominent figures were readily taken up as sales arguments. Thus Fritz Benscher, a very popular TV quizmaster of the time, was quoted: "Scrabble ought to be avail-

British Scrabble Champions

1971 Stephen Haskell
1972 Olive Behan
1973 Anne Bradford
1974 Richard Sharp
1975 Olive Behan
1976 Alan Richter
1977 Michael Goldman
1978 Philip Nelkon
1979 Christine Jones
1980 Joyce Cansfield
1981 Philip Nelkon
1982 Russell Byers
1983 Colin Gumbrell
1984 Michael Willis
1985 Esther Byers
1986 Viraf Mehta
1987 Nigel Ingham
1988 Margaret Rogers
1989 Russell Byers
1990 Philip Nelkon
1991 Philip Appleby
1992 Philip Nelkon
1993 Alan Saldanha
1994 Michael Willis
1995 No competition
1996 Andrew Fisher

World Scrabble Champions

1991 Peter Morris
1993 Mark Nyman
1995 David Boys

able on prescription". The editor of trade journal "Das Spielzeug" (Toys), Werner Nostheide, confessed: "I often play and enjoy playing Scrabble when travelling… Scrabble is never boring and one can play it again and again, for it has never-ending possibilities." And the initially rather sceptical publishing director of the German Book Guild in Darmstadt reported the result of his family game studies: "Now that I have dealt thoroughly with the aim of Scrabble and mastered the method of playing, the game has become one of our family favourites, because it is so enjoyable. Scrabble fever, as it were, has broken out with us…".[123]

The elaborate sales and advertising strategy of reaching customers via retailers, prominent figures and other opinion-makers paid off: Scrabble managed to establish itself in Germany as one of the most popular parlour games ever; within word games it is almost without rivals even up to this day. Unlike Britain, the USA or France, Germany did not develop a Scrabble movement which manifested itself in clubs and tournaments. Building on the positive experiences gleaned from British Scrabble competitions, Spear of Nuremberg also tried organising a German language championship. It was held for the first time in Nuremberg on 29th September, 1973. By the end of heats in ten German and Swiss cities, 34 participants had qualified for the final. Accompanied by considerable interest from the media, the title of the first German Language Scrabble Champion went to Ruth Schmidt from Frankfurt. A year later Fritz Wellmann from Hanover took the trophy and cash prize. These two remain to this day the only German-speaking Scrabble champions, for the competition was not continued. Clearly Spear had not been successful in establishing the tournament idea among the numerous German-speaking Scrabble-lovers – by 1975, after all, more than two million games had been sold in the Federal Republic.[124] Without the basis of a broad movement of organised players, the championship remained too much on

the level of a purely promotional event. Apparently German-speaking Scrabble players prefer to indulge their hobby within their own four walls and refuse to join the public "battle for words".

Scrabble was without doubt the motor for Spear's many years of success, both in Germany and in Great Britain. Other Spear's articles also sold better in the wake of the remarkably well-known crowd puller, of course. After all, on account of the high and the largely constant demand, no toy dealer could ignore Scrabble. The sales potential of the whole range increased because of it, offering as it did a wealth of family oriented games and activity ideas for all age groups, from toddler to grandparent. At the same time Scrabble's success opened up for the management a greater scope for investment in new production methods as well as in new games, which in turn helped to strengthen the position they had gained on the market. The large profits were invested in modern machines which could also be used to manufacture other products more efficiently. All of this considerably strengthened the group's competitiveness allowing it, against the background of such constant high profit margins, to get over unavoidable set-backs resulting from less successful innovation.

Going Public

Scrabble's great success and the popular "Basics" range, as the old tried and tested parlour and activity games were called by insiders, helped Spear to achieve both a solid financial basis and loyal customers. In England as in Germany, Spear's traditionally relied on specialist shops in its marketing strategy. Since the strength of the Spear range lay not in short-lived, extravagantly promoted fashionable articles but in a wealth of non-seasonal products, close co-operation with established specialist shops was sought. Regular visits by sales representatives were just as much part of the service as information events and training

Müller the Painter

The success of a game does not only depend on the idea it is based upon, but to a great extent also on the design of its game board, components and box lid. In view of the many competing products, design plays an important role in the customer's decision to buy a certain item. Nevertheless, games producers have only recently started quoting – alongside the game's inventor – the graphic artists whose creative ideas affect the presentation of a game and sometimes even an entire range of products. In the past, with very few exceptions, they remained unknown. It was the brand name that counted, not the individual style of one designer.

Spear was no exception. It was only with picture books and card games that the names of designers were given, following the tradition of book publishing, where the creative input of authors and illustrators had been recognised for much longer. In this context, the Nuremberg Toy Museum may consider itself lucky to possess documents showing the important contribution of one single graphic artist to Spear design. For more than five decades, from 1927 to 1980, Nuremberg graphic artist Gustav Müller (1899-1990) worked for J. W. Spear & Sons. Thanks to the accurate documentation of his extensive bequest by his daughter Anneliese Müller-Dupont, who kindly donated all pertinent documents to the Nuremberg Toy Museum, we can paint a picture of the man who always referred himself to as "Maler Müller" (Müller the Painter) right from the beginning of his professional career as a self-employed graphic artist.

Son of Georg Michael Müller and his wife Anna Elisabeth, Gustav Müller was born in Nuremberg on 16th November, 1899. He grew up in modest circumstances, for his father, an official in the lower echelons of the Royal Bavarian Railways could only just manage to make ends meet for his family of six. Little Gustav's gift for drawing and craft work became apparent very early on. One

Gustav Müller, 1925

of his primary school teachers therefore advised his parents to apprentice him to a scene-painter. In 1914 Gustav Müller started his apprenticeship with the largest firm in the trade at this time, "Royal Bavarian Court Scene-Painters Ober & Hartner" in Nuremberg. Being keen to learn as much as possible, he also took evening classes in drawing. His master even granted him permission to take part in day courses at the Nuremberg School of Arts and Crafts for two terms. After finishing his apprenticeship with flying colours in summer, 1917, the young journeyman applied for a scholarship to attend the Nuremberg School of Arts and Crafts. He was, however, drafted into the navy, and thus could not realise his plans. Seaman Müller did not return to Nuremberg to pursue his studies until the end of March, 1919.

In his unpublished autobiography, Gustav Müller reports on the sound education he received at the School of Arts and Crafts, while studying with professors Selzer, Schiestl and Körner: "My life only started having some purpose again in autumn, 1919, when the winter term at the School of Arts and Crafts started. I could dedicate myself from morning till night to drawing and painting, not only from plaster models, flowers and all sorts of stuffed animals, but also from live animals, since I had been given a free student pass for the zoo. I could also practice sketching, and drawing heads, figures and nudes, as well as learning all about creative graphic design, commercial art and font design. I took part in several competitions, with varying success, tried my hand at lithography, silhouettes, and linocut. By the time I left the School of Arts and Crafts in Flaschenhofstraße at the end of the summer term of 1922, I was familiar with most methods used in graphic art – with the exception of etching, woodcut and oil painting." For quite some time the young graduate from the School of Arts and Crafts considered enrolling at the Munich Art Academy, but his parents' financial means did not stretch that far. In addition he had reached the self-critical conclusion, that "as an artist I would not get all that far, since in my opinion I was lacking the necessary prerequisites, and above all the talent required."

For three years Gustav Müller tried to make ends meet by taking on all sorts of jobs. He hardly managed to keep his head above water. By coincidence, in 1925, he made the acquaintance of the publisher of the magazine "Jugendlust", who commissioned numerous illustrations from him for his publication over the next few years. For the first time, the young graphic artist had a more or less secure income. His financial situation improved further when he entered into a long-term co-operation with the "Nürnberger Bund" in 1926. This trade association organised a major trade fair every year and commissioned Müller to do all the lettering work – everything from small labels to huge banners. His proven competence in this field was later also to acquire him another major client: the Nuremberg Toy Fair, who regularly commissioned work, starting with the first Toy Fair in 1950.

Gustav Müller married in 1926, and in 1927 he established his own advertising studio under the name "Maler Müller". First contacts with J. W. Spear & Söhne were made in the same year. A minister, who was a friend of Müller's, had asked him to design an educational game he had thought up and to find a producer for this game in Nuremberg. After a few unsuccessful attempts, Müller presented the game to Spear: "They were not interested in the game, but as they liked the design, they immediately gave me a commission, and further jobs were soon to follow. In all those years Spear – in particular the English subsidiary, managed by Richard Spear, established in 1930 – has proven to be one of my best clients", Müller the Painter wrote in his autobiography, thus underlining the major importance of this co-operation which lasted for decades.

The very first commission was to design a brochure on table tennis, a sport which was experiencing a rapid rise in popularity at the time. Further jobs entailed firstly the design of newspaper advertisements, advertising posters and lettering for picture and colouring books as well as box lids for games. These graphic designs clearly matched the client's aesthetic ideas, and as a result Müller increasingly became responsible for the design of numerous parlour, card and activity games. To give just some examples: In the years 1929/1930, he designed box lids for "Kwiknit" and "Freut Euch des Webens" (Happy Weaving) as well as for the card games "Graf Zeppelin Quartett" (Count Zeppelin Happy Families), "Das schöne Deutschland" (Beautiful Germany) and "Fortschritt im Verkehr" (Traffic Progress). The designs for "Eile mit Weile"[1], Spear's version of "Ludo", and for "Ludo/Snakes and Ladders" (1931) were also provided by Müller. The versatility of "MM" – thus he initialled his designs – can also be seen from his design for pewter figures for dice games such as "Bonzo-Jagd" (Hunt for Bonzo) and "Reisespiel" (Travel Game, both 1929) and for the movable wooden figures for "Topscor" (1937).

At Spear's, new games were usually designed by several people. One of the many graphic artists provided the artwork for the games board and/or the title illustration, and Müller the Painter added missing elements, quite often only the lettering, especially for foreign language versions. Undoubtedly this method presupposed that the artist had a particular sensitivity for his colleagues' artistic "handwriting", an ability Müller did indeed possess. But there were also designs provided entirely by him. All components of "Die Autofahrt" (A Car Journey, 1935) and "Die Luftreise" (Air Travel, 1936) or "Starkholzspielzeug" (Wooden Toys, 1937), were, for example, designed completely by Gustav Müller. "Gliding", a game published by Spear in 1936, is special, because Müller the Painter was also the game's inventor. His passion for gliding and for model planes constructed according to his own designs came to the fore in this beautiful game.

Up until the company's "Aryanization" in 1938, Müller the Painter provided hundreds of graphic designs for J. W. Spear & Söhne. Although he had enjoyed excellent and close co-operation with Hermann and Richard Spear, he continued working for the games manufacturer in Höfener Straße after Hanns Porst had taken over. Porst even commissioned him to illustrate numerous newly developed games. Thus even terrible games such as "Kurs Ost-Nordost!" (Heading East-Northeast!, 1939), "U-Boote fahren gegen England" (U-Boats Attack England, 1940) and "Bomben auf England" (Bombs on England, 1940) were designed by the Nuremberg graphic artist who apparently had no problem adapting to his new client's wishes. This opportunist approach may be explained by his worries about his wife and two small children, but also by the fact that Porst managed to have Müller's draft into the army deferred until late autumn, 1940.

In April, 1945, Gustav Müller was taken prisoner by the Americans, but soon after his release in summer, 1945, he returned to his family in the destroyed city of Nuremberg. Overcoming great difficulties, he managed to build a makeshift home – which he had designed himself – in the suburbs of the city and to re-establish his business. His old business contacts with the Nürnberger Bund trade association and the Christian Herbart toy manufacturing company were re-established. Richard Spear, who obviously bore him no grudge because of his work for Porst, commissioned work from Müller the Painter as early as 1948.

During the 1950s, Müller the Painter continued to work for both Spear factories, in Enfield and in Nuremberg. From 1954 to 1958 his daughter, Anneliese, who had followed in his professional footsteps, worked for the Nuremberg company. Amongst others Müller the Painter designed the boxtops and sometimes game components for successful games such as "Denk fix"/"Tell Me" (1951/1956), "Das Flunderspiel"/"Floundering" (1952), or such Spear classics as "Die fliegenden Hüte"/"Flying Hats" (1955/1961) and "Angelspiel"/"Magnetic Fish Pond" (1952/1957). The most famous artwork provided by him proved to be his re-design of the German version of the Spear hit "Scrabble". In the years 1958/1959, Müller replaced the rather boring original American design – a burgundy box with a round logo in the top left-hand corner – by a stylised version of the game plan with broad lettering on a dark green background. Undoubtedly this clear classic design counts among the Nuremberg graphic artist's best works. In spite of several changes its influence can still be felt today, and it has left a lasting impression on millions of players.

Müller's co-operation with Spear Nuremberg ended in 1960. The management were relying on younger artists at the time and wanted to modernise games design – sometimes with doubtful success. Richard Spear however, kept his experienced company designer on. He went on commissioning work from him up until 1980. As a rule, Müller the Painter flew to England once or twice a year to discuss products and to make first rough sketches, and after his return produced the finished artwork within the space of a few weeks – promptly, reliably and always on friendly terms. He finally retired from business at the age of 81 years. From then on he only did "private" work, painting water-colours and oil paintings from sketches made in earlier years. Müller died in his home town of Nuremberg on 22nd July, 1990, after a short illness.

Undoubtedly Gustav Müller strongly influenced the graphical image of Spear and its products. This conclusion is certainly justi-fied, if only by the wealth of artwork he produced over more than five decades. When critically assessing his work, however, it is hard to identify one single artistic style. This certainly has much to do with his clients, who used him as a "Jack of all trades" – to design a newspaper advertisement here, and some lettering, a box lid or some game board there. Spear had no corporate design as no artistic director ensured a uniform image. The variety of the product range, which had steadily evolved over many years, was always mirrored in several design concepts which co-existed at any given time: old-fashioned design parallel to modern design, figurative representation parallel to abstract design, finely detailed work parallel to large, bold blocks of colour. In a way, Müller the Painter himself, also seems to have had problems in developing and pushing his own style. His doubts regarding his artistic talents may have stopped him from becoming truly distinctive. Rather, with the years, he kept adapting to the taste of the times, taking up suggestions from all directions and then rendering them in his meticulous craftsmanship. In the 1920s he designed newspaper advertisements in Bauhaus style, in the 1930s indulged in the Gothic print which was then in vogue, and in the 1950s underlaid his designs with fashionable pastel washes. Even the Flower Power era, with its bold colours and dissolving shapes, entered into his work, as can be seen in "Spearoscope" (1968). This flexibility was his strength and secured him work as one of the most popular and long-standing commercial artists. At the same time it also revealed a weakness, because it prevented him from creating designs with outstanding artistic quality which could point the way in games design.

Design for a company advertisement, 1927

---

1   *The figures given in brackets refer to the date the work was commissioned and may therefore not always coincide with the actual year of publication of the game in question.*

for sales personnel. This strategy was still adhered to as competition from supermarkets and mail order companies increasingly made itself felt — earlier in Britain than in Germany. Later on this led to problems, but until well into the 1970s the company fared quite well with this concept. Constant rates of growth confirmed their policies.

The concern was headed by a strong personality, in Richard Spear. His long years of experience, his extensive connections and his business instinct had helped the company to reach an excellent position in the games trade. He was an entrepreneur of the old school, a hard worker with a lot of self-discipline, who was nevertheless always mindful of keeping in touch at a personal level with his employees both on the production line and in the administration. Each day after lunch "Mr. Richard", as he was often called, made his rounds of the factory and personally checked how things were going. A family atmosphere in the factory was very important to him, an aspect also shared by his son and successor, Francis Spear. Both endeavoured to provide good working conditions and fair wages. If there were differences of opinion, a discussion was sought immediately, in order to resolve conflicts amicably. In this way, quite unlike many other British companies, industrial action could be avoided at Spear's of Enfield over several decades. Relatively low staff turnover and a high proportion of employees with 25 or more working years' service at Spear's are expressions of a good working atmosphere.

Changes in personnel at management level became necessary in the course of the 1960s. The leading figures – Richard Spear and Fritz Kahn in Enfield, and Edgar Stockhausen and Else Spear in Nuremberg – had been active in the toy trade for decades, and were nearing the age where they had to think of entrusting the management to younger people. Tragically, Fritz Kahn could no longer participate in this generation change: He died in a traffic accident on 13th June, 1963. In Fritz Kahn, the concern lost a manager of many years' standing who had helped to build up the factory at Enfield and particularly to expand export, especially to the USA.

Kahn's death led to the appointment of two new directors: George Hanna (born 1923) was now responsible for marketing and sales, and Francis Spear (born 1931) became production director. Both had worked in various positions within the company since 1949, and both were to contribute considerably to its continuity. George Hanna continued working at executive level until his retirement in 1983 as a result of ill health. In his very important position he had a considerable share in the successful development of the company. "Jock", as he was often called, was exceptionally popular and respected with the staff and in trade circles. His door was always open for all his employees. With Francis Spear, who over the years had concerned himself above all with the technical side of games production, the fourth Spear generation joined the management of the company in 1963. Ten years later he finally took over the position of managing director from his father. In spite of his age, however, Richard Spear was still there to help whenever necessary.

In the meantime, essential changes had taken place in the company's legal form. As is the case in every family concern, Richard Spear, too, asked himself how the existence of the company could be safeguarded financially after his retirement from business life, and at the same time how the family's claims could be dealt with fairly. At the beginning of the 1960s he had considered selling the concern, and entered into negotiations with various interested parties. Indeed in September, 1964 a preliminary agreement to this effect was reached, but it was cancelled again. Instead, as a better alternative, preparations were made to go public in the following year on the London Stock Exchange, for in the meantime Spear had reached a size which made conversion into a public company possible. A large proportion of the capital remained in family hands: 35 per cent of the shares were sold, a tenth of these being purchased by employees and friends of the family. When the Spear shares were first traded on the London Stock Exchange on 17th January, 1966, the price rose by almost forty per cent on the first day! This was a clear sign of the City's trust in the solidity of the company.

The conversion to a public limited company only applied to the English parent company. The legal status of the associate in Nuremberg remained unaffected. A far-reaching change in personnel occurred in 1970, however, when Edgar Stockhausen and shortly thereafter Else Spear retired after reaching the age of seventy. 41 year-old business school graduate Gerhard Paul became the new managing director, having joined Spear in Nuremberg in 1966. Initially he had been responsible for the improvement of production planning. This also included the introduction of a basic data processing system without which administration would in the long run have become unmanageable.[125]

Paul was a man with great organisational talents who sought to the best of his ability to modernise the company which was partly out-dated and frequently relying on stop-gap measures. New factory extensions were built, and in 1973, a large capacity warehouse was opened.[126] The product range was revised, too. There were two main points of emphasis: the area of family games was extended, and the activity games were given new momentum. Especially mind games and games of strategy appealed to Gerhard Paul ("I enjoy making things which are meant to be enjoyed"). Thus, for example, "Momox" (1972) and "Janus" (1975) appeared, both fine games by the well-known Frankfurt games inventor Rudi Hoffmann. In the context of the "do-it-yourself" movement, "Nuremberg Hobby Kits" were developed in 1971. These bargain-price sets, packed in "see-through" bags, offered everything children or adults needed to produce useful little consumer articles such as greeting cards, napkin sets, ovencloths or raffia coasters, at little expense. Some of them had already been part of the Spear's range for a long time, and in their new get-up these products proved quite successful as impulse purchases on the counters of the retail shops.

Against the backdrop of a boom in the whole toy trade, Spear of Nuremberg found itself on a course of expansion in the 1970s, thus emulating its parent company in Enfield, which was going through a period of even more rapid growth. In the decade between 1968 and 1978 the number of employees in the UK doubled from 314 to the historical maximum of 662.[127] Together with the roughly 110 Nuremberg employees, therefore, almost 800 people were working for the group, one hundred years after the founding of the company – even more than in the best times between the wars.

With regard to production technology the most important innovation in the 1970s was the start of plastic moulding at Enfield. Since wooden Scrabble tiles, which traditionally were produced

Gerhard Paul (left), manager of Spear (Nuremberg) at the company stand, handing out prizes to the winners of a games competition on the occasion of the Nuremberg Toy Fair, 1977.

in Germany, could not be imported in the necessary quantities because of import restrictions, plastic tiles had already been dominating most markets for a long time. They were more uniform than the wooden ones and cheaper to produce. In addition, they had the technical advantage that they could be printed better by machine. Scrabble tiles and other plastic parts were obtained from various suppliers in the London region. When one of these companies came up for sale in 1973, Spear's management purchased the concern and integrated its production plant into their factory. The new department was extended to become a modern and highly efficient part of the company.

The high rate of growth in the "golden" 1970s presented great problems for the management.

The overheated economy in Britain led to a high rate of inflation, production and storage space became scarce, skilled workers were really hard to find and there were even temporary difficulties in obtaining raw materials. Factory extensions had been built in 1955 and 1970, but by 1973 the capacity of the site, which measured just 5,000 square metres (1.25 acres), was completely exhausted. In this respect they could only look enviously across at Nuremberg, where still enough land was available which had not been built on, on an area five times as large. Since at this time planning and building permission in Greater London was very hard to come by, the company management considered the complete transfer of the business to one of the "New Towns" which were created in various parts of Britain at the time. At the last moment, however,

Overview showing the various stages of development at Spear's (Enfield)

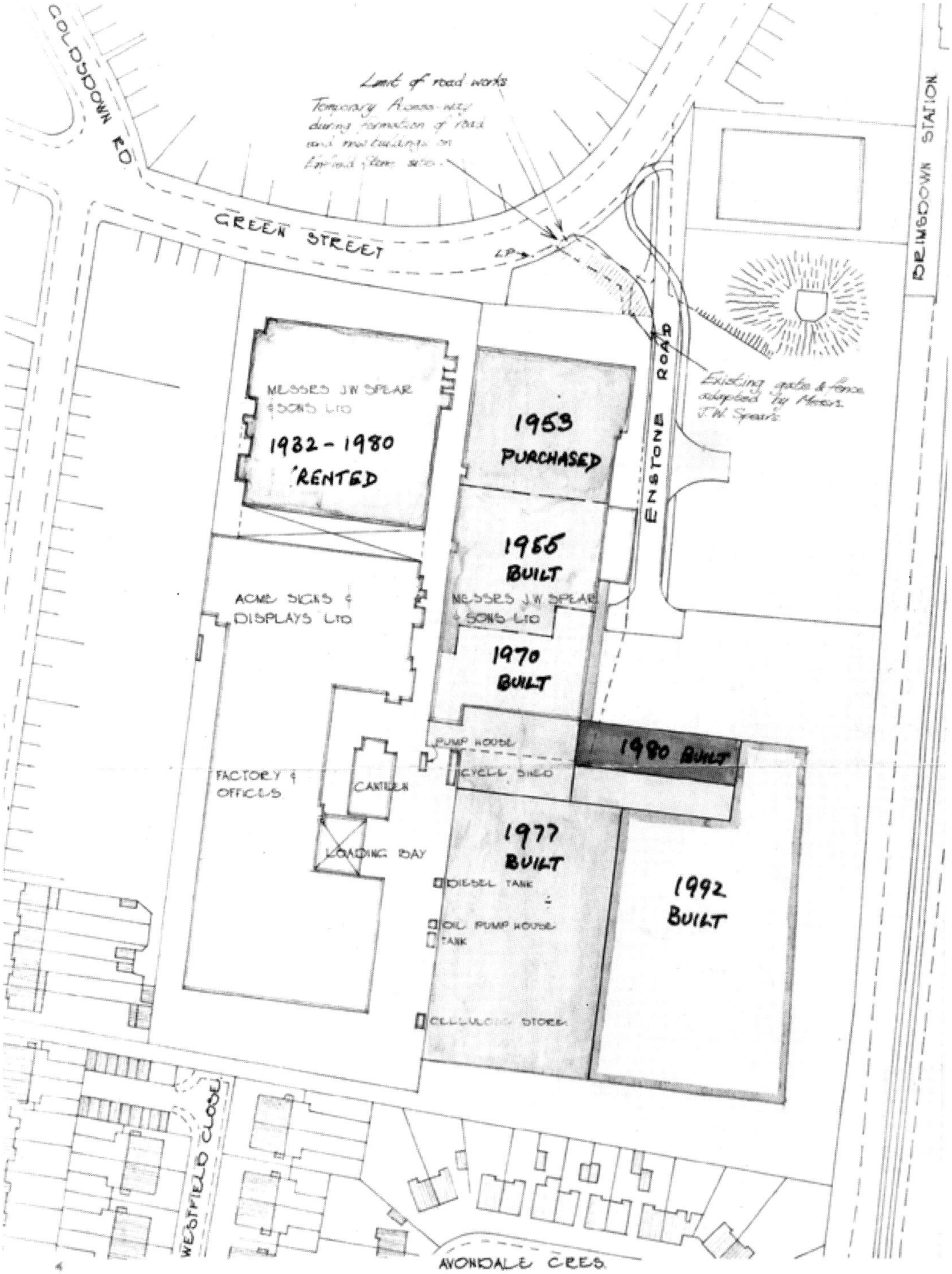

Aerial photograph from 1976, showing the former premises of the Enfield Stone Company in the foreground. Immediately afterwards, construction of a new Spear's factory was started on this site. The older Spear's buildings can be seen centre right.

they succeeded in purchasing the adjacent, dilapidated factory and site they had long tried in vain to acquire. Since these 16,000 square metres (4 acres) of land were already zoned for industrial use, Spear were finally granted planning permission for their desired building scheme.

A long-term development plan was drawn up and gradually carried out. Initially the construction of a new factory, which was completed at the end of 1977, took priority. In 1980 the company moved into Richard House, its new administration complex. Finally, in 1992, a large warehouse for finished products followed. All the new buildings were equipped to the most modern standards and made possible a much more efficient production and administration process. Ironically, however, Spear could never again achieve a

record which had been attained in 1977, the year before the opening of the new factory: In that year some six million games had been produced and sold!

The popular, hand-sawn Victory jigsaws from Gerald J. Hayter's company in Bournemouth contributed quite considerably to the positive development of these years. In September, 1970 Spear had bought the successful concern from the childless Hayters, who thus wanted to ensure the continuation of their life's work. Sale of the jigsaws was taken over by Spear under the unchanged brandname of "Victory", and product development and manufacture remained under Mr. Hayter's management in Bournemouth. It was agreed that he could work there as long as he wished, in spite of his advanced age. During

G.J. Hayter & Co., Bourne-mouth: A view of the factory's packing room, around 1965

Using the delicate saws with their thin sawblades required concentration and great skill. This photo was also taken around 1965.

Victory – G.J. Hayter & Co Ltd, Jigsaw Puzzles

In the parliamentary election campaign of 1910, Colonel Nicholson, Conservative Party candidate for East Dorset, had an unusual idea for recommending himself to his electorate: He had produced from his photograph a one hundred piece jigsaw puzzle and distributed it among the citizens of his constituency. He could hardly have known that, as well as promoting his own political career, he would also influence the future life of a boy who was, at that time, just eight years of age. Gerald Hayter, a farmer's son from Kingston Lacy, was one of the recipients of the election gift. He was so enthusiastic about this wooden jigsaw that he soon began using a fretsaw to produce all sorts of household and décor articles, and later also his own jigsaws.

At the age of 16, Gerald Hayter began his working life as a trainee with Lloyds Bank in Chirstchurch, Hampshire. His salary was so modest that he began to improve his meagre budget by selling jigsaws he had made himself mainly using second hand ply wood and old calendar pictures. This hobby developed into a fairly lucrative sideline. During his holidays, Hayter cycled to the toy shops in the surrounding area in order to bring in orders for his goods which – shortly after the victorious ending of the First World War – he named "Victory" jigsaws. When he got married in 1924, his wife, Nellie, gave him all the support he needed for the gradual building up of his small business. With his parents' help a workshop was fitted out in a garden shed, and gradually he even succeeded in selling his precisely sawn jigsaws to London shops. The business grew and in 1928 premises were rented in Bournemouth.

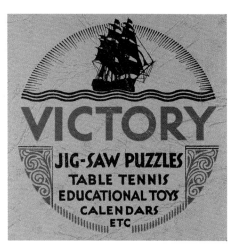

Company logo, around 1937

In 1932, at the height of the world economic crisis, Gerald Hayter took a bold step. He gave up his secure position at the bank in order to be able to devote himself completely to his own business. Production was now taken up on a larger scale in a factory building in Boscombe, near Bournemouth. Thanks to untiring work and high quality craftsmanship, Victory goods gradually became known to the many British jigsaw enthusiasts. Soon even members of the Royal Family counted among the customers of the south coast jigsaw factory. King George VI always had his own table with Victory jigsaws at Sandringham Castle, and the future Queen Elizabeth and Princess Margaret found jigsaws from Boscombe under the Christmas tree every year.

The concern was reorganized and expanded in the years following the Second World War. Up to 120 workers now painstakingly produced by hand the popular plywood jigsaws, which took up historical, geographical, technical, cultural and natural history themes in countless variations. The range included simple jigsaws for small children and for educational purposes as well as extremely sophisticated puzzles of 1,000 pieces or more. Since the latter were mostly delivered without any picture to work to, quite a few jigsaw enthusiasts may have found their skills stretched to the limits. Whether the customer from Northern Ireland, who had a 10,000 piece puzzle made to order, was ever able to enjoy the completed picture, will remain a mystery forever.

Gradually other articles were also incorporated in the range, such as table tennis bats, board games and educational games, supplementing G. J. Hayter's main products. A 1950s catalogue with all of 35 pages displays a great wealth of goods and explains why Victory products enjoyed such high regard, not only in Britain, but also in the USA and numerous other countries around the world. In the best way possible Hayter combined quality hand-made articles with a stimulating game idea still popular among all age groups and social classes today. Many older jigsaw-lovers, who nowadays are forced to make do with modern puzzles punched from card, will no doubt miss such inscriptions as "approximately 500 pieces", which recall those days of skilled handwork – when you could never be sure, even in a specialized concern such as Gerald J. Hayter, whether just 491 or 512 pieces would come out of a sheet of plywood.

This account is based on various newspaper articles and reports on Gerald Hayter and Victory jigsaw puzzles from the Spear Archives as well as on conversations with Francis Spear.

the 1970s these high-quality Victory jigsaws sold very well, but in the 1980s overseas competition grew more and more. In view of the high production costs arising from work predominantly done by hand the wooden jigsaws, unlike the considerably cheaper punched card products, ultimately were no longer viable. For this reason Spear's management most reluctantly closed the Bournemouth concern in 1988, a business which had written a very British chapter in games history.

In 1978 Spear of Enfield celebrated its company centenary, and a year later Nuremberg followed suit. The occasion was celebrated both in England and in Germany. Two special trains took the complete British staff to Portsmouth where they enjoyed, together with their colleagues from the Victory Jigsaw Puzzle factory, a glittering party which lasted well into the night. In Nuremberg the management invited a select circle of VIPs and business friends to an entertaining formal dinner in the banqueting hall of the old imperial castle. Quite in keeping with the medieval surroundings, Sir "Spearitus", a knight in full armour, officiated in the capacity of resident ghost and host. In the presence of the English management, speakers from the world of politics and business used the opportunity to praise the company as "pioneer of the trade".[128]

The Wild Eighties

"Spearitus" was more than just a party gag: He was the symbolic figure of a new advertising strategy planned by the Nuremberg company , which had been renamed Spear-Spiele GmbH in 1978. In a playful way he was also to make clear to the German public, once and for all, how to pronounce that English name.[129] The large-scale advertising campaign, which was meant to improve sales with its innovative catalogue design, competitions and new sales displays, was badly needed, for after several "golden" years the whole trade found itself in a severe crisis, affecting companies at an international level.

The Spear group's turnover and profits had already fallen off towards the end of the 1970s.

Then, in March 1980, it was announced that one of the trade's leading concerns, the Anglo-American toy group Dunbee Combex Marx (DCM) was going into receivership. The news shocked the trade, being an unmistakable sign that even the large concerns could no longer escape the pressures of the general recession. One of DCM's subsidiaries was the Dutch company SIO (Speelgoed Industrie Overijssel).This business produced wooden toys and had been licensed by Spear to manufacture and sell Scrabble in the Netherlands since 1955. Since Spear were looking for possible investments abroad at this time, they entered into purchase negotiations. Under pressure from SIO's banks, who were pushing for a quick sale and were threatening to close the business otherwise, a hurried examination was carried out. The result was that Spear's

Three generations of Spears, Portsmouth, 1978.
Back row (from left to right): Gerhard and Margaret Paul, John Estall, Timothy Spear, Gerald Hayter, Margaret Greene, Francis Spear, George Hanna, Ruth Estall.
Front row (left to right): Margaret Hanna, Susan Spear, Richard Spear, Sally Spear, Nellie Hayter

management decided to buy the struggling concern in March 1980, at a price of £889,000.[130]

As Francis Spear stated in retrospect, the purchase of SIO was a "bad decision, as Spear did not have the personnel or the experience to run a distribution company in a foreign country".[131] The numerous problems in connection with SIO took up a great deal of his time. In spite of intensive efforts neither the British parent company nor the Dutch management succeeded in getting SIO back on the road to success. To crown it all a disastrous fire destroyed the SIO wooden toy factory at Vroomshoop in eastern Holland. Unfortunately it was then discovered that the factory was underinsured.

In August, 1983 the SIO affair came to an inglorious end: Spear was obliged to dispose of the concern for a nominal sum, this having, of course, a significantly negative effect on their own balance sheet. In this year, for the first (and last) time since the opening of the factory in Enfield in 1932, the group made a loss. And for the first time ever in the company's history a managing director was then appointed who was not a member of the Spear family. David Smith took over from Francis Spear, who became non-executive chairman of the company, responsible for overseas subsidiaries, and continued to be involved in manufacturing.

The purchase of SIO had been part of a plan for Spear to meet the conditions of the coming single European market by building up its own continental distribution network. To this end, in 1981 Spear joined with the French Habourdin family, which enjoyed an excellent reputation within the French toy trade. Habourdin had previously distributed Scrabble in France and thus already had connections with Spear. Together they founded Habourdin International, a marketing company which was to distribute both Spear products and those of other manufacturers, in France and French-speaking countries. Although

Spear's shares in this company had to be sold again in the wake of the SIO crisis of 1983, they continued to work together. The companies merged in 1989, which contributed substantially to the group's considerable success in the last years of its existence.

The turbulent year of 1981 also brought with it a far-reaching change for Spear-Spiele GmbH. The business had been modernised and rationalised under the management of Gerhard Paul, but now as a result of the general recession in the toy market parts of the expanded production plant lay unutilised. Sales stagnated and profits fell. When the old-established Fürth games manufacturer and Spear competitor L. Kleefeld & Co. also got into economic difficulties, the two companies merged. Spear took over the shares of the limited partner who was retiring for reasons of age, and at the same time the concern was converted into a limited company. The previous boss, business school graduate Herbert Kreppner, remained managing partner.[132] Kleefeld's production plant was transferred from their headquarters, which were just about one kilometre from the Spear factory, to Höfener Straße. It was hoped that because of the extraordinarily similar production processes the plant could be more efficiently used to capacity, to the benefit of both parties. Furthermore it was agreed that both companies would retain their product development and sales organisation for their own articles.

Although the games range of the two companies was very similar, their marketing and production policies differed considerably. At this time Spear had a relatively stable range of some 100 articles, the various Scrabble products being by far the best-sellers. The launching of new games every year played a rather secondary role. Because of the large standard range, production followed a carefully worked-out plan which aimed at a minimum of machine changes. Kleefeld, on the other hand, had no comparable winners in its range and

Nürnberger Spielefabrik L. Kleefeld & Co

The Nürnberger Spielefabrik (Nuremberg Games Factory) was founded by businessman Ludwig Kleefeld in Fürth in 1884.[1] Under the company trademark, the cloverleaf, the concern manufactured mainly parlour and activity games and picture cubes. As well as the usual drawing, sewing, embroidery, weaving and painting sets which belonged to the core of every range of activity games, there were also many original parlour games and games of skill. Kleefeld specialised in modern motifs from the world of technology and of sports.

The appeal of many Kleefeld articles lay in the use of mechanical devices which brought elements of skill and luck into play. The car game "In flotter Fahrt" (Speeding Along, 1911) for example, had a toy car with propeller which could be moved around the course with the aid of a blow-pipe. The betting game "Tip-Tip" (1908) consisted of a punched box-inlay with a letter of the alphabet beneath each of the holes. At the start of the game, each player had to note down a short word. By means of a sprung lever on a small metal typewriter a ball was then catapulted into the box, where it landed on one of the letters. If the noted word contained this letter, the player either received a reward or, if it did not, had to pay a fine.

From 1907 the concern was headed by Leopold Bomeisl, son-in-law of the company's founder. In 1915 his brother Moritz joined the company. Under their management Kleefeld became one of the leading German producers in the games trade. In 1926 the company, which at the time had between 150 and 180 employees and exported world-wide, moved to prestigious premises of the Fleischmann & Bloedel Nachf. J. Berlin AG toy factory. The range was expanded considerably over the years, but the original lines – parlour and activity games and picture cubes – were maintained. Only conjuring sets, table tennis, table croquet, cut-out sheets and jolly jumpers were added, as can be gathered from the 1937 catalogue. On 52 pages, it lists several hundred articles, many of them available in English, French, Dutch, Portuguese or Spanish language versions.

At the beginning of 1938 Kleefeld also offered "Monopoly", the "new, interesting and topical parlour game for adults and mature

Company founder Ludwig Kleefeld, 1909

young people", as an advertisement in the "German Toy Gazette" proclaimed. This best-known of all business-world games had come onto the German market in 1936, but had sold rather badly. The game was obviously out of place in National Socialist Germany, and is even said to have been banned during the war, since it apparently seemed "unsuitable for the education of Germany's youth, because of its emphasis on speculation".[2]

The Bomeisl brothers were given no further opportunity, though, to popularize this game, which was to become so successful in post-war Germany, the land of the "economic miracle". The National Socialist persecution of the Jews forced them to give up their business. The company was "Aryanized" and in 1939 passed into the hands of wooden toy producer Max Herbart from Steinach, in Thuringia. Leopold Bomeisl and his wife, Marie, emigrated to Rotterdam in the summer of the same year. The couple were arrested by the Gestapo there in 1942 and deported to Sobibor, where both were killed.[3] Moritz Bomeisl survived the Nazi terror and the war years. After the business was returned he continued to run it until his death in 1951. Thereafter, his wife, Auguste, and her brother-in-law, Dr. Leonhard Kreppner, were responsible for the fate of the concern so rich in tradition. Dr. Kreppner's son Herbert took over its management in 1966 and headed the company until March, 1997. The connection with Spear's Games was established during this time. Following the closure of the Nuremberg Spear factory in 1984, L. Kleefeld & Co. GmbH moved back to Fürth, where it had been founded, and today it is still operating successfully as a marketing company under the name of Klee-Spiele GmbH.

1 We thank Herbert Kreppner of Fürth for valuable information and documents concerning the company history.
2 On the history of Monopoly compare: Dan Glimne/Barbara Weber, "Monopoly", in: Spielbox, 4/95, pp. 10 - 14 and 5/95, pp. 4 - 8.
3 Fürth Municipal Archives, Aryanization files, AR 33, Nr. 149; Fürth Book of Remembrance, edited by the Committee for the Remembrance of Fürth Shoah Victims, Fürth 1997, p. 61

Richard Spear, around 1975

with great confidence. In 1981 – according to the advertising – the "MS Spearitus" (a display device in the form of a ship provided to specialist customers) steered off at full steam into the "Spear-Spiele-Spaß" (Spear-Games-Fun). The following year the sales motto was: "Bei uns blühen die schönsten Spiele-Ideen" (The finest games ideas blossom in our garden), but the desired riches did not roll in. The profit situation of the Nuremberg company so rich in tradition worsened steadily, and the appointment of a second director – Reinhold Weber, already responsible for marketing and sales since 1979 – could not remedy that either. Against the backdrop of the bitter losses of the crisis year 1983, the parent company decided the same year to close the original Nuremberg factory at the end of 1984 and to produce only in the modern factory at Enfield in future.

The Kleefeld shares were sold to managing director Herbert Kreppner, and the factory site was also disposed of and some of the machines transferred to Enfield. The considerably reduced Spear Games range was still distributed along with Klee games in 1984, before Nuremberg company Apex Spiel + Hobby GmbH took over the task in 1985. Some of the sales staff were taken over by Apex; the roughly sixty remaining were made redundant. After 85 years games production in the historical factory complex in Höfener Straße came to an end on December 31, 1984.

Richard Spear did not experience this sad end of an epoch. He had died on 6th August, 1983, after a long illness. He had to a very high degree determined the varied fortunes of the Spear company in Germany and in England for half a century. He died the undisputed head of his family, and in him the company lost its popular "old boss" and the whole games trade a knowledgeable and highly respected man, who had been an entrepreneur heart and soul. His life's work had given the name Spear's Games a fine reputation all over the world.

was thus considerably more flexible in taking up new variations of products. This also meant more frequent adjustments to the production plans. A further difference consisted in the fact that Spear traditionally only supplied specialist shops, and Kleefeld the wholesale and export trades. These company philosophies were hard to reconcile which led to frequent clashes over the production plans. In any case, the hoped-for savings did not occur and the profit situation continued to worsen.

The Nuremberg "Spearers" launched into their second century of games production in 1980

Finished product warehouse at Spear's (Nuremberg)

External view of the company buildings at Höfener Straße, 1976. The low building replaced the old factory buildings which were destroyed during the war.

New administration building at Enstone Road, Enfield, 1981

End-Game at Enfield

The hard, but, in the group's interest, obviously unavoidable consolidation measures put the concern, which had been struggling since the end of the 1970s, back on the road to success. In 1984 and 1985 satisfactory results could be achieved. Turnover and profits increased, though they did not reach the high level of the 1970s. But in both the following years difficulties started anew which were mainly of a structural nature. Traditionally, Spear had worked closely with independent toy dealers, who valued the company's wide range. This alliance was reflected in various awards from the British Association of Toy Retailers, which were presented to Spear for, among other things, their non-seasonal range. But the specialist shops were finding it harder to hold their own against the competition of the large supermarket and discount chains, which for their part were only interested in "cherry-picking" a few items from what was a large selection, and then only, if these were extensively advertised in the media. Even Scrabble sales stagnated, albeit still at a high level. It was the great era of "Trivial Pursuit", that amazingly popular game of knowledge which indeed badly affected Scrabble for some years.

The company tried to counteract these negative developments in two ways. The previous dependence on specialist shops was reduced by promoting new sales outlets using shop chains. At the same time the presentation of many games was gradually adapted to prevailing tastes and the range modernised by development of new products. The company logo was given a bright yellow and red frame which was designed to attract greater customer attention. In 1986, as part of a large advertising campaign, a mobile day-nursery, which was meant to tempt parents into specialist shops with their children, went on tour across Britain. The motto was "Come into our little World", and above all was supposed to introduce a new game, which came onto the market in the same year with the title "Little World of Scrabble". This was an ambitious learning-game project which had been devised with the co-operation of university educationalists. The idea of the game was to introduce children to the world of reading and writing on the basis of Scrabble with books and letter game sets. As innovative as this approach might have been, the high expectations were not fulfilled.

"Rummikub", produced under licence and based on the card game Rummy, was considerably

more successful. It had already been introduced in 1984 and sold well for years. Just as for Scrabble, public competitions were organised for this game. The company entered new territory with so-called audio games such as "Go fetch it!" (1985) and "Chartbuster" (1986). In these games the attraction lay in the combination of board game and audio cassette, which contributed game instructions and background music.

Scrabble, the undisputed hit, was also redesigned, in 1988/89. The box and game plan design was modernised and new Scrabble products such as an electronic timer and a reworked Junior Scrabble with double sided game plan were introduced. Indeed the "new" Scrabble returned

once again to the top position among the best-selling games. It experienced a renaissance at the beginning of the 1990s, leading to a rapid rise in the sales figures and thus also in the Spear group's profits. In 1991, for example, with total sales of £27.3 million, profits of £2.53 million before tax could be realised. This corresponded to a growth in profits of 80.5 per cent compared to the previous year![133]

This positive economic development reflected the intensive modernisation efforts of the previous years, which had been considerably accelerated by changes in management. After the previous managing director David Smith had left the company in 1986, Francis Spear managed the

company temporarily, once again. Michael Bucher, president of Habourdin International, joined the concern shortly afterwards, first as marketing consultant, and then as marketing director. In January, 1989 he was appointed managing director. The concerns merged in May, 1989.

Bucher introduced a wealth of measures which modernised Spear further. The advertising budget was increased considerably. Two million pounds were invested in advertising for eight selected main products in 1990 alone, a record sum for the company. In the same year fifty new products came onto the market. "We've shed our old image", the 1990 catalogue announced under the picture of a gloriously colourful Spear butter-

fly which had emerged from its cocoon.[134] This cut both ways, though, for within the company, the new management also carried out unpopular measures which severely shook up what until then had been a predominantly family atmosphere. As a result of rationalisation the number of employees decreased from 453 in 1987 to 241 in 1994.[135] The shareholders could rejoice, however: Their shares continued to rise steadily up until the sale in 1994.

For Spear's, the increasing international interweaving of the whole trade with regard to the single European market led to a co-operation with Dutch games manufacturer Hausemann en Hoette (Jumbo). This family concern was roughly

OUR GAMES DON'T NEED ANY PLUGS.

There are no electronic 9-days-wonder games in Spears exciting range for 1980. Just boxes full of fun for all the family at real value-for-money prices.

Full page, full colour ads like this will be appearing in Family Circle, Mother, Woman & Home, She, Radio Times, Look-In, My Weekly and Woman's Weekly – backed up by big spaces in the News of the World and Sunday Express.

WE'RE PUTTING THE FOCUS ON 'FOCUS'.

The never-get-board game. Focus is Spears fast-moving and exciting new game of skill and strategy for 10 year olds upwards and we're launching it in time for Christmas in the Sunday Times, Sunday Express and Games & Puzzles!

Ring 01-366 0261 and we'll make sure you're well stocked for the Christmas rush!

A TREEFUL OF GAMES FOR THE PRICE OF A SPACE INVASION.

£46.00   £47.70

SPEAR'S GAMES (VICTORY)
The best name in games since 1878.
J.W. SPEAR & SONS LTD. (INCORPORATING G.J. HAYTER & CO. LTD.), PO BOX 49, ENFIELD, MIDDLESEX EN3 7SF.

Spear advertisement in British trade journals, 1980. Emphasising the family character of Spear's games with their traditional outlook and low prices, the company takes a stance against the growing influence of expensive electronic games competition on the market.

the same size as Spear and had a similar product range. Before the Second World War it had distributed Spear's games in the Netherlands, but after the war it had set up its own production. After the sale of SIO in 1983, Jumbo had taken over the sales of Scrabble in the Netherlands. When Spear's German Scrabble distributor Apex had to cease trading in 1989, Jumbo also took on the German market. As a countermove Spear

took over sales of Jumbo products in Great Britain and France. The close co-operation between Jumbo and Spear expressed itself not only in the area of joint product development, but also in the fact that both companies sent a representative to the board of the partner concern.

In the 1990s Francis Spear and his second wife, Hazel, who had worked for Spear since 1968, began to think about what would happen after their retirement from business life. Francis had a son and a daughter from his first marriage. Neither they nor any other family member, however, showed ambitions to take an active part in the company. Thus various possibilities for securing the company's future were considered, among them mergers with other games manufacturers. The family shareholders and the Spear trustees, who together owned roughly forty per cent of the share capital, became convinced that the best solution would be to sell the company. This was to go ahead in 1996, the year in which Francis Spear would reach the age of 65 and would retire from business.

Francis Spear's preferred partner was the American giant Hasbro. The concern held the Scrabble rights for the USA and Canada and had possessed an almost 27 per cent share in Spear since 1990. Co-operation with Hasbro, under its president, Alan Hassenfeld, had always been very satisfactory. For the Spear family it was comforting to have financially strong business associates who accompanied their business ventures with goodwill, but without influencing these directly, not even expecting to be represented on the board of directors, as would have been quite normal in these circumstances. At the same time the large Hasbro block of shares was good protection against accumulation of shares by unknown investors, even if only relatively few shares were available for trading as a result.

In summer, 1993, first private talks began between Alan Hassenfeld and Francis Spear regarding a later take-over. Spear's Games were attractive to Hasbro for several reasons: The concern was on the ascendant. Its profits had tripled since 1989, and within Great Britain it held a sixteen per cent share of the games market. With around forty per cent of the market share, Hasbro was itself by far the largest games supplier in Britain, but of course the purchase of the world rights to the classic Scrabble especially appealed to the international concern. On the part of the Spear family, the future of the company was seen as being well looked after with Hasbro, above all because the group, incorporating among others the two large American games manufacturers Milton Bradley (since 1985) and Parker Brothers (since 1991), possessed substantial know-how and experience. Further, the expanding American concern had the reputation of dealing fairly with the staff of the companies they took over.[136]

For various reasons, Francis Spear thought it advisable to bring forward the proposed sale of the company. In December, 1993, Hasbro consulted Spear's board of directors for the first time. They expressed interest in a take-over and asked for confidential information essential for the drawing up of an offer. When it became known that they had in mind an offer only slightly over the trading price for the shares at the time (£ 5.50), Hasbro's approach was rejected by the majority of Spear directors. A veritable business thriller ensued, causing a sensation in trade and financial circles on both sides of the Atlantic.[137]

Without consulting the board of directors, the Spear trustees, who represented a majority of the family's holdings, entered into negotiations with Hasbro and agreed to the sale of their share capital at nine pounds per share, a price which lay more than twenty per cent above the highest price from the last stock exchange quotations. The trustees were permitted, however, to withdraw from this agreement if a higher bid was publicly made within three working days of its

announcement. In spite of intensive efforts by Spear board members, bankers and legal advisers, who considered the bid too low, it seemed impossible to find a potential buyer who would step in against Hasbro within such a short time. But ten minutes (!) before midnight, on the day the deadline expired, a written offer was received in London from the American toy concern Mattel (Barbie, Fisher Price Toys): Mattel offered £10 per share. The race for Spear was still on.

Tough negotiations resulted in the weeks which followed. The battle between the American arch rivals, who at different times both claimed to be "the world's largest toy manufacturer" was extensively commented upon in the press: "Barbie and Sindy fight for favours of Spear", according to the Daily Telegraph and "Babes battle for Scrabble maker" in the Express.[138] Ultimately Hasbro raised its offer to £11, and Mattel followed, offering 50 pence more. Thus the battle of the giants was decided: on 12th July, 1994, Mattel's bid was accepted, and with this offer even Hasbro was prepared to sell its shares.

Nuremberg Toy Fair, 1988: Francis and Hazel Spear receiving a certificate of honour, thanking them for 25 continuous years of presence of J. W. Spear & Sons at the Toy Fair.

At the end of the day all shareholders (including Hasbro) profited from this battle for Spear, which had driven the price up considerably: the transaction amounted ultimately to £62 million.

Generally it was thought that Mattel had paid this very high price in order to get onto the games market in which up to then the concern had only played a secondary role. Hasbro had achieved a turnover of $915 million with games world-wide in 1993, against Mattel's mere $50 million.[139] Was the Spear take-over an attempt to improve this weak position? Initially it seemed so. Production continued normally; it was agreed that Francis and Hazel Spear be allowed to go on working for Spear until Francis reached retirement age in June, 1996. This, however, was not allowed to happen. The great-grandson of the company's founder and his wife were pressurised into leaving the concern early. Both had their final day at work for the company on 17th March, 1995. Under such circumstances and after so many years of working for the company, the leave-taking was very painful: the farewell party with the staff was a sad occasion for those present. In numerous telephone calls to the local press employees vented their displeasure at the unworthy treatment of the Spears, who were very popular in the company.[140]

Seven months after the Spears had left, Mattel announced that they wanted to close the factory in Enfield by the end of the year. Production of Spear's games was to be transferred to Peterlee in northern England, where a toy factory belonging to Mattel subsidiary Fisher-Price already existed. Roughly 150 staff members were directly affected by the closure, but all Enfield mourned the closing of this business, which had given many families in the district work for over six decades. A series of articles in the local press once again showed how much Spear had been part of local economic and social life. In several articles former employees expressed their disappointment and anger at the enforced closure of a factory which

for many had been more than just a place to earn money. "Spears was like one big, happy family", was the banner headline in the Enfield Independent, and moving memories from former employees were printed, unanimously conjuring up the harmony of old times.[141]

This situation fuelled public outrage, when the new company management made Hazel and Francis Spear stand in the cold outside a locked factory gate for hours on the last day of production, when they wanted to join the remaining employees in taking leave of the place where they had worked together for many years. While inside the factory an official ceremony was going on, the Spears stood outside the gate and handed out leaflets announcing that they had set up a private foundation which could among other charitable causes benefit needy former company employees. One worker expressed what many were thinking: "I can't understand why they weren't allowed in. The Spear family made this company. They were good to their workers and to see them standing on the other side of the gate I could have cried, they looked just like prisoners on the outside looking in. But we are having a workers party and they're invited to that – it will be our chance to say goodbye."[142] And that is just what happened a few days later: "The roof rose that night to Tina Turner's 'Simply the Best'", Hazel Spear recalls the memorable party and continues, full of gratitude: "The affection and loyalty of the Spear employees during a very difficult time has and will always leave a lasting memory on Francis and myself."[143] Since then, two successful reunions of former employees have taken place, hosted by Francis and Hazel Spear in their home.

Some weeks after the factory closure the production plant was dismantled and part of it transferred to Peterlee. But it soon emerged that this factory was lacking the know-how for the complicated work with paper and card. Only plastic had been processed here up until then and

games production by its nature required quite different processes and knowledge. In summer, 1997, this factory was also closed and the Spear's games which Mattel still offers today – above all Scrabble – are manufactured outside Great Britain. Only time will tell what will happen to the brand name Spear and whether it will indeed be kept on or will soon continue to exist only in people's memories.

In any case the time had certainly come to look back with this book on a family concern which made games history. That this was possible in such depth at all is especially due to Francis Spear, for he has preserved his sense of tradition – unlike so many other persons responsible in the toy trade. Along with his wife, former export manager Norman Thompson and former Scrabble champion Anne Bradford he established

a foundation which in the meantime has set up the Spear Games Archives at his home. It was opened on 17th June, 1996, Francis Spear's 65th birthday, with a wonderful reception and in the presence of numerous guests from the toy trade from all over the world. In a well-ordered manner, the Archives present well over 1,500 games and documents from the turn of the century to the most recent past. They are a veritable treasure trove for all who want to track down the cultural history of games in the industrial age using the example of the Spear company. It is hoped that this book will inspire a great many interested people to do just that.

Plate 1
Spiele-Sammlung. 3 beliebte Spiele, around 1935
Compendium of Games, around 1970
Compendium of Games, around 1955

Marion Faber

Compendium of Games

Having some games in the house and using them more or less frequently in the family circle or with friends is not unusual, even today. When TV and print media were not yet monopolising our leisure time, family homes and meeting places for young people offered a variety of popular games. No holiday home or youth hostel was complete without a classic games compendium in a cardboard or wooden box containing rule books and components for nine men's morris, draughts, chess, dominoes, halma and ludo. After all, parlour games were designed to bring people together and maybe to help them to get to know each other better through shared personal experiences.

As early as 1889, the new company J. W. Spear & Söhne advertised its games compendiums in the "Guide to the Toy Industry", although at the time parlour games still held much lower priority than other items of their product range. The compendiums contained dice games, dominoes, cards, draughts and chess pieces, and represented the basic set of board and other games which could be found in any middle-class household. A chess board with chess pieces owned by Jacob Wolf Spear shows that this game was popular particularly in bourgeois circles. It is a simple wooden set for everyday use with pieces resembling the English Staunton type ones, which to this day are preferred in tournament chess because of their stability and clear shapes. The chess board was probably made by Hartwig, Spear and Bergmann around 1870. During the 1870s and 1880s many international chess tournaments took place, eventually leading to the first official world championships in 1886.

The history of games shows that games production has always reflected the ideas of its time, and incorporated social and artistic influences or educational trends. Technical progress or politics could sometimes also play a part. Even nowadays, the games industry offers many new parlour games every year - mirroring contemporary realities, events and dreams. Thus games topics around the turn of the century, for example, reflected progress in aviation, the discovery of the North Pole and the Boy Scout Movement. In this way games companies made good use of the momentum generated by technical and social developments. Aeroplanes and zeppelins and pioneers such as Lilienthal, the Wright brothers, Blériot, and Graf Zeppelin, hit the headlines and became idols which were quickly taken up by the tin toy and games industries. Amundsen's and Peary's adventurous Arctic expeditions were reflected in games and youth literature world-wide. The reform movement which started around the turn of the century and aimed at helping city dwellers to escape from the big towns and their conflicts was represented in the games topics of Boy Scouts and rambling.

The game industry has always been keen on taking up current trends as quickly as possible. Thus during the World Wars, propaganda type games were published in Germany (and elsewhere), focusing on the topics of warfare and war heroes. Some games showed the almost natural inclusion of war in everyday civilian life – dealing, for example, with issues such as air raid shelters and energy saving – and always fuelling hatred of the enemy. Special games versions for soldiers at the front or in military hospitals were developed, which were small enough to be posted in a standard forces' letter. These games – mainly chess, draughts, halma, nine men's morris and dominoes – were made entirely from cardboard. Even the play pieces had been replaced by cardboard counters.

When in the 1920s the USA became the world's most powerful industrial nation and a political, social and cultural role model for Western countries, this development influenced the worlds of fine art, music and literature, but also city life and the entertainment industry. Games of chance such as poker and roulette, as well as one-armed bandits and betting on horses and greyhounds held considerable appeal for many people, especially in the difficult economic climate. Contemporary films such as Fritz Lang's "Dr. Mabuse, the Gambler" (1922) also conjured up the world of casinos and gambling clubs. Monte Carlo was considered the Mecca of gamblers world-wide and was the setting for dramatic stories about money lost and won, in parlour games such as "Bombs on Monte Carlo" (Germany, 1931) or "Gambling in Monte Carlo" (France, 1932). Many impulses for games and toys came from the world of film. It was, for example, considered very smart to try one's luck with the "harmless" version of roulette at home, with an aeroplane instead of the usual small ball indicating the winning number. Charlie Chaplin and popular comic heroes such as Bonzo, Mickey Mouse and Donald Duck figured in dice games and took over the nurseries in all sorts of guises: as soft toys or toys made from tin or celluloid.

Scrabble was a true novelty on the games market when it was launched after the Second World War. In addition to its high entertainment value, this crossword game followed the trends of the time by also including a learning component. The number of learning games showed a marked increase until the mid 1970s. This development may be seen as a parallel to contemporary educational policies striving to create equal opportunities for all children in their schooling and professional training. Sophisticated family and adult games became much more important in German-speaking countries from that time on, resulting generally in much wider acceptance of games within the population. People increasingly wanted to enjoy leisure time and life in general, and a certain trend towards a more playful approach to life was also noticeable. This climate proved fertile ground for a major increase in the range of games for adults. More people than ever played games in Germany. This trend was reflected in average annual growth rates of 10 to 12 per cent for the games industry. Games associations and professional games critics established themselves in the 1970s. A jury consisting of journalists and games experts was established in 1978 by the association

"Game of the Year". In order to provide some orientation for the playing public this group selected the best of the many new games launched every year. Games archives, museums, magazines and regular meetings of game inventors and players followed in the 1980s and also influenced the games scene in Austria and Switzerland. Various games "fashions" have been observed since then: from games of knowledge and strategy, to dice craze, quiz mania and detective games. The popularity of parlour games decreased rapidly with the advent of new electronic games towards the end of the 1970s and early 1980s, winning over mainly the young people. It is maybe no coincidence that the end of Spear's Nuermberg games production fell into this period. But in spite of all new possibilities offered by our digital media age, traditional board and card games have managed to hold their ground quite well up to the present.

A look back on a century of games history shows that the most successful games were those based on clear and original ideas with few, concise rules and a pleasing design. Games promoting speed, memory, powers of language, manual skills and presence of mind have always sold rather well. Apart from a small, well-defined nucleus of chess players, only a fairly small section of the general public play games which promote strategic thinking, judgement and powers of combination. The various qualities expected of a good parlour game lie somewhere between these two extremes. Nowadays nearly all games have a narrative framework and offer topical games equipment conjuring up a different world for the players. People who play a lot and are forever on the look-out for exciting new ideas prefer complicated games with sophisticated rules. They are particularly interested in using their minds more efficiently, stretching their creativity to its limits and planning to translate play strategies into their lives and professional situations. The large majority of "occasional players", however, prefer family games which have high entertainment value, are easy to understand and suitable for all ages.

While the games industry, particularly in the 20th century, has always been keen on taking up new ideas, an astonishing number of titles were kept in the product range for a very long time. This is particularly true for Spear's games. Some games which figured in their 1920s and 1930s catalogues can be traced to the 1960s and later. The basic recipe for success with Spear's has always been a healthy mix of tried and tested classics and topical novelties which were designed with a wide, international public in mind and therefore did not address any political or religious topics. The broad variety of games offered constitutes a fascinating reflection of the cultural history of an entire era. On the following pages the "Compendium of Games" sets out to introduce the main sections of the comprehensive Spear's range. The selection is based on the usual classification of games into those involving strategy, chance, activities, learning, patience, cards and manual skills. At the same time information is given about the origins of various types of games.

Note on the captions of the colour plates

Titles of games are given in the original language of the depicted game. English translations and additional information on inventors and artists are provided in brackets where necessary. The titles of actual English equivalents are given *in italics*.

Plate 2
Chess set owned by Jacob Wolf Spear. The board was presumably made by Hartwig, Spear & Bergmann of Sonneberg around 1870.

Games of Tactics and Strategy

Chess certainly ranks highest among those games which need neither dice nor other elements of chance. There are many theories concerning its origins, but hardly any material to back them up. Most chess researchers assume that India is the country where chess originated. Most probably, forerunners of chess existed in this country in the early centuries of the Christian calendar, and perhaps even earlier. Chess is not documented in old Sanskrit texts until the 7th century AD, however. In the early Middle Ages the game made its way to Europe via Persia and Arabia. Since then it has risen from being a pastime for aristocrats and clerics into a most demanding game for all strata of society and even to a competitive sport.

All classical games compendiums, in addition to having a chess set, contain games of nine men's morris, draughts and halma. Nine men's morris is among the oldest games known to humankind: finds in Bronze Age graves in Ireland date this game of strategy to about 2000 BC. Draughts in its classical form is much younger. Written documentation and pictorial representations of the game only became common about 1500 AD, mainly in Spain and France. In the course of the following centuries, draughts developed into one of the most popular games ever, mainly in Britain and the USA. The youngest among the group of traditional games of tactics is halma. It was invented in 1883 by English surgeon George Howard Monks and soon after was published in the USA. "Chinese Chequers", a variation of halma, became very popular in the late 1920s, particularly in America. Whereas the normal variation is played on a chequered game board and with the usual halma pieces, the Asian-influenced variety is played with small coloured balls on a game board in the shape of a six-pointed star.

Spear, like almost any other games producer, offered these standard board games in its general range. They sold well, but in the context of a "renaissance of game playing", particularly in Germany in the 1970s, many adults were looking for new ideas in the field of strategy games. After many years of abstinence, Germans had obviously become keen to play and wanted to follow the economic miracle with a "games miracle". Spear reacted by intensifying co-operation with well-known game inventors such as Rudi Hoffmann and Alex Randolph. In the early 1970s, Rudi Hoffmann was considered Europe's most important games inventor and produced several very successful games of strategy for Spear, among them "Momox", published in 1972, which challenges concentration and memory. In 1975 "Janus" was added to the range, a game which demands clever strategic planning. In 1988 "Janus" was re-published, this time by Franckh-Kosmos Verlag, and was only discontinued in 1996. Both games are based on the principle, that tiles be put down as profitably as possible and that tiles already put down must be skilfully removed again.

Rudi Hoffmann had a further series of very original games published by Spear, among them "Schmugglerjagd" (Hunt for Smugglers, 1965/66), "Bist du sicher?" (Are You Sure?, 1971), "Hamstern" (Hoarding, 1972), "Jag und schlag" (Hunt and Hit, 1973) and "Figuro" (1973). He maintained that games should claim the status of works of art. And indeed his games are outstanding in their unified presentation, in respect of idea, rules and aesthetics. A graphic artist by trade, he usually worked out his game concepts in great detail before offering them to games publishers.

Alex Randolph, probably the world's most well-known professional games inventor, works in a very similar way. An American living in Venice, Randolph is the "spiritual father" of more than 100 games, among them classics such as "Twixt", "Sagaland" and "Incognito". He, too, designs, draws and tests his new games entirely by himself. Spear only published two of his games: "Stop" (1977) and "Jago" (1985), which was a new edition of "Wörterklauer" (Word Thief, first published by Ravensburg in 1975). The game of strategy "Stop" is reminiscent of "Wolf und Schafe" (Fox and Geese), a very old variation of draughts: four police cars have to surround a gangster's car in the tangled web of streets in a very colourful little town in this simple and beautifully produced game.

Plate 3
Halma, around 1960
(box design by Gustav Müller)
Mühle und Dame, 1926
[Nine Men's Morris and Draughts]
Mühle- und Damesteine,
around 1935 [draughtsmen]

Plate 4
Chinese Chequers, 1956

Plate 5
Momox, 1972
(invented by Rudi Hoffmann)

Plate 6
Janus, 1975
(invented by Rudi Hoffmann)
Stop, 1977
(invented by Alex Randolph)

Dice Games and Games of Chance

Dice – whether used for games of chance or for oracles – count among humankind's oldest toys. They were known to the Sumerians five thousand years ago and can be found in almost all cultures of the world, in various natural or geometric shapes. Whenever dice are combined with a game board or counters the mere chance aspect of the game may be modified, depending on the rules: sometimes possibilities arise which also allow tactical playing, as in the games of pachisi and backgammon which both originated in the Orient. Whereas backgammon has been played in Europe since the 11th century, Pachisi probably did not arrive until the 17th century, when it was introduced by English travellers.

The Indian national game of pachisi is the model for similar race games which became popular in the USA and Europe during the last third of the 19th century. This applies, for example, to "Parcheesi" which was developed by either John Hamilton or Albert Swift in the USA and sold to New York company E.G. Selchow & Co. (later Selchow & Righter) in 1867. Up to this day it has remained one of the world's most popular games. Very simplified versions appeared in Britain in 1896 under the title "Ludo" and in Germany in 1912 as "Mensch ärgere dich nicht" ("Man, don't get upset"). It was to become the best-known of all German family games. Josef Friedrich Schmidt, a clerk with Munich's municipal administration, who had originally made "Mensch ärgere dich nicht" by hand for his three sons, founded his own company for the commercial exploitation of his product, a company which over the years developed into one of Germany's most important games producers (Schmidt Spiel + Freizeit).

In Britain Ludo became a generic title used by all games manufacturers. In Germany, on the other hand, Schmidt had the sole right to use the name "Mensch, ärgere Dich nicht". The linguistic acrobatics performed in the 1920s and 1930s in order to find a title that might be equally catchy were quite amusing. This title could almost be said to have created a fashion, sometimes even being used as inspiration for games titles which did not even have the same game idea. Around 1925 Spear brought out a version entitled "Der Mann muß hinaus" (The man must go out), which was very similar to the Schmidt original and only varied in small design details. A further development of the game, "Home you go", was far more original in its design.

"Fang den Hut", first published by Otto Maier Verlag in Ravensburg in 1927, did not inspire quite so many similar German titles. The game's idea, however, and the original, clear Bauhaus design of the running men with their colourful hats found countless imitators. Spear followed with their own versions, named "Wer hat, der hat" and "Coppit & Cappit".

"Snakes and Ladders" was very popular, particularly in the English-speaking world. This game with its high "moral content" – the ladders depicting the path of virtue and the snakes being the embodiment of vice – was first published in England by F. H. Ayres in 1892. At that time Ayres still used a circular game board with 100 squares, which was later replaced by the more popular rectangular version created by R. H. Harte. The game was based on an ancient religious Indian game – the symbolic content being more and more superseded by cheerful childlike picture motifs.

In addition to the predominant race games played with dice and based on older versions, the 19th century produced its very own game ideas. One of these is "Glocke und Hammer" (Bell and Hammer), as well as its predecessor "Thron und Hütte" (Throne and Cottage), which both reflect the reality of middle class life around 1800. Viennese publisher and art dealer H. F. Müller is supposed to have invented "Bell and Hammer" and contributed considerably to its distribution. The game, with its highly original card auction at the beginning, had already found its way to Britain by 1816. Spear had it in their product range from the 1890s until the Second World War.

Plate 7
Die Windmühle. Ein neues Spiel
(kleinste Ausgabe), 1926
[*Dutch Roulette*, small edition]
Roulette, 1926
[Roulette with spinning top]
Spear's Lustiges Tivoli Spiel.
Verbesserte Ausgabe,
around 1930
[*Spear's Comical Tivoli Game*,
improved edition]

Plate 8
Volando "Flying Roulette",
around 1935
(Manufactured at the
Spear Works Enfield)

Plate 9
Glocke und Hammer,
around 1920
Glocke und Hammer,
around 1930
[Bell and Hammer]

Plate 10
Royal Parcheesi, around 1920
(J. W. S. & S. Bavaria,
export version)
The Game of Parcheesi, 1930
(Manufactured at the Spear
Works Bavaria, export version)

Plate 11
Det lystige Klatrespil,
around 1930
(J. W. S. & S. Bavaria, export
version for Denmark)
[*The Climbing Monkeys*]
Snakes and Ladders, 1964

Plate 12
Das Gänsespiel
(Prachtausgabe), 1913
[*The Game of Goose,
Edition de Luxe*]

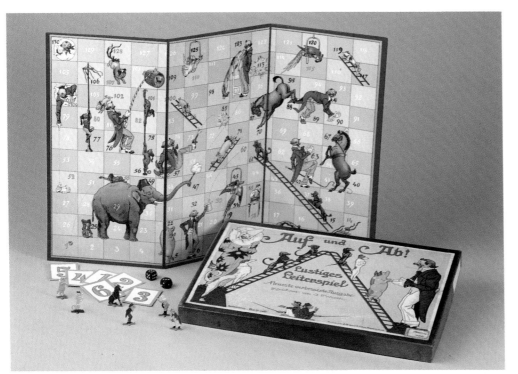

Plate 13
Auf und Ab!
Lustiges Leiterspiel.
Neueste verbesserte
Ausgabe, gezeichnet
von J. P. Werth, around 1922
[*Up and Down!*
The New Ladder Game]

Plate 14
Das Gänsespiel, 1933
[*The Game of Goose*]
Das neue humoristische
Gänsespiel, around 1920
[New Comical Game
of Goose]

Plate 15
Home you go!
A family fun game,
1968–1984
Spear's Coppit.
A "fun-from-start-to-end"
game, 1964–1984
(boxes and boards of both
games designed by
Gustav Müller)

Plate 16
Wer hat, der hat!, 1938
(box and board designed by
Gustav Müller)
Nimm's leicht!, 1965
[Ludo]

Race Games and Money Games

Most classical dice games may be traced back to a few basic patterns. Two main groups may be distinguished: games where – as in pachisi – the opponents must be obstructed or thrown out, and spiral or circular games where in the course of the game players may land on various events squares which help or hinder them, but cannot stop their opponents. The game of goose provides the basic pattern for this second group of games. Although the first written mention of this game only dates back to 16th century Italy, examples may be traced back to the very beginnings of civilisation. Games in the shape of a spiral representing a curled-up snake can be found in Egypt as early as the third millennium BC.

The Spear range contains a great number of spiral and circular race games, differing only in the choice of subject and in design. It says a lot for Spear's innovative and clever strategic thinking that they took up current affairs and trends of the time in the fields of technology, sport, culture and everyday life and quickly transformed them into race games with appropriately designed play pieces, even before the First World War. In the wake of the general aviation craze, for example, Spear published exceptionally beautiful games such as "Flug im Aeroplan" (Aeroplane Flight) and "Eine Reise im Luftschiff" (Journey in a Zeppelin). Explorers' expeditions were reflected in games such as "Die Entdeckung des Nordpols" (The discovery of the north pole). The rapid development of the motorcar in the 1920s and 1930s was accompanied by a wealth of car and traffic games. After the Nürburgring course was opened in 1927, car and motorcycle race games became fashionable at Spear's. The triumphs of the Mercedes Silberpfeil cars, inspired Spear's games such as "Der große Preis von Deutschland" (German Grand Prix).

Speed and mobility promised greater freedom than ever. The citizens of the Weimar Republic lived through moving times in the word's truest sense. Those who could afford it travelled – by motorcycle, car, railway or plane. Spear's games such as "Harz-Reise" (Travels through the Hartz Mountains), "Die Rheinreise" (Journey along the Rhine) or "Die Schweizer Reise" (Swiss travels) took up the theme of such travel experiences. Those wanting something more exotic chose "Die Orientreise" (Oriental travels) whose box lid boasted a very appealing, atmospheric picture, leading thoughts to the legendary Orient Express train.

The predominant feeling of the times was also expressed in peoples' attitudes to movement and to sports activities. The Spear's games themes of gliding, canoeing and football expressed the leisure activities of the time, while horse and greyhound races, including betting, which had long been traditional pastimes for the more affluent members of society, particularly in Britain, were represented by "Steeplechase" and similar games. In the "Golden Twenties" in Germany, horse-racing was still a topic, even beyond the world of games.

In their range of traffic and race games, Spear published some very fine box lids and game boards, with highly dynamic and very striking designs. The high quality of poster and advertising art of the time clearly influenced the work of many graphic artists creating designs for various games publishers. Unfortunately – with the exception of Müller the Painter – very little is known about the illustrators working for Spear. Around 1920, the company published two fairy tale games with drawings by Otto Kubel and the chicken game "Gluck Gluck!" by J. P. Werth. Both artists were renowned children's book illustrators of their times.

Against a backdrop of stock market speculation and banking, economic activities have been an important topic of the 20th century. When "Monopoly" was published in the USA in 1935 and became available in a German language version a year later, Spear countered in 1938 with the banking game "Handel und Wandel" which centred around the buying and selling of businesses. In the 1960s a stock market game called "Flutter" was published: share values of six imaginary companies rose and fell according to the throw of a die and the "bulls" and "bears" tried to make their fortunes by timely buying and selling.

Plate 17
Die Entdeckung
des Nordpols, 1910
[*The Game of North Pole*]

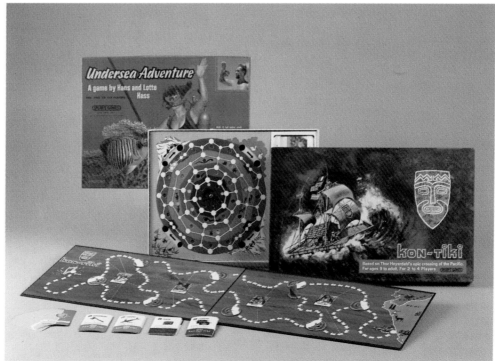

Plate 18
Kon-Tiki. Based on Thor
Heyerdahl's epic crossing of
the Pacific, 1967–1973
Undersea Adventure.
A Game by
Hans and Lotte Hass,
1967–1971

Plate 19
Ein Flug im Aeroplan.
Ein Gesellschafts-Spiel.
Spear's große Ausgabe, 1910
[*The Aerial Contest*]
Eine Reise im Luftschiff.
Aktuelles Gesellschaftsspiel,
1909
[*A Voyage through the Clouds*]

Plate 20
Die Schweizer Reise,
around 1925
[*Swiss Travels*]

Plate 21 ▷
Ein Flug im Aeroplan:
extragroßer, vierteiliger
Spielplan, 1910
[*The Aerial Contest*]

In ein Gewitter geraten,
zurück nach No. 37.

In starkem Regen,
zweimal mit Würfeln
aussetzen.

Durch Wind begünstigt,
fährt sofort nach No. 73.

Im vollen Fluge, rückt
sofort nach No. 76 vor.

Um Zusammenstoss
mit einem Aeroplan
zu vermeiden, zurück
nach No. 52.

Wird durch Anstossen
an den Leuchtturm de-
fekt und scheidet aus
dem Spiele aus.

Begegnet einem Luft-
schiff, einmal mit Würfeln aussetzen.

Mit einem Dampf...
wer die Zahl 6 w...
Dampfer aufgeno...
nach 3 maligem...
weiterspielen, son...
S...

Plate 22
Eine Ferienreise, 1939
(board designed by
Gustav Müller)
[Holiday Travels]
Die Luftreise, 1939 (box and
board designed by
Gustav Müller)
[*A Journey by Air*]

Plate 23
Das Bergrennen, 1932
[The Mountain Race]
Das Motorradrennen.
Ein spannendes Spiel, 1932
[*On the Dirt Track*]

Plate 24
Die Autofahrt, around 1925
[*The Children's Joy Ride*]
Die Feuerwehr, 1932
[*Fighting the Fire*]

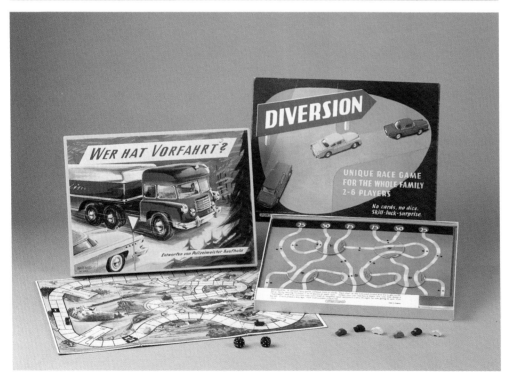

Plate 25
Wer hat Vorfahrt? Entworfen
von Polizeimeister Kaufhold,
1957
(box and board designed by
Gustav Müller)
Diversion. Unique Race
Game for the Whole Family,
1962

Plate 26
Ausziehen – Laufen – Los! Segelflugspiel, 1936
(invented and designed by Gustav Müller)
[Gliding]
Paddelfahrt. Ein lustiges Gesellschaftsspiel für Jung und Alt,
around 1930
[Canoeing]

Plate 27
Rail Race. A Novel Travelling Game, 1946

Plate 28
Pfadfinder-Spiel.
Neueste Ausgabe, 1914
[Boy Scout Game]
Mit Rucksack und Laute,
around 1925
[With Rucksack and Guitar]

Plate 29
Durchs Bayernland.
Ein Reisespiel, 1926
[Journey through Bavaria]
Die Rheinreise.
Neue Ausgabe, around 1922
[Journey along the Rhine]
Harz Reise, around 1925
[Travels through the
Hartz Mountains]

Plate 30
Die Orientreise, around 1922
[Oriental Travels]
Im Fluge um die Erde, 1932
[A Flight Round the World]

Plate 31
Eislaufen, around 1925
[Skating]

Plate 32
Hindernis-Lauf, 1932
[*The Great Obstacle Race Game*]
Spears Pokal-Fußball-Spiel, 1925
[*Playing for the Cup*]

Plate 33
Spears Hunderennen.
Das fesselnde Spiel, 1932
[*Greyhound Racing.
The Great Game*]

Plate 34
Das Wett-Rennen.
Mit Totalisator
(Prachtausgabe),
around 1925
[*The Grand National Steeple
Chase. Edition de Luxe*]

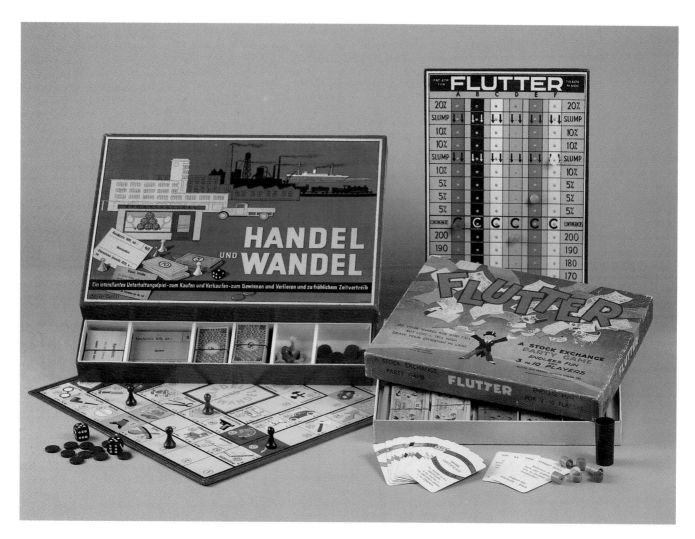

Plate 35
Handel und Wandel. Ein interessantes Unterhaltungsspiel, 1938
[Buy and Sell] (board designed by Gustav Müller)
Flutter. A Stock Exchange Party Game, 1957–1964

Plate 36
Gluck Gluck!
Lustiges Hühnchenspiel von
J. P. Werth, around 1922
[*Little Chicken*]
Die Bremer Stadtmusikanten.
Gezeichnet von Otto Kubel,
1926
[based on
"The Travelling Musicians",
a Grimms' fairy tale]

Plate 37
Der Weg zur Schule.
Ein lustiges Hindernis-Spiel,
around 1925
[On the Way to School]
Die Schul' ist aus!, 1937
[School's out!]
(box and board designed
by Gustav Müller)

Plate 38
Katz und Maus.
Ein lustiges Fangspiel,
around 1920
[*Cat and Mice*]
Der Wolf und die 7 Geißlein.
Gezeichnet von Otto Kubel,
1933
[based on "The Wolf and
the Seven Kids",
a Grimms' fairy tale]

Plate 39
Peterchens Mondfahrt …
Nach dem gleichnamigen
Märchen von Gerdt von
Bassewitz, 1967
[based on a German fairy
tale by Gerdt von Bassewitz]
Pünktchen und Anton.
Nach dem Buch von
Erich Kästner, 1967
[based on a German child-
ren's book by Erich Kästner]

Plate 40
Beschäftigung für kleine Leute, 1933
[Bead Pictures and Sewing Cards]
Kindergarten Compendium. 5 Popular Pastimes for Kiddies,
1954–1965

Activity Games

Friedrich Fröbel (1752-1852), the father of the kindergarten, had a very strong influence on preschool educational theory with the activity games he developed. Recognising that a child's abilities develop in stages, he created an entire system of activity toys which remains effective up to the present day. Fröbel's holistic view of playing was one of the reasons that child's play became much more highly regarded in society as well as in educational practice at that time than it had been at the beginning of the 19th century.

Pre-school education following Fröbel's methods was acknowledged and practised nearly everywhere in Europe and North America. Various games publishers in Germany produced activity and Fröbel games of all kinds for nearly a century. While nowadays only specialist shops supplying kindergartens sell games based on the original Fröbel system, up until the 1960s numerous games publishers offered not only parlour games in their product range, but also activity games based on Fröbel.

Spear was no exception. On the contrary: for decades the company was extremely successful in marketing activity games. Since in the field of activity games the name Fröbel itself stood for games of a specific type and quality, other important companies such as Otto Maier in Ravensburg, A. Sala and Werner & Schumann in Berlin took up the production of Fröbel games and used the great educator's name in their advertisements. Fröbel games enjoyed a fine reputation and in the customer's mind stood for good materials and high-quality educational content.

Quite a few activity games on the market which claimed Fröbel's name as a kind of trademark interpreted his original ideas rather liberally. Strictly speaking, the term Fröbel games only applies to a very clear-cut group of two- and three-dimensional toys. Firstly, the group contains the so-called Fröbel "Spielgaben" (gifts), i.e. ball, cylinder and cube. By systematically subdividing those three-dimensional shapes, sets of building bricks are compiled which can be used by playing children to construct imaginary objects or reconstruct objects seen in their immediate surroundings. The development of these "gifts" make Fröbel the "father" of sophisticated sets of wooden building bricks. The group of genuine Fröbel games furthermore contains some activity games invented by him, based on two-dimensional shapes, lines and dots. They encompass mainly tiles in various geometric shapes, little sticks of varying length and beads and other round shapes as connecting elements.

In Fröbel's system, playing with geometric structures is followed by other games which in free combination offer new possibilities for activities. Thus children can gain many varied experiences from pricking, tying knots, plaiting, folding, threading and sewing. Especially when working with paper, folding and plaiting can exercise manual dexterity and creativity in many different ways.

The many activity games using Fröbel's name were usually based on the production of practical objects or toys. Spear offered a very varied selection of games for boys and girls, in response to parents who wanted to promote their offspring's creative talents and manual skills. These games also offered children the possibility of busying themselves alone. Numerous activities were offered — from the "Kindergarten Compendium" to a construction kit for building a greenhouse or a loom for weaving a scarf. The materials used were also very varied: wood, card, paper, wool threads, felt, raffia, straw, glue, wire, clay, cork, textiles or threads. Usually each activity game contained a ready-made sample which could be used as a pattern for further work.

Among the most strikingly beautiful games offered are "Körbchenflechten" (basket making) and "Möbelflechten" (furniture making): pre-punched card shapes were assembled into pretty basket shapes or delicate doll's furniture, using small wooden rods and paper strips. The "Sonnenstrahlen-Schablonen" (sun-ray stencils) were among the most original kits: punched patterns were laid on top of photographic paper and then exposed to the sun, producing simple photograms. Using ordinary stencils made from oiled paper, the possibilities for drawing and painting on paper were practically limitless. Using just paper and glue and various cutting and folding techniques, many practical photograph albums and colourful little boxes could be formed, with "Freut euch des Klebens" (Happy pasting). Wool winding sets containing card and thread could make a great variety of decorative articles.

A large section of the activity games for girls was intended to teach them textile working techniques and thus to prepare them for needlework lessons in school or supplement these lessons. As a preliminary step for small children, sewing cards with pre-punched holes were offered which were then embroidered with coloured thread. Girls usually enjoyed sewing more, though, when they could make new articles for their dolls. For this purpose Spear offered complete doll's outfits in open boxes with paper lace around the edges or in little lockable suitcases inspired by the French doll's trousseaux. The baby doll dressmaking sets usually contained several finished or partly finished textile articles, as well as sewing patterns and handicraft tools. Thus cutting out, sewing or embroidering doll's clothes became "child's play". Older girls could busy themselves with embroidery kits complete with needles, threads and an embroidery frame, just like their mothers'. Typically enough, Spear produced one of its embroidery kits under the motto "Just like Mother" – the illustration on the lid depicting a charming smiling girl sitting near her mother's picture with an embroidery frame.

To this day, the "Knitting Nancy" is used for teaching children how to knit. An item much less known today is the "Fleißknäuel" (Knitting Nancy's Surprise) which contained a small reward for the industrious little child who knitted up all the wool. Spear enjoyed exceptional success with their weaving and knitting devices in various sizes and price ranges. The "Luise" loom and the "Kwiknit" device were practical to use and constructed not only with children, but also with adult users in mind.

Suitable activity games for boys such as puzzles and hammer and nail games were also developed:

colourful wooden tiles and sticks could be arranged into pictures and nailed onto a fibreboard. Printed plywood for work with a fretsaw was designed to give ideas for useful craftwork to fathers and sons alike. Building bricks were rather a neglected area in the Spear range up until the 1920s. In 1931, however, Spear established itself rather well in this sector, when it introduced "Figuba", a set of wooden building bricks. The set consisted of colourful squares, circles, rectangles, wheels and tiny additional components which were assembled using little connecting rods, giving the completed buildings or figures very good stability. "Figuba" was also offered with additional wool-spun wire which could be used as arms and legs for the figures, giving them a particularly life-like appearance. In the following year Spear added "Baut mit!" (Build with us!), a set of wooden building bricks, to its product range. This consisted of coloured, drilled beams of varying lengths, as well as wheels and round stoppers, which could be combined into all sorts of objects using round connecting rods. Special topic kits for assembling a clock or a greenhouse were also part of the Spear range.

In 1938 "Baufix" was launched; its fired clay tiles were supplied in two sizes and could be firmly connected by way of small interlocking knobs – very much like the Lego bricks of later years. But the big breakthrough in the field of building bricks came with the launch of "Brickplayer" on the English market. This universal model building set consisted of clay bricks of various standard sizes as well as additional roof and window parts which could be assembled into all sorts of buildings using mortar and could later on be dissolved using plain water. This unusual construction kit was ideally suited for building on model railways and became one of the most popular toys of the 1950s.

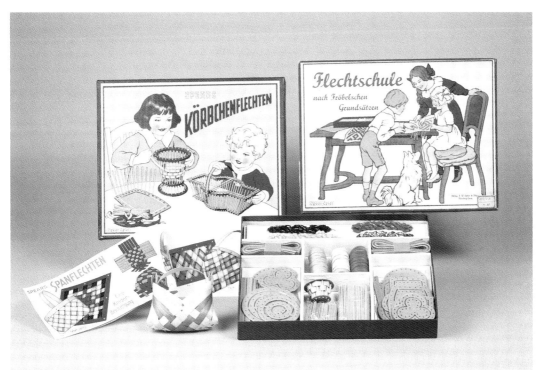

Plate 41
Spears Spanflechten
(Muster und Anleitung),
1933
[Chip Basket Making,
sample and instructions]
Spears Körbchen-
flechten, around 1930
[Basket Making]
Flechtschule nach
Fröbelschen Grund-
sätzen, around 1925
[Paper Plaiting according
to Fröbel's principles]

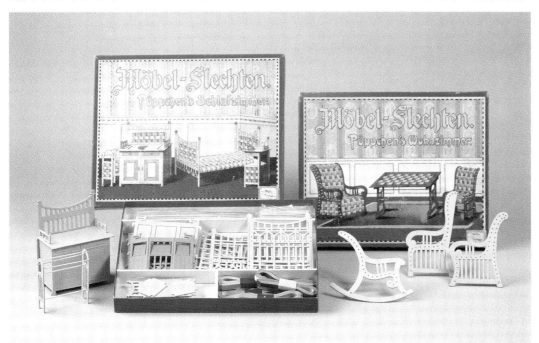

Plate 42
Möbel-Flechten.
Püppchens Schlafzimmer,
around 1920
[*Dolly Dimple's
Bed Room*]
Möbel-Flechten.
Püppchens Wohn-
zimmer, around 1920
[*Dolly Dimple's
Drawing Room*]

Plate 43
Sonnenstrahlen-Schablonen, 1933
[Photogram Stencils]
Complete Stencil Set, around 1935
(Manufactured at the Spear Works, Enfield)
Fröhliche Stempelei, 1934
[Merry Stamping]
Spearoscope, 1971
(designed by Gustav Müller for Spear's Games in 1969)

Plate 44
Wellenbilder. Ein Klebespiel, 1937
[Picture Pasting]
Ausschneide- und Klebearbeiten, around 1925
[*Picture Cutting and Pasting*]
Freut Euch des Klebens, denn Ihr braucht keinen Leim –
nur Wasser, around 1930
[*Useful Things of Cardboard and how to make them*]

Plate 45
Moderne Schalen.
Anfertigung hübscher
Geschenke durch
Kinderhände, 1938
[Modern Bowls]
Bunter Schmuck, 1957
(designed by
Anneliese Dupont)
[Colourful Ornaments]

Plate 46
Wickel-Blumen.
Nähkarten zum Sticken
und Wickeln, 1934
[Wool Lacing and
Sewing Cards]
Lerne spielend Flechten
und Knüpfen, 1938
[Plaiting and Braiding]
Spannflott. Spears
Spann- und Knüpf-
Rahmen, 1933
[Braiding frame]

Plate 49
Spear's Scatty Scroll
"The Hits" for Trendy
Teenagers to Trim and Make,
1967
Dressing Doll (prototype),
1957

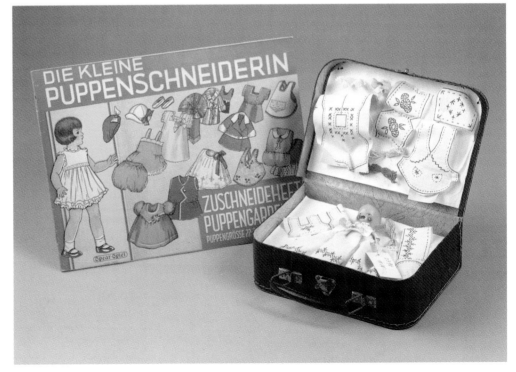

Plate 50
Die kleine Puppen-
schneiderin, 1933
[The little dress maker;
dress patterns]
Puppenausstattung und
Stickkasten mit
Biskuloid-Baby, 1939
[Doll's trousseau and
embroidery set with baby
doll in small suit case]

Plate 51 ▷
Puppenmütterchens
Nähschule, 1937
[Making Dolly's Dresses]

Plate 52
Strickflott, 1954 [*Kwiknit*]
(box designed
by Gustav Müller)
Spear's Fleißknäuel, 1955
[*Knitting Nancy's Surprise*]
Kwiknit. Spear's Improved
Knitting Apparatus
Size No. 4, around 1935
(Made at the Spear Works
Bavaria, boxed in England)
Strick-Peter.
Zum Stricken von Wolltieren,
Blumen u.s.w., 1932
[*Knitting Peter*]

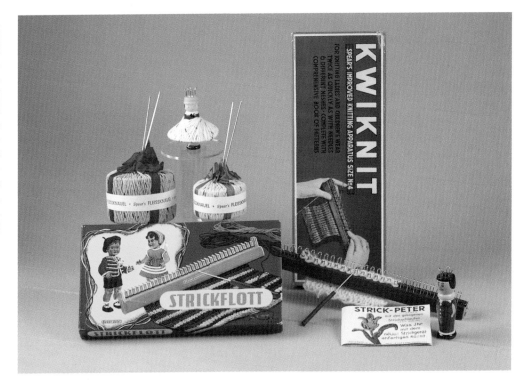

Plate 53
Spear's Weaving Loom
Size 3, around 1955
Freut Euch des Webens!,
around 1930
[*Simple Weaving Outfit*]
Spear's Kinder-Webstuhl, 1933
(box designed
by Gustav Müller)
[*Weaving loom for children*]

Plate 54
Pyramid Cubes
"Familiar Objects",
10 blocks, 1926
Pyramid Cubes
"New Children Scenes",
11 blocks, 1926
(pictures by Irma Graeff)
Kartenhäuser.
Ein lustiges Bauspiel, 1933
[*Card Houses.*
New Edition]

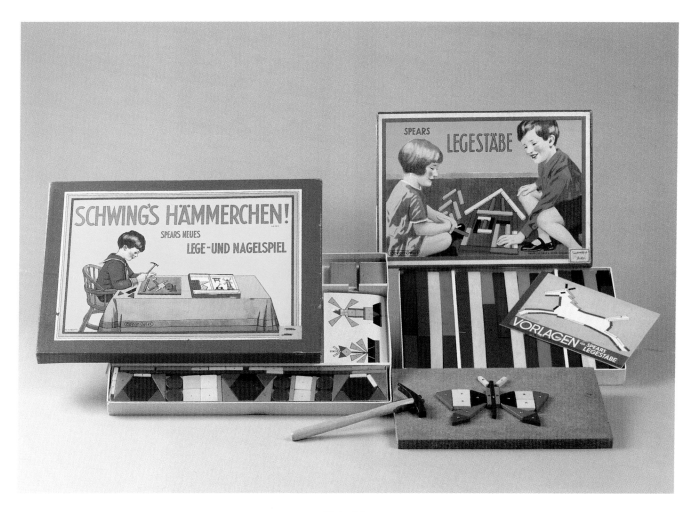

Plate 55
Schwing's Hämmerchen. Spears Neues Lege- und Nagelspiel, 1937
[*Tile Pictures with Hammer and Nails*]
Spears Legestäbe, 1933
[Stick Laying]

Plate 56
De kleine Klokken-
maker, 1938
[Little Clock Maker]
(J. W. Spear & Söhne,
Nürnberg,
export version for
the Netherlands)
Boys' Own Model
Building, 1937
(Manufactured at the
Spear Works Bavaria,
boxed in England),
Gewächshaus zum
Selbstbauen, 1938
[Greenhouse
Construction Kit]
(all boxes designed
by Gustav Müller)

Plate 57
Contemporary
Brickplayer Kit B.,
1959–1964

Denk fix
Ein lustiges Frage -Spiel
mit 1000 Antworten

Spear-Spiel
26301

¡PENSAD PRONTO!
Jocoso cuestionario de 1000 preguntas.

JUEGOS SPEAR

26301
1.—

QUIZ · TELL · ME · GAME
MADE IN ENGLAND

NAME OF A TOWN
Le nom d'une ville

A FILM STAR
Une étoile de cinéma

NAME OF A MEMBER OF PARLIAMENT
Le nom d'un homme d'Etat

PENSATE RAPIDAMENTE!
UN QUESTIONARIO DIVERTENTE
CON 1000 RISPOSTE.

GIOCHI SPEAR

26301
1.—

DENK FIKS!
Een vroolijk vraagspel
met 1000 antwoorde

SPEAR'S SPELEN

DERNIÈRE ÉDITION DE
«PENSEZ VITE!»
avec de **nouvelles questions.**
Un joyeux questionnaire à 1000 réponses.

Learning, Quiz and Word Games

All civilised societies attach great value to education and knowledge – in their own right and as a means of professional qualification. Thus most parents try to teach their children as early as possible, and in a playful way, in order to prepare them for learning in school. Games as domestic teaching aids are very popular not only for teaching the "three Rs", reading, writing and arithmetic, but also for conveying other types of knowledge and for memory training.

Lotto and other lottery games started appearing as learning games for children towards the end of the 18th century. Thus the simple principle of those games of chance found its way into the nursery. Bingo, a variation of number lotto, became a very popular family game during the 19th century, mainly in Britain and the USA. The irresistible attraction of the play idea is vividly illustrated by the fact that up to this day public lotteries and bingo halls attract many adults, sometimes luring them with considerable prize money. But lotto learning games are also an interesting pastime for smaller children. The games are usually based on the principle that pictures or figures on cards or chips are drawn and called up by a games master, and must then be identified and located on their cards by the players. In the more sophisticated versions, the children must know their multiplication tables or have some knowledge of grammar, geography, world or natural history in order to be able to compete.

Spear produced many lavishly designed lotto games. One of them is the "Natural History Lotto", published in 1904, with its majestic lion on the box lid. The "Stamp Game" and the "Picture Postcard Game" are based on very original ideas: in the latter, small, very realistically designed picture postcards must be placed in an album.

The basic equipment for "learning-by-playing" consists of teaching clocks, arithmetical toys, reading games and school games. Spear offered all of these over several decades, and they were all very instructive, beautifully coloured and available in handy sizes. "Dolly's School", for example, contained a blackboard complete with stand, pupils' slates with little sponges, jotters, timetables and wall charts. The various children's post office games also offered everything children needed for their role on either side of the counter: as post office customers or clerks. The "Tiny Town Post Office" even came with a pretty lithographed half mask sporting the hat of an English post office clerk!

Entertainment and learning were ideally combined in question and answer games which even managed to amuse teenagers. "Denk fix" (Tell me) was launched around 1930 and was to become one of the longest-running international hits, available in most important European languages. Round about this time several publishers came out with battery-powered electric question and answer games. In 1931 two Berlin companies launched the games "Lichtra" and "Electra", in which a small light bulb lit up, when the correct answer was given. They were a further development of earlier games such as "Miraculum" which worked mechanically using a magnetic indicator needle. Spear added to this range of electrical and magnetic games in the 1950s with "Electric Contact Quiz" and "Magihara". The first quiz games were introduced in Germany around 1960, in the wake of popular television quiz shows.

Virtuoso lettercraft and intellectual enjoyment of word creation are Scrabble's main attractions. Here, you are completely lost without profound knowledge of words. This explains the game's immense popularity, particularly in Britain, the cradle of the crossword puzzle. It is less well known, however, that between 1928 and 1940 quite a few other crossword games were on the market in various countries. In Germany, in addition to the "Pulok" games, there were "Multikrux" and "Kreuzwort-Rätsel-Löser" (Crossword Puzzle Solver). "Krewo" was produced in Switzerland, "Typ Dom" in Austria and "Wordy" in the USA. But in spite of similar game elements, none of these games could rival Scrabble's success.

Plate 58
Denk fix, 1939
¡Pensad Pronto!, 1933
Tell me. The Grand Quiz Game, 1960
Pensate rapidamente!, 1933
Denk fiks!, 1933
Pensez Vite!, 1933

Plate 59
Der Tag des Kindes.
Spears Lehruhr mit Bildern,
1932
[Educational Clock Face]
Toyland ABC. The "Victory"
Word Building Set. A Set of
Cut-Out Wooden Letters,
around 1955
Spears Lesespiel, 1932
[Spelling Board]

Plate 60
Tiny Town Post Office,
around 1950
Kinderpost, 1933
[Post Office Set]
Die kleine Feldpost, 1915
[Little Forces' Post Office]

Plate 61 ▷
Kasperl-Theater, 1930
[Punch and Judy show]
(prototype designed by
Gustav Müller)
Neues Kasperl-Theater,
around 1925
[Punch and Judy show]

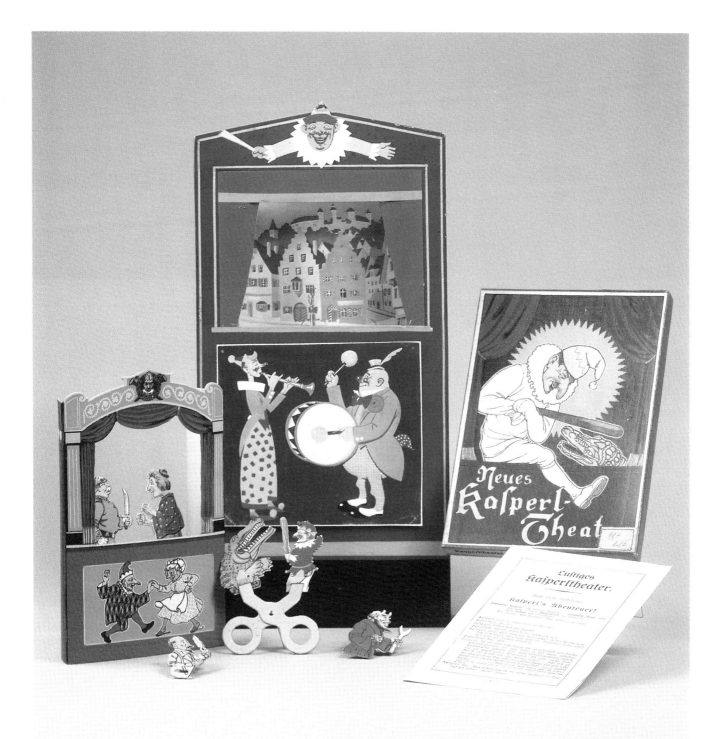

Plate 62
Spear's New Trunk Lotto,
1930
(Manufactured at the
Spear Works Bavaria,
export version)
Bingo for your Home,
1966–1981
Bingo, 1982

Plate 63
The Little Teacher
Dolly's School, 1930
(Manufactured at the
Spear Works Bavaria
boxed in England)
Der kleine Schaffner
(Schaffnergarnitur), 1926
[Conductor Game]

Plate 64
Tierlotto, 1931
[Animal Lotto]
(label by Willy Tiedjen,
picture cards
by Walter Heubach)
Wohin gehört's?
Ein neues Spiel, 1910
[Picture Lotto]
Durch die weite Welt.
Ein lehrreiches Spiel
für die Jugend, 1932
[Transport Lotto]

Plate 65
Ansichts-Karten Spiel,
1906
[*The Game of Picture
Postcards*]
Briefmarken-Spiel.
Ein neues Lottospiel
für die Jugend, 1910
[*The International Mail*]
Naturgeschichtliches
Lotto, 1899
[*Natural History Lotto*]

Plate 66
Magihara antwortet auf jede Frage, 1954
(box designed by Gustav Müller)
Gewußt wo … Ein Spiel zum Kombinieren und Konzentrieren.
Nach der beliebten, gleichnamigen Fernsehsendung, 1960
[based on a quiz show on German TV]
Electric Contact Quiz. Lights up your party, around 1953

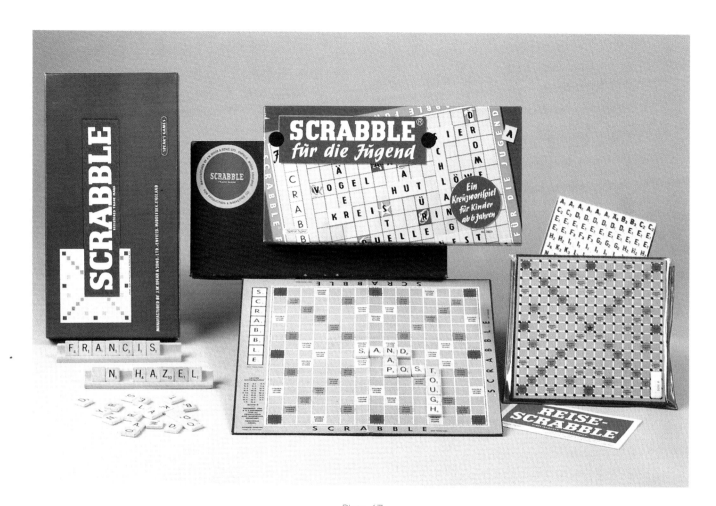

Plate 67
Scrabble, 1960 (Manufactured by J.W. Spear & Sons, Enfield)
Scrabble, 1955 (Manufactured by J.W. Spear & Sons, Enfield)
Scrabble für die Jugend, 1959
[*Scrabble for Juniors*]
Reise-Scrabble, 1963
[*Travel Scrabble*]

Puzzles and Games of Patience

You need a lot of time if you want to have a go at a puzzle or a game of patience. And while playing you can enter a very concentrated and almost absent state of mind. Small children are fascinated by the task of placing tiles, balls or other elements in such a way that they form patterns, mosaics or pictures. Most games manufacturers have always offered a wide selection of items catering for toddlers. Picture cubes and other cube games are a universal toy for very small children, introducing them to first basic building principles and increasing their combination skills in putting together various pictures. Spear did not start production of picture cubes until the 1920s.

Nuremberg was a major centre for picture cube production, since the pictures glued onto the cubes as well as those used as a guide could be cheaply produced by the numerous local lithographic printers. The unfinished wooden cubes were mainly bought in from sawmills in the Thuringian and Bavarian Forests. The market leader in this specialised field of toy production was J.A. Kithil. They offered a very wide selection of picture cubes with up to 54 cubes, even including cubes on castors made from sheets of plywood with metal wheels and pictures on both sides. Spear's range contained similar games: the stand-up toy and puzzle game "Starkholz-Spielzeug" (Solid Wood Toys) had railway cars, bridges and signals which could be combined to form a toy landscape and then, when being put back into their box, also acted as a puzzle.

To this day jigsaw puzzles remain the most common puzzles. The first documented puzzles of this kind were created by London cartographer and copperplate engraver John Spilsbury around 1760, when he pasted his maps on wood and then sawed them apart along the political boundaries. The puzzle craze spread across Europe like wildfire. Cutting complicated shapes became much more simple and accurate with the invention of the mechanical jigsaw in 1870. From the early 20th century puzzles were increasingly fashioned from card, too, and could be punched in a single machine operation. Most Spear puzzles produced in Germany consisted of strong cardboard lined with colourful chromos. These "Picture Making Games" for children were part of the Spear range from 1904, with two, four or six jigsaw puzzles in each box.

The range of topics and the number of pieces increased, as more and more adults began showing an interest in jigsaw puzzles. As early as 1912, S. Resnován & Co Berlin (Trademark "Zeitvertreib"), the oldest German jigsaw puzzle makers, produced jigsaw puzzles with between fifty and three thousand pieces for adults. They were immensely popular in the elegant salons of railway trains and steam liners of the time, but during the First World War were also supplied en masse to military hospitals. The rise of the German jigsaw puzzle industry was paralleled by absolute jigsawmania in Britain and the USA. German-English publisher Raphael Tuck opened a subsidiary in Berlin in order to supply the German market with his latest London-made "Zag-Zaw-Puzzles" and other brainteasers. The late 1920s brought a new jigsaw craze all over Europe. In the wake of the world economic crisis, in some countries organisations were set up where home-made jigsaws could be had on loan. In England, G. J. Hayter & Co of Bournemouth produced their high-quality "Victory" wooden jigsaw puzzles which Spear (Enfield) kept in their range under the same name after taking over the company in 1970. Spear (Nuremberg) had also continuously supplied jigsaws with a marked increase in the 1970s.

Metal Chinese puzzles have always been among the classic games of patience. The player has to disentangle various parts which seem to be permanently connected to each other. The most famous puzzle of this kind, the "Nürnberger Zankeisen" (also known as "Chinese Rings" or "Nuremberg Trifle"), has its origins in China, where it was already widely known in the first millennium AD. The early 20th century brought a marked increase in metal Chinese puzzles. At the same time, cheap glass top puzzles became very popular. In such puzzles, small balls or other objects had to be manoeuvred to particular positions in the base of a small box.

Plate 69
Picture cubes:
Transport, 1939
Gute Freunde.
Spear's Kubus-Spiel,
around 1930
[Good Friends]
(pictures by Willy Tiedjen)
Fairy Tales, 1935
(pictures by Otto Kubel)

Plate 70
Spear's Magnetic Pictures.
A creative toy
for the very young,
1966–1972
Starkholz-Spielzeug.
Aufstellspiel Eisenbahn
Legespiel, 1938
[stand-up game /
plywood puzzle]
(boxes of both games
designed by Gustav Müller)

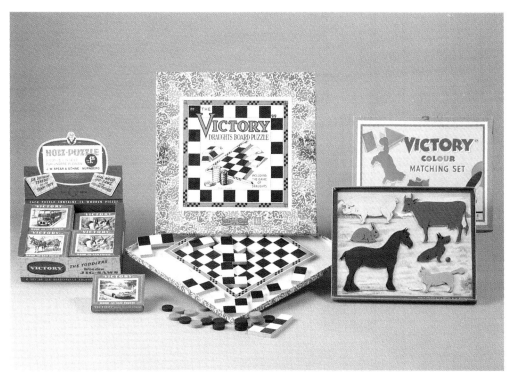

Plate 71
Display box "Victory"
Wooden Jig-Saws,
around 1975
(for sale in Germany)
The "Victory" Draughts
Board Puzzle Including
the Game of Draughts,
around 1965
"Victory"
Colour Matching Set,
around 1965

Plate 72
Glass top puzzles: Auto-Pech
[*The Unfortunate Motorists*]
(1933), Die Fee (1933), Das
Pflaumenparadies (1939),
Pierrot and Pierrette (1933),
Herzen fischen (1933)
Wer kann's? Spear's Metall-
Geduldspiele, 1933
[*Spear's Wire Puzzles*]
(box designed
by Gustav Müller)
Hexenkette, 1939
[Wire Puzzle]
(box designed
by Gustav Müller)

Card Games, Children's Books and Paper Toys

Spear entered the world of children's and family card games in 1899 with the game of "Schwarzer Peter" (Black Peter or Old Maid). The 1904 company catalogue listed this game in a large size edition as a game with "25 pretty cards, cork in metal container and play bowl". The piece of cork which was blackened with soot was used to paint a black moustache on the player who was left holding the "Schwarzer Peter" card at the end of the game. "Schwarzer Peter" was not issued as a card game with special cards until roughly 1860. Its origin is closely linked with the division of African territory among the European colonial powers of that time, the German Reich having joined the ranks of those powers in the mid 1880s. Black people and people with dark skin moved to the centre of public interest, but at the same time also became targets of "white scorn". Seen in this context, the equation of "loser" and "Black Peter" is a typical expression of the spirit of those years. When Germany lost its colonies after the end of the First World War, the game of "Black Peter" also changed in appearance. Now the "Black Peter" card in the Spear range showed a banjo player, a black cat, a boy or a chimney sweep.

Whereas "Old Maid" has hardly been played at all since the 1960s, games of "Happy Families" are still popular family card games. They probably date back to around 1840. But a similar type of card game was presumably played before then, using standard playing cards. The first Happy Families published by Spear, in 1903, had the topics of poets, composers and flowers and consisted of 40 or 60 cards. Since Happy Families were mainly used to convey knowledge to young children and teenagers, the subject range was very wide indeed. Quite often book illustrators were involved in designing cards. In the 1920s Spear published a whole series of Happy Families which boasted a very high artistic standard and were very well printed. In 1929 the company bought the rights to B. Dondorf's family card games and parlour games, and could thus significantly increase its range of first class Happy Families games. In the 1930s Spear also sold, in addition to these colourfully illustrated cards, some monochrome card games produced in the autotypy technique using photographs. Among those were mainly travel and traffic Happy Families such as "Die Schweiz" (Switzerland), "Weltflug-Quartett" (Flight around the world) or "Mit Graf Zeppelin um die Erde" (Around the world with Graf Zeppelin). After the Second World War Spear (Germany) no longer produced Happy Families, however.

A separate department in the Spear concern produced picture and colouring books, mainly in the 1920 and 1930s. The company brand name "Was ihr wollt" (What You Will) boasted about 140 titles around 1930. Spear even had a book warehouse in Berlin and a distribution warehouse for booksellers in Leipzig. The books in the range were mainly made from strong cardboard, often not bound, but zigzag folded. They were geared entirely to pre-school children and catered to prevailing tastes in matters of content and presentation. Fairy tales and animal stories, and subjects from children's immediate environment were the main topics. Spear succeeded in winning rather famous authors and illustrators for its series. Sometimes picture book illustrations were also used, unaltered, for picture cubes and jigsaw puzzles. The basic principles for picture books also applied for colouring books: clear blocks of colour, simple shapes and naïve everyday scenes.

Spear also proved extremely skilful in such sidelines of games production as dressing-up dolls and jumping jacks. In 1910 the company catalogue listed dressing-up dolls with elegant dresses, hats and all sorts of fashion accessories. In the 1920s these dolls had simple names such as "Robert", "Lieschen" or "Annemarie", had their hair cut in a bob and preferred casual clothing. At the same time, Spear produced jumping jacks of excellent artistic quality, in the shape of highly imaginative animals or other figures. They were made from card or thin wood, were available in various sizes, and the customer could choose from bears, Chinese dolls, clowns, Red Indians, Easter bunnies or Father Christmas.

Plate 73
Happy Families:
Dichter Quartett, 1926
[Poets]
Handwerker-Quartett.
Entworfen von
Friedrich Petersen, 1914
[Craftsmen]
Der Lebenslauf.
Ein lustiges Quartettspiel
von Frau Prof. Dr. H. Fernow,
around 1925
[Course of Life]
Fortschritt im Verkehr.
Quartettspiel, 1933
[Transport]
(box designed
by Gustav Müller),
Mit "Graf Zeppelin" um die
Erde. Ein Quartettspiel,
1930 [Zeppelin]
(box designed
by Gustav Müller, 1930)
Weltflug Quartett.
12 wichtige Luftverkehrs-
strecken mit 48 Original-
aufnahmen bearbeitet von
Walter Mackenthun, 1933
[Air Travel]
Display for Spear's Happy
Families designed
by Gustav Müller, 1928

Plate 74
Weltreise-Quartett,
1913
[Happy Families:
A Journey around
the World]

Ausreife
Im Reiſebureau
Spiel auf Deck
Abſchied von Genua
Im Speiſeſalon

Ausreife
Abſchied von Genua
Im Speiſeſalon
Im Reiſebureau
Spiel auf Deck

Ausreife
Spiel auf Deck
Abſchied von Genua
Im Speiſeſalon
Im Reiſebureau

Ausreife
Im Speiſeſalon
Im Reiſebureau
Spiel auf Deck
Abſchied von Genua

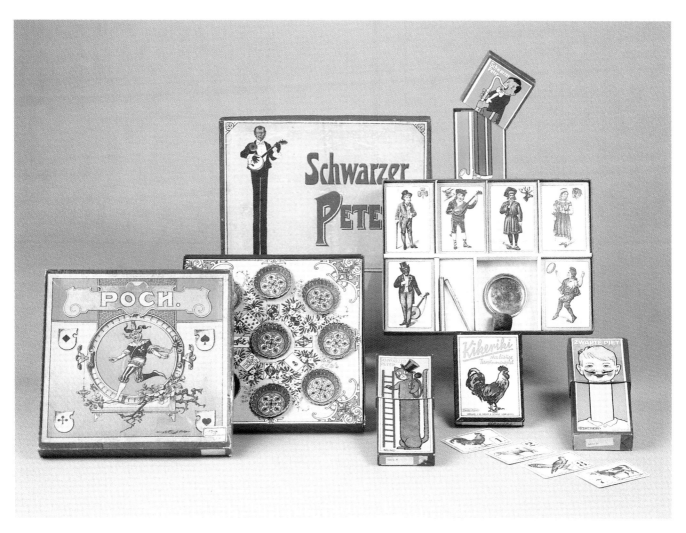

Plate 75
Card games:
Poch, 1904 [no English equivalent]
Schwarzer Peter (große Schachtelausgabe), around 1910
[*Black Peter, large edition*]
Schwarzer Peter, 1934 [Old Maid in sliding box with cat motif,
designed by Gustav Müller]
Schwarzer Peter, 1931 [Old Maid in sliding box]
Kikeriki, das lustige Tierstimmenpiel, 1932 [card game based on
animal sounds, box designed by Gustav Müller]
Zwarte Piet, around 1930 [Old Maid in sliding box,
export version for the Netherlands]

Plate 76
Picture books:
Bei Spiel und Arbeit, 1937
[At Work and Play]
Rund um die Welt,
around 1930
[Around the World]
Meine Lieblings-Spielsachen,
1923
[My Favourite Toys]
Steh Schneemann steh!,
1930
[Snowman]

Plate 77
Picture and colouring books:
Das goldene Malbuch
(pictures by Gustav Müller),
1937
Strecke frei!
(pictures by C. Lindeberg /
text by Hans K. Meixner),
1937
Drinnen und draußen
(pictures by Aunt Irma /
rhymes by
Carola Kellermann), 1930
Brumm und seine
Kameraden, 1937

Plate 78
Jumping figures,
around 1928
(two prototypes, only the
duck was produced by
Spear's)

Plate 79
Paper dolls:
Das blonde Fränzchen, 1939
Hannelore mit ihrem lieben
Bobbi und ihren schönen
Kleidern, 1939
Das Mode-Püppchen mit
seinen eleganten Kleidern
und Hüten, 1913
[*Dolly Dimple with all her
New Dresses and Hats*]
Die kleine Annemarie mit
ihren Kleidern, around 1925
[*Little Gladys and her
Pretty Frocks*]

Plate 80
Das Angelspiel.
Große
Prachtausgabe,
around 1904
[*The Game of
Magnetic Fish
Pond. Edition
de Luxe*]

Games of Skill and Sports

When Spear launched one of its most successful games of skill, "Die Fliegenden Hüte" (Flying Hats) in 1901, parlour games using mechanical contraptions had just become fashionable. Other games publishers had also read the signs of the times, and followed suit, "inventing" very similar games. Within the year the Berliner Spielefabrik Hermann Pohl & Co. Nachf. announced their game "Springende Clowns" (Jumping Clowns), just in time for Christmas business. The idea was exactly the same: with a light tap of the finger, players catapulted small clown shapes (rather than cardboard hats) into the numbered holes on the game board.

About one third of all games in Spear's 1904 catalogue can be summed up under the heading of mechanical or sports games. This was obviously a response to the customers' wishes of the time. Magnetic fishpond, tiddley winks, table tennis: these Spear specials were very popular even then. Spear continued its successful streak with "Hoki Poki" (Piggeries), launched in 1907. In this game, hungry pigs have to be manoeuvred up a ramp towards their troughs by means of a simple but ingenious mechanical contraption. The game was to be a bestseller until well into the 1930s. Spear (Enfield) published a very similar game under the name of "Barrola": using a sort of pastry wheel, little barrels had to be manipulated along a pivoted ramp and dropped on a tray with holes, different scores being associated with these holes.

The ball plays an important part in many sports or games of skill. As early as the end of the 18th century the educationalist J.C.F.Gutsmuths recommended that young people should exercise and relax their bodies by playing all sorts of ball games. In the 1830s Fröbel praised the ball as an ideal toy for children. Many painters and graphic artists have portrayed all kinds of ball games in their works, seeing these games as an expression of life itself. Many parlour games, games of chance, of patience or of skill would be impossible without the use of small balls, and many sports rely entirely on the use of a ball of some description.

In this context it is remarkable that Spear, in the early 1930s, produced many games of skill with balls, which could be played on the table in the home. In "Triambolo", the ball had to be thrown in such a way that it bounced back off the table and then fell into one of the holes in the box. One game of skill which thrilled grandchildren and grandparents alike – at least that is what the picture on the box lid suggests – was "Brückenspiel" (Cuebridge). Using a small cue, the players had to roll balls under the arches of a bridge in such a way that they rested exactly underneath.

Around the turn of the century public interest in sports and outdoor activity games also grew in Germany – following the example of Britain, home of sports, and also using English terminology. Lawn tennis and football were not only played as serious adult sports, but were also very popular in the various children's playgrounds in larger cities. Since Nuremberg games producers were always keen to bring out novelties, they soon launched sports games for domestic use. Spear was one of the first German manufacturers to come out with table tennis sets, as early as 1901, in no less than 27 different editions and nine price categories. Some boxes even included a "ball catcher" to spare players from bending down to retrieve balls: these consisted of a long wooden rod with a crown of metal claws to grip the elusive celluloid ball.

"Snipkick" was Spear's 1904 contribution to the growing German football craze. In 1910 this was complemented by the original "Blow Football". In this game, as the name suggests, a blow pipe was used to shoot celluloid balls across the table and manoeuvre them past mobile goalkeepers into wire goals. The subject of football was also taken up in the 1925 dice game "Pokal-Fußball" (Cup Football) and in the 1930s in the game of "Schuß!Tor!" (Shoot! Goal!) with movable figures. In England Spear marketed the same game under the title of "Topscor". Football was definitely an "in" topic of the time. Between the wars other companies also published games of table football: for example "Hurra … Tor!"

(Hurray … Goal!) by Meto (Cologne), "Tipp-Kick" by Edwin Mieg (Schwenningen), "Hipp-Hipp-Hurra" by Kibri (Böblingen) or "Rapid" by Christian Herbart (formerly Kleefeld, Nuremberg).

Although Spear featured table croquet in their sports games range right from the beginning, this game never became as popular as the skittles game which still is the centre of activity in many a cheerful gathering today. "Spear's finely enamelled skittles" were available in presentation packs with particularly large skittles for playing outdoors or with beautifully painted smaller skittles as table games. Customers could choose between simple versions in two colours and more elaborate skittles "dressed up" as scouts, soldiers, clowns or sailors.

Around 1910 the toy industry started reflecting the time's preoccupation with physical exercise and picked up fashion trends by launching a great wealth of ball and catching games. The games were mainly aimed at entertainment and movement, rather than building muscles. Spinning tops, balls, parachutes and other flying objects take first place: hurled into the air and then caught using nets, forks, sticks and all sorts of other implements. In addition to well-known "old" catching games such as cup-and-ball or diabolo, games named "Pipifax", "Angelo", "Vola", "Baloneto", "Kubalett" or "Gabelo" were launched. In spite of their excellent play value, they were much less popular after the Second World War. In their place scooters and bicycles became best-sellers and were therefore produced in great variety.

Spear offered various games of quoits for training physical skills indoors. The adult version consisted of a small wooden peg and rings fashioned from "especially strong hemp rope with coloured wooden sleeves". For children they thought up charming "nose" quoits. In "Radscha, der kluge Elefant" (Rajah, the clever elephant) a big papier mâché elephant's head protrudes from the centre of a disk, catching the rings with its long trunk while bowing elegantly. The comic strip dog "Bonzo" performs its favourite trick: it balances a bone on its nose, and the rings have to be thrown over this bone.

Conjuring must surely be the monarch of all games of skill and dexterity. Even Goethe gave his grandson a present of a conjuring set in 1830, because he considered conjuring tricks to be an adequate means of acquiring physical and mental dexterity. It is astonishing that most larger conjuring sets for children also contain the kind of apparatus used even by great magicians. In order to make things disappear, for example, you need a box with a false bottom, dice which fit one into the other, tubes consisting of various parts or the beautifully and precisely turned ball-shaped boxes which are masterpieces of Nuremberg wood-turning skill. As early as the 19th century Nuremberg had the edge as far as the production of this type of wooden conjuring apparatus was concerned, with the workshops of C. Baudenbacher or C. Vierlinger.

After buying the wooden toy manufacturer's Baudenbacher in 1919, Spear offered conjuring sets in its range for quite some time. In the same year it registered the trademark "Hokus Pokus". In 1924, conjuring sets of 20 different sizes were offered, ranging in price from 50 pfennigs to 9.65 marks. These sets were marketed under varying names such as "Zauber-Apparate Marke Hokus Pokus" (Hokus Pokus conjuring sets), "Spear's Conjuring Tricks" or "Hokus Pokus. Zauberkiste für Liebhaber" (Hokus Pokus Conjurer's Box for Connoisseurs). The last conjuring set from Spear's Nuremberg factory came out in 1981 under the name of "Hokus-Pokus-Bastelei" (Do it yourself Hokus Pokus) and was based on an idea supplied by famous magician Wittus Witt. It did not offer ready-made conjuring apparatus, but rather sheets of card from which the utensils had to be assembled.

Soap bubbles are much simpler in comparison, but equally fascinating. Their perfect shape, their rainbow colours and their short, but vivid life cycle have fascinated people for centuries. Play with the miraculous bubbles appears in many a painting or drawing. Soap bubbles were offered in presentation packs from the turn of the century on. From about 1904 until the 1930s Spear brought joy to countless children with its imaginatively packaged "Billy Bubbles" which had a soap face, legs fashioned from clay pipes and arms made from straws.

Plate 81
Hütchen auf den Kopf!
Das lustige Geschicklichkeits-
Spiel, 1932
[*Kappinoddles*]
Die fliegenden Hüte,
around 1918
[*The Flying Hats*]
Die fliegenden Hüte.
Original-Ausgabe mit
Zelluloid-Hüten, 1939
(box designed
by Gustav Müller)

Plate 82
Hoki-Poki!
Die hungrigen Schweinchen,
around 1920
[*The Piggeries*]

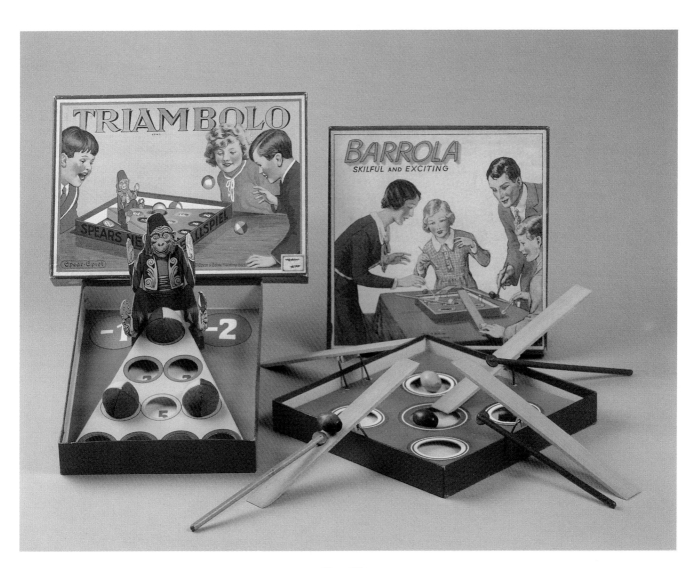

Plate 83
Triambolo. Spears neues Ballspiel, 1933
[*Triambolo*]
Barrola. Skilful and Exciting, 1934
(Spear's Games made in England)

Plate 84
Spears fein lackierte Kegel "Clowns mit spitzer Mütze",
around 1935
Spears fein lackierte Kegel "grün-gelb-weiß lackiert",
around 1935
Figurenkegelspiel "Soldaten", around 1935
[Spear's Enamelled Fancy Skittles, various designs]

Plate 85
Tisch Tennis, 1902
[*Table Tennis*]

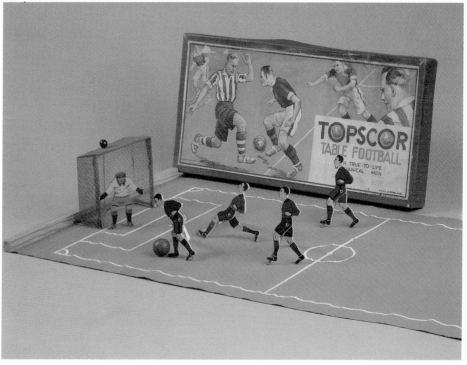

Plate 86
Topscor
Table Football with
true-to-life mechanical men,
1938
(Made at the Spear Works, Enfield)

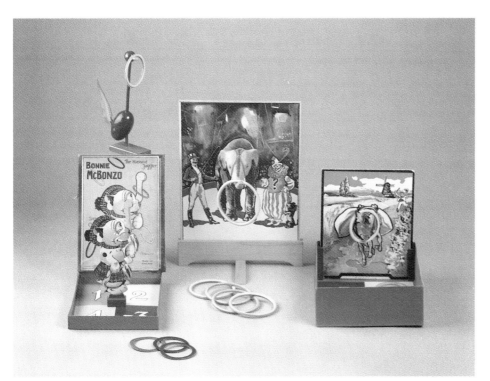

Plate 87
Bonnie Mc Bonzo.
The Hieland Juggler, 1936
(Manufactured at the Spear Works,
Enfield)
Gog der Gänserich.
Lustiges Ringwerfen, around 1930
[*Gay Mr. Gander*]
(wooden goose only)
Radscha. Der kluge Elefant, 1933
[*Rajah Ring Toss Game*]
Whoa-Neddy!, 1930
(Manufactured at the Spear Works
Bavaria, designed in England)

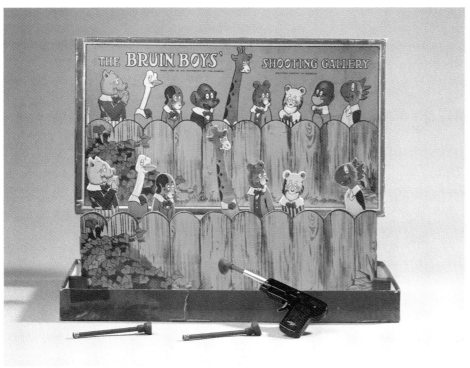

Plate 88
The Bruin Boys' Shooting Gallery,
around 1935
(Manufactured at the Spear Works,
Enfield)

Plate 89
Tiddledy Winks,
around 1925
Spears vier verschiedene
Knips-Spiele, 1933
[*Spear's Compendium
of Tidley Winks*]
Knips- oder Flohspiel
"Fliegenpilz", around 1950
[Tiddly winks with
mushroom shaped cup]
Wupp. Das lustige Fangspiel,
1952 [Hustle]
(box designed by
Gustav Müller)

Plate 90
Das Brückenspiel, 1926
[*Cuebridge*]
Wer will in mein Häuschen?
1926
[*Goal Skittles*]

Plate 91 ▷
Hans Purzelbaum, 1933
[*Rumble Tumble Tim*]
Glida, 1933 [*Glida*]
Ri-Ra-Rutsch. Das fesselnde
Spiel, 1933
[*The Jolly Game of
Rumble Tumble*]

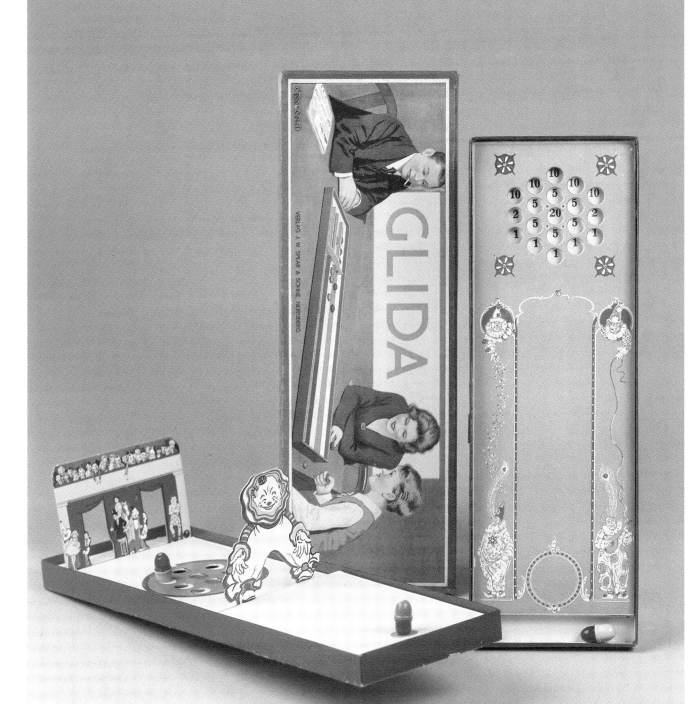

Plate 92
Hokus Pokus. Zauberkiste für Liebhaber, 1939
[Hokus Pokus Conjuring Set]
Zauber-Apparate. Marke Hokus Pokus, around 1925
[Conjuring Tricks, Hokus Pokus brand]
Spear's Conjuring Tricks, 1930
(Manufactured at the Spear Works Bavaria)

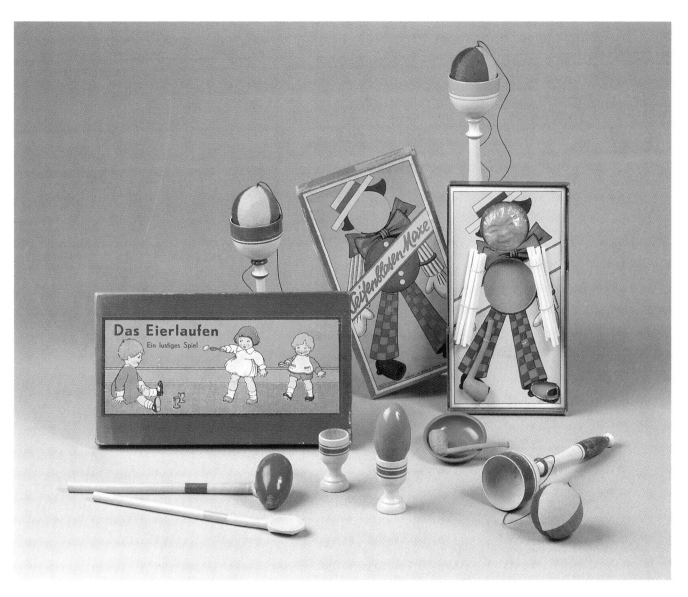

Plate 93
Das Eierlaufen. Ein lustiges Spiel, around 1930
[*The Egg and Spoon Race*]
Fangbecher, around 1930
[*Cup and Ball*]
Seifenblasen Maxe, 1933
[*Billy Bubbles*]

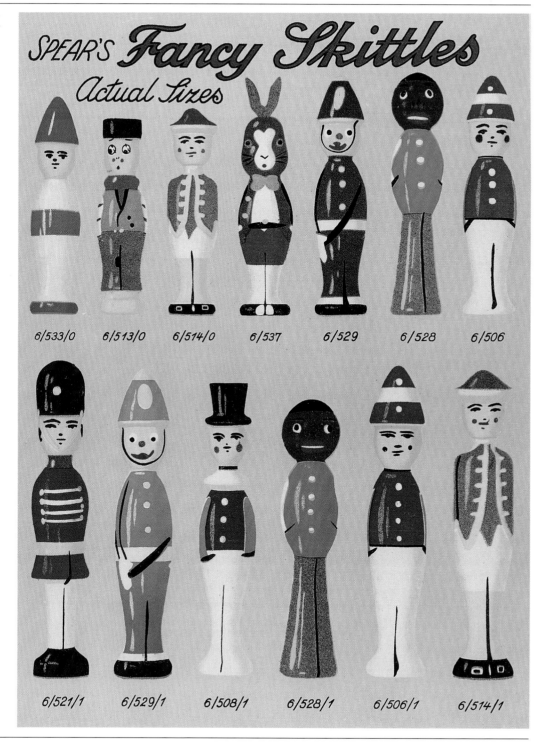

SPEAR'S *Fancy Skittles*
Actual Sizes

6/533/0 6/513/0 6/514/0 6/537 6/529 6/528 6/506

6/521/1 6/529/1 6/508/1 6/528/1 6/506/1 6/514/1

Markus Schicker

Spear Company Trademarks

Legal protection of new products, processes and trade names against unrestricted imitation has not only promoted economic activity in the industrial era, but is one of its main prerequisites. In the first half of the 19th century leading industrial nations such as Britain and France were already offering efficient protective legislation to their inventive engineers and entrepreneurs. In rather more backward Germany, because of the country's political fragmentation, a unified protective law could only be formulated after the founding of the German Empire, with the Imperial Patent Office in Berlin monitoring compliance with this legislation from 1877 onwards.

In the context of the otherwise rather sparse source material regarding industrial production of toys, patents and registrations of trademarks are important aids for the historical pin-pointing of individual products as well as giving clues to the general development of a company. This is why the relevant publications issued by the German Patent Office were systematically searched for material relating to the Spear company. As was to be expected, the company's importance is reflected in a large number of applications for protection filed, especially in the field of registered trademarks. Thus in the hundred years between 1894 – the years of publication of the first "Waarenzeichenblatt" (Registered Trademark Gazette) – and 1995, in Germany alone (no research was carried out in the UK) more than 300 registered trademarks could be identified.[1] The protected marks were words or images, i.e. mainly games titles such as "Die fliegenden Hüte" (Flying Hats, 1899) or "Ludo" (1912), lettering such as "Spear's Games" (1913) or "Was ihr wollt" (1914), but also included complete box designs, such as, for example the packaging for "Blow Football" (1911) or "Bist du sicher?" (Are you sure? 1972). The majority of the registrations were applied for between 1910 and 1938 and thus coincides more or less with the years when the company was at the height of its importance in Germany.

The research findings are compiled in the following listing which is subdivided into five columns:

1. **Number:** the increasing numbers in this column represent the register number of the registrations in question. It is the only unambiguous means of identifying a specific registered trademark – particularly in cases of duplication.
2. **Registered trademarks:** This shows the individual words or images registered as trademarks.

3. **Application:** Lists the date when the application for protection of the trademark was filed.
4. **Registration:** Gives the date of registration and thus the beginning of protection of the trademark.
5. **WZB:** Lists the page of the relevant issue of the "Warenzeichenblatt" (Registered Trademark Gazette) where the protected word(s) or image(s) are listed. The year of issue may be obtained from the registration date listed in column 4.

The registration of trademarks is a good indication of the development of the product range and thus greatly facilitate dating of individual items, but unfortunately there are some pitfalls. Application for protection and registration as trademark, for example, do not give a reliable indication of the date the relevant article was launched on the market with the title given. Sometimes protection was applied for in advance and in some cases was never used – or used very much later. The registration of the word trademark "Was ihr wollt" is a good example for this: The trademark was registered in May 1914, but the first advertisement for the games compendium of the same name was not placed in the trade journals until 1919. The opposite case could also happen, the best example being the registration of the "couchant lance with shield" as trademark for the company J.W.Spear & Söhne in June, 1910. This trademark had already been in use since 1904, at the latest, when the first company catalogue known so far was published.

Quite apart from these restricting considerations, it can, however, be assumed that in the 1920s, at the latest, Spear developed a certain routine in their applications for the registration of trademarks. It seems that the company applied for protection of all its important new products on a regular basis. The entries for the 1920s and 1930s thus represent quite a reliable indication for the dating of individual items. And in any case, the list offers a point of reference for all those cases where further sources of information – such as advertisements, catalogues or company documentation – are not available.

1 The great majority of entries concerning Spear can be found in the original "Großgruppe" (major group) resp. "Warenklasse" (goods classification group) 35: "Spiele und Spielwaren" (Games and Toys) which in 1968 in the course of adaptation to international standards was included in the new class 28. Between 1944 and 1950, no new issues of the "Warenzeichenblätter" were published, incidentally. On the general topic of the development of trademarks cf. Rudolf Busse, Warenzeichengesetz: nebst Pariser Verbandsübereinkunft und Madrider Abkommen, Berlin 1990.

NO	REGISTERED TRADEMARK	APPLICATION	REGISTRD.	WZB	NO	REGISTERED TRADEMARK	APPLICATION	REGISTRD.	WZB
41732	Die fliegenden Hüte	08.05.1899	12.01.1900	158	183534	The lost heir	15.07.1913	07.11.1913	2961
55140	*Graphic sign:* Der fidele Emil!	24.05.1902	17.07.1902	673	183768	Multum in Parvo	29.03.1913	11.11.1913	3219
62101	Cetro	22.05.1903	19.08.1903	1129	184214	*Graphic sign:* Schwarzer Peter	23.06.1913	21.11.1913	3282
63765	*Graphic sign:* [Snipkick]	08.09.1903	21.10.1903	1472	184292	*Graphic sign:* The Game of			
77693	Zillograph	06.02.1905	27.03.1905	679		Red, White and Blue	22.04.1913	22.11.1913	3283
85666	Hoki-Poki	12.12.1905	26.02.1906	474	184691	Wer weiß es?	03.10.1913	29.01.1913	3283
85830	*Graphic sign:* The Piggeries				184922	Tiny Tots	06.06.1913	04.12.1913	3283
	(The latest craze)	30.12.1905	05.03.1906	474	184923	Chi va piano va sano	15.07.1913	04.12.1913	3284
104303	*Graphic sign:* USA Lotto	21.02.1907	15.01.1908	131	184924	Es war einmal	03.10.1913	04.12.1913	3284
130981	*Graphic sign:* Spear-Schutzmarke				184925	Japtoss	03.10.1913	04.12.1913	3284
	(lance)	19.04.1910	09.06.1910	1192	185644	Toy Town	10.05.1913	16.12.1913	272
138229	*Graphic sign:* Art Needlework	15.11.1910	22.12.1910	157	185755	Chessindia	16.06.1913	17.12.1913	273
140385	*Graphic sign:* Blow Football	24.11.1910	20.02.1911	544	185972	Unsere Jungen in Wald			
145537	*Graphic sign:* Der Irrgarten	10.05.1911	14.06.1911	1349		und Flur	27.10.1913	24.12.1913	273
156199	Ludo	06.01.1912	15.03.1912	643	185973	Wie Du mir so ich Dir	27.10.1913	24.12.1913	273
160663	Parcheesi	11.04.1912	15.06.1912	1474	187302	Tittlebats	03.10.1913	19.01.1914	566
161592	Wohin gehört's?	07.05.1912	04.07.1912	1799	187483	Wer will unter die Soldaten?	06.11.1913	22.01.1914	567
163810	Globe Trotters	26.02.1912	12.09.1912	2150	188743	*Graphic sign:* Spear's Games,			
165198	Blumenflirt	02.05.1912	11.10.1912	2416		Made at the Spear Works,			
168728	Tiny Town	07.11.1912	21.12.1912	221		Bavaria	15.07.1913	13.02.1914	860
168828	Attack	02.11.1912	27.12.1912	221	188744	Der kleine Lehrer	15.07.1913	13.02.1914	861
168829	Laripino	09.11.1912	27.12.1912	221	188745	Wer kriegt die Braut?	27.10.1913	13.02.1914	861
168830	Weltgrößen	14.11.1912	27.12.1912	221	188895	Crokinole	10.05.1913	16.02.1914	811
168982	Pfefferkuchen	19.09.1912	30.12.1912	222	188986	*Graphic sign:*			
168983	Lebkuchen	19.09.1912	30.12.1912	222		Lustiges EinMalEins	06.06.1913	17.02.1914	862
169453	Trop grande hâte est				189123	Buttercup	15.07.1913	19.02.1914	862
	cause de retard	13.11.1912	11.11.1913	222	189124	Ri-Ra-Rutsch	15.08.1913	19.02.1914	862
169815	Schutzmann	02.11.1912	20.01.1913	491	189859	Happy Families	11.11.1913	06.03.1914	863
169816	Slipping the slip	04.11.1912	20.01.1913	223	190221	Derby	15.07.1913	13.03.1914	1217
169817	Nain jaune	04.11.1912	20.01.1913	223	190506	Die kleinen Franzosen	11.11.1913	19.03.1914	1218
169886	Was tun?	07.12.1912	20.01.1913	223	191329	Knacknüsse	12.12.1913	02.04.1914	1219
171208	Conturo	13.12.1912	17.02.1913	736	191535	Steeple Quoits	23.10.1913	06.04.1914	1219
171209	Was bist du?	27.12.1912	17.02.1913	736	192079	Right away	05.01.1914	07.04.1914	1548
171210	Leap Frog	09.11.1912	17.02.1913	736	192924	Crack Regiment	23.12.1913	01.05.1914	1549
171890	Lebenslauf	27.12.1912	28.02.1913	738	192925	Rosycheeks	23.12.1913	01.05.1914	1550
175548	Most haste least speed	27.03.1913	21.05.1913	1610	194231	Der kleine Juwelier	05.01.1914	25.05.1914	1905
175549	Alabama Coon	28.03.1913	21.05.1913	1610	194232	Was Ihr wollt	21.02.1914	25.05.1914	1905
177322	*Graphic sign:*				194900	Glücksglocken	21.11.1913	05.06.1914	1906
	Die kleine Weberin	22.04.1913	24.06.1913	1913	195042	Prinzess	11.12.1913	08.06.1914	1907
177876	Stets voran	29.03.1913	04.07.1913	1913	195043	Fleur de Lys	23.12.1913	08.06.1914	1907
178681	Dolly Dimple	09.04.1913	17.07.1913	2147	195714	Hopla	28.11.1913	22.06.1914	2201
178790	Hâte-toi lentement	29.05.1913	18.07.1913	2180	198444	Nations & Flags	12.12.1913	22.08.1914	2718
180239	Wer muß es haben?	10.05.1913	04.09.1913	2407	198860	Perdra	27.02.1914	15.09.1914	2718
180805	For Dainty Fingers	26.05.1913	17.09.1913	2682	199988	Wunderfische	17.03.1914	03.11.1914	2990
182386	Snipkick	09.07.1913	16.10.1913	2959	204460	Glücksfische	27.02.1914	03.07.1915	874
182387	Der verlorene Passagier	15.08.1913	16.10.1913	2959	212514	Jumpkins	28.02.1916	14.09.1916	969
183045	*Graphic sign:*				213136	Royal Ludo	20.01.1916	06.10.1916	1092
	[Koffer-Lotto / Trunk Lotto]	26.06.1913	30.10.1913	2960	213137	Warum?	05.09.1916	06.10.1916	1092

218329	Wie es Euch gefällt	23.04.1917	20.06.1917	845
218330	Der kleine Gernegroß	23.04.1917	20.06.1917	845
218683	Mit Laute und Rucksack	10.05.1917	03.07.1917	846
219220	Wer zuletzt lacht,			
	lacht am besten	08.06.1917	03.08.1917	958
219221	Ende gut, alles gut	08.06.1917	03.08.1917	958
220605	Schwuppdiwupp	07.06.1917	26.10.1917	1304
220765	Gluck Gluck	02.05.1917	05.11.1917	1304
221248	*Graphic sign:* Ludo oder			
	Wer Pech hat!	19.07.1917	01.12.1917	1402
225103	Rausschmeisser oder			
	Ärgere dich nicht!	15.04.1918	05.07.1918	688
226350	Spear	15.04.1918	24.09.1918	952
226646	Schuster bleib bei			
	deinem Leisten	01.07.1918	08.10.1918	953
227191	*Graphic sign:*			
	[Dog with girl]	26.08.1918	31.10.1918	1074
227406	Am Scheideweg	13.08.1918	07.11.1918	1074
227548	Die springenden Hüte	31.07.1918	16.11.1918	1089
228273	Die goldene Brücke	01.07.1918	30.12.1918	54
228274	Herzblättchen	15.04.1918	30.12.1918	54
228400	*Graphic sign:*			
	[Harlequin with crocodile]	11.07.1918	06.01.1919	54
228401	Glücksringe	21.08.1918	06.01.1919	54
229819	Ueber Stock und Stein	26.09.1918	26.02.1919	317
230389	Tischlein deck dich	13.12.1918	22.03.1919	461
230981	Durch Dick und Dünn	19.12.1918	12.04.1919	608
230982	Länder und Leute	16.01.1919	12.04.1919	608
232011	Däumling	07.10.1918	14.05.1919	609
232012	Kribbel – Krabbel	03.02.1919	14.05.1919	609
232935	Zwick und Zwack	07.10.1918	10.06.1919	769
233299	Wer wagt, gewinnt!	13.02.1919	18.06.1919	903
233311	Sag mir, was ist das?	11.03.1919	19.06.1919	903
233591	Wickel Wackel	03.02.1919	24.06.1919	903
234847	Knuddelmuddel	03.03.1919	29.08.1919	1152
236178	Holterdipolter	20.05.1919	03.10.1919	1343
236179	Abwarten und Tee trinken	20.05.1919	03.10.1919	1343
236255	*Graphic sign:* Ludo oder			
	Wer Pech hat!	22.04.1919	04.10.1919	1343
239493	Hokus Pokus	07.04.1919	06.12.1919	1822
241258	Wichtikus	30.05.1919	23.01.1920	377
241710	Hansel Schluck	07.04.1919	30.01.1920	377
244302	Sirius	19.06.1919	17.03.1920	904
248030	De Flygande Hattarna	31.01.1920	03.06.1920	1464
248031	Wenn der Mensch Pech hat	03.02.1920	03.06.1920	1464
248032	Hänschen und Fränzchen	21.02.1920	03.06.1920	1464
248033	Das Wandern ist des			
	Müllers Lust	24.03.1920	03.06.1920	1464
248034	Hat ihn schon	24.03.1924	03.06.1920	1464
248035	Kissemurre – Lustigkurre	24.03.1920	03.06.1920	1464
249458	Nöff! Nöff!	24.03.1920	30.06.1920	1847
249586	*Graphic sign:* Was Ihr wollt	21.01.1920	13.07.1920	1827
250376	Tag till Lekstaden	24.03.1920	16.08.1920	1848
250681	Flying Jack	21.02.1920	20.08.1920	2109
251641	Kisse missarna	24.03.1920	06.09.1920	2110
251642	Farbror Lekkamraten!	25.03.1920	06.09.1920	2110
251895	Die hüpfenden Hüte	30.03.1920	10.09.1920	2355
253696	Spearino	26.04.1920	09.10.1920	2646
255275	*Graphic sign:*			
	[Flying Hats]	22.04.1920	05.11.1920	3048
256191	Les Chapeaux volants	29.05.1920	24.11.1920	3049
256192	Durch die Blume	08.06.1920	24.11.1920	3049
256857	Klipp Klipp	24.03.1920	08.12.1920	3050
257506	Kleider machen Leute	23.06.1920	21.12.1920	143
257507	Durch die Wälder			
	Durch die Auen	21.06.1920	21.12.1920	143
257775	Fang mich	25.05.1920	27.12.1920	143
257776	Der Mann muß hinaus!	13.09.1920	27.12.1920	143
261501	Hennypenny	04.10.1920	08.03.1921	700
262631	Lefo	16.08.1920	23.03.1921	1110
264389	Rollaway	25.06.1920	29.04.1921	1421
264450	Dont worry!	19.11.1920	30.04.1921	1454
268080	Mopperl	08.06.1920	29.06.1921	2022
268081	Wer zuerst kommt,			
	mahlt zuerst	14.04.1921	29.06.1921	2022
268082	Crazy Gussie	19.11.1920	29.06.1921	2022
268829	Such mich	25.05.1920	02.08.1921	2327
275629	Jack und Jane	19.11.1920	21.11.1921	3556
275689	Erstens kommt es anders,			
	zweitens als man denkt	06.06.1921	22.11.1921	3556
279376	Knock out!	06.06.1921	06.02.1922	476
279407	Buy a bungalow	06.06.1921	06.02.1922	496
282161	Wer kauft das Haus?	06.06.1921	13.03.1922	1189
285101	Catch that Fly	29.12.1921	29.04.1922	1585
285681	Hütchen flieg!	07.10.1921	08.05.1922	1922
291220	Der Lausbub	18.05.1922	01.09.1922	2978
294604	You never can tell	01.07.1922	20.11.1922	3507
294605	Rausschmeisser	10.07.1922	20.11.1922	3507
295368	Epsom	17.06.1922	07.12.1922	181
295369	Des Einen Leid –			
	des Andern Freud	17.06.1922	07.12.1922	181
298602	Carrots	30.10.1922	02.03.1923	659
304585	Tweedledum and Tweedledee	12.04.1923	04.08.1923	1705
305954	*Graphic sign:* Royal Ludo	03.11.1922	15.09.1923	1953
307199	Neck and Neck	11.07.1923	23.10.1923	2225
320389	The Girl who would			
	a-travelling go	26.05.1924	06.09.1924	2015
320947	Spear's Games	16.06.1924	15.09.1924	2169

322143	Say it with Flowers	26.05.1924	07.10.1924	2300
322144	Um Nasenlänge	07.06.1924	07.10.1924	2301
328269	Ludo Imperial	20.10.1924	06.02.1925	628
328981	Sweet Wedding Bells	22.11.1924	19.02.1925	757
329944	Wer will in mein Häuschen?	12.12.1924	07.03.1925	896
333355	Irrgarten	19.02.1925	08.05.1925	1426
336542	Laß mich in Ruh!	12.02.1925	18.07.1925	2032
340314	Pokal	09.01.1925	08.10.1925	2651
341974	The Hidden Treasure	01.07.1925	23.10.1925	3005
349569	Fleurt	11.11.1925	18.03.1926	1089
356069	Graphic sign: [Clown profile]	20.05.1926	24.08.1926	2231
356169	The Piggeries	20.05.1926	26.08.1926	2231
356319	Hoki Poki	20.05.1926	30.08.1926	2371
360079	Je bent er nog niet	03.07.1926	26.11.1926	2956
363003	Das Tierkonzert	20.11.1926	29.01.1927	477
365397	Graphic sign: [Quoits with clowns]	22.12.1926	12.03.1927	891
365986	Strick-Liesl	04.10.1926	23.03.1927	1064
365987	Piccaninny	04.10.1926	23.03.1927	1064
368181	Houdt er den moed maar in	21.01.1927	07.05.1927	1457
369022	Naseweis	05.03.1927	20.05.1927	1583
372977	Totem	16.05.1927	18.08.1927	2392
375524	Schau hinein	10.06.1927	18.10.1927	2883
376115	Ons eigen Land	30.06.1927	01.11.1927	2884
380476	Komm mit!	29.08.1927	23.01.1928	459
381162	Royal Ludo	04.11.1927	02.02.1928	599
381163	Stunts	12.11.1927	02.02.1928	599
382937	Coppit & Cappit	04.10.1927	07.03.1928	862
382938	Wie es Euch gefällt	04.11.1927	07.03.1928	862
382939	Ende gut, alles gut	04.11.1927	07.03.1928	862
382940	Wer zuletzt lacht, lacht am besten	04.11.1927	07.03.1928	862
383083	Ganz wie Mama	12.12.1927	08.03.1928	853
383540	Gluck Gluck	04.11.1927	17.03.1928	997
383541	Sieben auf einen Schlag!	21.12.1927	17.03.1928	997
383773	Spira	19.12.1927	23.03.1928	997
383774	Sei fleißig!	21.12.1927	23.03.1928	997
384363	Spier	16.01.1928	04.04.1928	1134
388371	Winzli – Wusch	24.03.1928	22.06.1928	1789
389067	Freut Euch des Klebens!	02.03.1928	07.07.1928	1915
392393	Hat over Hat	04.06.1928	02.10.1928	2424
392838	Rundherum (class 32)	01.03.1928	12.10.1928	2418
398889	Freut Euch des Webens	16.08.1928	19.02.1929	660
398890	Woolly Pictures	24.10.1928	19.02.1929	660
399228	Ocean	16.01.1928	26.02.1929	649
399640	Graphic sign: [polar bear]	24.03.1928	06.03.1929	766
400040	Rundherum (class 35)	13.07.1928	14.03.1929	766
400113	Luise	06.07.1928	16.03.1929	879
400777	Flecht – Flink	19.12.1928	02.04.1929	990
401373	Strick – Flott	19.12.1928	15.04.1929	991
401958	Annemarie	14.06.1928	25.04.1929	1117
403916	Däumling	05.03.1929	06.06.1929	1456
403917	Tischlein deck dich!	13.03.1929	06.06.1929	1456
404424	Die goldene Brücke	15.04.1929	18.06.1929	1559
404895	Denkfix	08.04.1929	01.07.1929	1663
404896	Der kleine Gernegroß	15.04.1929	01.07.1929	1663
406386	Zug um Zug	10.06.1929	06.08.1929	1867
408494	Herzblättchen	16.04.1929	09.10.1929	2238
408961	Knuddelmuddel	10.06.1929	18.10.1929	2352
408985	Wer wagt, gewinnt	28.05.1929	18.10.1929	2352
408986	Wickel Wackel	28.05.1929	18.10.1929	2352
408987	Kribbel Krabbel	28.05.1929	18.10.1929	2352
408988	Graphic sign: [Old Maid with saxophone player]	31.05.1929	18.10.1929	2352
408989	Kwiknit	05.06.1929	18.10.1929	2352
410419	Doppelmoppel	08.06.1929	13.11.1929	2478
411549	Triambolo	05.10.1929	09.12.1929	94
413277	Nesthäkchen	08.06.1929	16.01.1930	429
413846	Whoa	28.10.1929	29.01.1930	430
414525	Abwarten und Tee trinken	15.11.1929	13.02.1913	539
414526	Wichtikus	15.11.1929	13.02.1930	539
414527	Holterdipolter	15.11.1929	13.02.1930	539
417755	Googly Golly	03.01.1930	30.04.1930	1072
420545	Was bringt uns die Zukunft	23.01.1930	27.06.1930	1604
420639	Graphic sign: Knetschule	10.05.1930	30.06.1930	1604
421577	Hänschen und Fränzchen	16.04.1930	22.07.1930	1698
422036	Spearino	07.06.1930	02.08.1930	1816
425138	Fang mich	09.07.1930	29.10.1930	2336
425139	Durch die Blume	21.07.1930	29.10.1939	2336
430078	Hütchen auf den Kopf!	27.11.1930	05.03.1931	653
430079	Hansel Schluck	10.01.1931	05.03.1931	653
430080	Crazy Gussie	26.01.1931	05.03.1931	653
430081	Don't worry!	26.01.1931	05.03.1931	653
430082	Jack and Jane	26.01.1931	05.03.1931	654
431613	Skittlewinks	21.02.1931	10.04.1931	865
433479	Winapenny	07.03.1931	26.05.931	1175
433699	Tornado	11.04.1931	30.05.1931	1175
434337	Wie boft?	07.03.1931	12.06.1931	1359
434788	Woolly Willie	28.02.1931	23.06.1931	1361
434912	Hoppityhop	02.05.1931	26.06.1931	1455
435874	Wer kann's?	13.12.1930	21.07.1931	1629
436785	Einmal hin und einmal her	01.06.1931	24.08.1931	1728
436786	Springinsfeld	23.06.1931	24.08.1931	1729
436787	Freud und Leid der Kinderzeit	23.06.1931	24.08.1931	1729
437287	Knetflink	28.01.1931	09.09.1931	1817
437405	Kennst du dein Vaterland?	13.03.1931	14.09.1931	1817
438405	Herzenfänger	24.07.1931	16.10.1931	1990
438619	Strickflott (class 23)	25.07.1931	22.10.1931	2047

Number	Title	Date 1	Date 2	Value
438629	Wer zuerst kommt, mahlt zuerst	12.08.1931	23.10.1931	2070
439308	Eins zwei drei!	12.08.1931	10.11.1931	2165
440019	Snippety Snip	01.07.1931	30.11.1931	2261
440020	Erstens kommt es anders, zweitens als man denkt	22.09.1931	30.11.1931	2261
440469	Dominino	26.01.1931	14.12.1931	65
441418	Rosen, Tulpen, Nelken, Blumen, die nicht welken	24.08.1931	14.01.1932	233
441419	Bunte Reihe	27.08.1931	14.01.1932	233
441976	Figuba	28.02.1931	01.02.1932	314
442503	Volando	18.12.1931	18.02.1932	467
442587	Kijk uit!	25.06.1931	22.02.1932	467
442861	Schwing's Hämmerchen!	02.01.1932	01.03.1932	467
442932	Glida	12.01.1932	03.03.1932	544
443059	Augen auf!	12.01.1932	08.03.1932	544
443631	Sonnenstrahlen	19.10.1931	29.03.1932	613
443835	Quintro	08.02.1932	04.04.1932	695
444487	Strick-Peter	31.07.1931	25.04.1932	747
445740	Graphic sign: 5 in einer Reihe	14.04.1932	01.06.1932	1004
445789	Baut mit!	19.04.1932	02.06.1932	1005
447104	Tipotip	04.06.1932	14.07.1932	1230
447365	Marvolette	11.06.1932	23.07.1932	1300
448329	Der Lausbub	04.07.1932	10.09.1932	1439
448330	Zegt het meteen	04.07.1932	10.09.1932	1439
452060	Hamertje Tik	24.11.1932	09.01.1933	221
452061	Ringschling	28.11.1932	09.01.1933	221
452498	Schipp-Schipp	13.12.1932	21.01.1933	303
452695	Blumenflirt	25.06.1932	26.01.1933	303
453825	Graphic sign: Kugel und Ei, die lustige Kneterei	26.01.1933	28.02.1933	463
454872	Spannflott	07.11.1933	30.03.1933	612
456847	Jobalo	17.02.1933	29.05.1933	1008
460050	Es war einmal	09.08.1933	10.10.1933	1531
460051	Ri-Ra-Rutsch	09.08.1933	10.10.1933	1532
461308	Für helle Köpfe	09.10.1933	23.11.1933	1752
461389	Füg's ein	21.08.1933	25.11.1933	1752
462376	Ôte-toi de là, que je m'y mette!	18.11.1933	04.01.1934	181
462959	Wo fehlt ein Knopf?	21.08.1933	25.01.1934	256
462960	Qui tarde est pris	02.12.1933	25.01.1934	256
464329	Glücksvogel	27.01.1934	17.03.1934	534
465126	Graphic sign: Seifenblasen Maxe	19.12.1933	17.04.1934	676
465315	Greif zu!	22.02.1934	24.04.1934	676
465562	Plumps!	23.01.1934	02.05.1934	742
469373	Glücksschleife	19.07.1934	27.09.1934	1341
470170	Rinn ins Eck	22.09.1934	26.10.1934	1481
475009	Die fette Neun	13.12.1934	18.04.1935	665
475010	Multisnip	07.01.1935	18.04.1935	665
479015	Graphic sign: Wacklwack	29.06.1935	27.09.1935	1308
479123	Graphic sign: Wörternageln	05.06.1935	01.10.1935	1371
480211	Graphic sign: Schliess ab!	29.06.1935	11.11.1935	1505
489655	Je bent er nog niet	07.10.1936	03.12.1936	44
496842	Aus allen Ecken	18.08.1937	19.10.1937	1295
499244	Wer hat – der hat!	15.10.1937	14.01.1938	197
500529	Handel und Wandel	07.01.1938	05.03.1938	458
501374	Kreuz und Quer	28.01.1938	06.04.1938	600
503443	Bango-Bingo	23.02.1938	25.06.1938	953
507177	Besetzt	31.08.1938	03.02.1939	292
507178	Soja	28.09.1938	03.02.1939	292
507179	Glücksringe	29.09.1938	03.02.1939	292
511037	Strick-Flott	02.01.1939	11.05.1939	904
512021	Baufix	28.09.1938	31.05.1939	1031
519910	Peng!	23.11.1939	18.03.1940	430
519911	Warum nicht?	08.12.1939	18.03.1940	430
520695	Wortklaubereien	08.02.1940	25.04.1940	552
520845	Und ob!	04.01.1940	07.05.1940	613
	class 35 entries transferred to Spear-Spiele-Fabrik Hanns Porst	31.12.1940		1672
41732	Die fliegenden Hüte			1672
178790	Hâte-toi lentement			1672
184923	Chi va piano va sano			1672
220605	Schwuppdiwupp			1672
239493	Hokus Pokus			1672
256191	Les Chapeaux volants			1672
257776	Der Mann muß hinaus!			1672
305954	Graphic sign: Royal Ludo			1672
320947	Spear's Games			1672
365986	Strick-Liesl			1672
381162	Royal Ludo			1672
382939	Ende gut, alles gut			1672
382940	Wer zuletzt lacht, lacht am besten			1672
400040	Rundherum (class 35)			1672
400113	Luise			1672
404895	Denkfix			1672
425139	Durch die Blume			1672
430078	Hütchen auf den Kopf!			1672
435874	Wer kann's?			1672
437287	Knetflink			1672
437405	Kennst du dein Vaterland?			1672
441976	Figuba			1672
442861	Schwing's Hämmerchen!			1672
443059	Augen auf!			1672
443835	Quintro			1672
445789	Baut mit!			1672
448329	Der Lausbub			1672

452060	Hamertje Tik			1672
453825	Graphic sign: Kugel und Ei,			
	die lustige Kneterei			1672
460051	Ri-Ra-Rutsch			1672
461308	Für helle Köpfe			1672
461389	Füg's ein			1672
462376	Ôte-toi de là,			
	que je m'y mette!			1672
462959	Wo fehlt ein Knopf?			1672
462960	Qui tarde est pris			1672
464329	Glücksvogel			1672
465126	Graphic sign: Seifenblasen Maxe			1672
465315	Greif zu!			1672
465562	Plumps!			1672
469373	Glücksschleife			1672
470170	Rinn ins Eck			1672
489655	Je bent er nog niet			1672
496842	Aus allen Ecken			1672
499244	Wer hat – der hat!			1672
500529	Handel und Wandel			1672
501374	Kreuz und Quer			1672
507177	Besetzt			1672
507178	Soja			1672
507179	Glücksringe			1672
511037	Strick-Flott			1672
512021	Baufix			1672
519910	Peng!			1672
519911	Warum nicht?			1672
520695	Wortklaubereien			1672
520845	Und ob!			1672
531997	Spear-Spiele, aber richtig!	25.05.1940	21.04.1941	1028
533668	Fang mich	11.10.1940	07.06.1941	1342
	Company name altered to			
	Porst-Spiele-Fabrik			
	Hanns Porst on	31.07.1941		1485
537443	Porst-Spiele	07.05.1941	09.10.1941	2138
	Company name altered to			
	Porst-Spiele-Fabrik on	15.11.1941		2161
543703	Hälmchen	29.10.1941	25.03.1942	713
543704	Helmchen	29.10.1941	25.03.1942	714
628554	Hâte-toi lentement	23.12.1950	21.10.1952	2778
628555	Spear's Games	23.12.1950	21.10.1952	2779
666935	Scrabble	20.07.1953	22.11.1954	3568
702736	Kreuz und Quer über			
	Land und Meer	11.08.1956	17.05.1957	1036
744130	Gute Fahrt!	06.04.1960	29.12.1960	216
744162	Wer kann's?	13.09.1958	29.12.1960	216
744163	Spear-Spiel			
	Wer hat Vorfahrt?	06.04.1960	29.12.1960	216

804248	Nimm's leicht	31.07.1964	18.05.1965	1759
835337	Multipuzzle	29.09.1966	21.07.1967	1867
865973	Spearoscope	14.02.1969	11.02.1970	496
890510	Memox	24.12.1971	11.02.1972	842
890511	Colormix	24.12.1971	11.02.1972	842
893688	Graphic sign: Deck ab!	17.02.1971	23.05.1972	1604
894310	bist Du ... sicher?	05.02.1971	14.06.1972	1784
899020	Graphic sign: bist Du ... sicher?	17.02.1971	02.11.1972	2968
959593	Momox	02.09.1976	27.06.1977	2242
	transferred to			
	Spear Spiele on	30.12.1978		3594
959593	Momox			3594
	transferred to			
	Spear Spiele on	15.02.1979		437
628555	Spear's Games			437
744162	Wer kann's?			437
744163	Spear-Spiel			
	Wer hat Vorfahrt?			437
835337	Multipuzzle			437
	transferred to class 28			
	Spear Spiele on	15.02.1979		446
41732	Die fliegenden Hüte			446
365986	Strick-Liesl			446
400040	Rundherum (class 35)			446
404895	Denkfix			446
442861	Schwing's Hämmerchen!			446
997533	Spearitus	15.06.1979	07.02.1980	1012
997534	Graphic sign: [Knight Spearitus]	15.06.1979	07.02.1980	1011
1027937	Graphic sign: Scrabble	28.10.1981	19.01.1982	659
1062136	Scorpion	13.08.1983	12.04.1984	1717
1066691	Satanix	13.08.1983	06.08.1984	2917
1067066	Scrabble People	07.03.1984	16.08.1984	3083
	transferred to			
	J.W. Spear & Sons (UK) on	14.08.1985		2395
628555	Spear's Games			2395
744162	Wer kann's?			2395
835337	Multipuzzle			2395
997533	Spearitus			2395
997534	Graphic sign: [Knight Spearitus]			2395
1062136	Scorpion			2395
1097139	Scrabble	10.07.1985	01.10.1986	3307
1149679	Junior Scrabble	01.03.1989	14.11.1989	4910
1149680	Rainbow Scrabble	02.03.1989	14.11.1989	4915
1150573	Spear	13.12.1988	29.11.1989	119
39400693	Scrabble	08.11.1994	14.03.1995	1960

J. W. SPEAR & SÖHNE, FUERTH, Bayern.

Adresse für Telegramme: „Spearson".

Inhaber mehrerer Patente.

Fabrik von **Kurz-**, Spiel- und Schreibwaaren. Federhalter Patentstifte, **Automatic-Pencils**, Radirgummi, Mal- u. Zeichen-Vorlagen, Stickmuster, **Abzieh-Bilder**, Chromo- und Heiligen-Albums. Schattenspiele. Schreibmappen. **Zusammenlegb.** Papierkörbe. Lampenteller.

Die neue
Victoria-Büchertasche
(ges. geschützt),
elegant, practisch, leicht, dauerhaft
und billig in Calico, Leder oder
Wachstuch.
Dominos, Schach- und Damenbretter, Rennspiele, Glocke- und Hammer-, Lotto- u. verschiedene andere Spiele.
Spielmagazine.
Gratulationskarten.
Probesendungen gegen Nachnahme oder Aufgabe von Prima-Referenzen.

Wir empfehlen uns auch zur Besorgung aller Nürnberger Artikel gegen mässige Provision. — Verkauf nur an Grossisten.

Zur Messe in Leipzig, Peterstr. 26 II (Schletterhaus).

Advertisement from the "Guide" (April 1887) with first trademark.

Lance used as company logo for English games presumably since 1899, definitely since 1904. Registered trademark in 1910. Used well into the 1930s.

„Was ihr wollt".

Registered trademark in 1914, used from around 1919 until 1933 at least.

SPEAR'S GAMES

First used in 1923, registered trademark in 1924, discontinued in 1982.

Spear-Spiele

Trademark used from around 1926 until 1966.

Spear-Spiele

Trademark for German games, 1967–1979.

Spear-Spiele

Die Spielmacher.

Trademark for German games, 1979–1984.

SPEAR'S SPELEN

Holland
N.V. Agentuur en Commissiehandel
v/h A. A. van der Kolk
Heerengracht 252, Amsterdam

JEUX - SPEAR

Comptoirs d'Echantillons et Représentations:
En France:
Etablissements Marcel Bernheim,
29 Blvd. St. Martin, Paris.
En Belgique:
E. Denys, 6, Place du Samedi, Bruxelles

JUEGOS SPEAR

Lieferungen für
Spanien und Lateinamerika
durch Exporthäuser

SPEAR'S SPEL

Schweden
Uno A. Riese & Co.
Stadsgården 14-16 (Drottsgården)
Stockholm 11

SPEAR'S SPIL

Dänemark
Alfred Dittmann, Kompagnistræde 21, 1
Kopenhagen K
Norwegen
C. A. Erichsen, Nytorvet 5, Oslo

GIOCHI SPEAR

Rappresentante per l'Italia:
Ditta G. Pansier, Milano (120),
Viale Piave 12

*Trademarks as used from the late 1920s onwards
(Spear ad from "German Toy Gazette", 1931).*

Trademark since 1983.

Annotations

The Players' Century (pp. 8–23)

1 Spiele zur Uebung und Erholung des Körpers und Geistes, für die Jugend, ihre Erzieher und alle Freunde unschuldiger Jugendfreuden (Games for the Exercise and Recreation of Body and Mind, for Young People, for Educators and All Friends of Innocent Youthful Pleasures), Schnepfenthal 1796, p. 27

2 Gutsmuths, p. XI. In both 1802 and 1803, an edition of the almanach was published: Spielalmanach für die Jugend, Frankfurt/Main (reprint edited by Horst Kunze, Leipzig/München 1975), each almanach encompassing 12 games, corresponding in sequence to the months of the year.

3 Ibid, p. VIII

4 Ludwig Fertig: Zeitgeist und Erziehungskunst. Eine Einführung in die Kulturgeschichte der Erziehung in Deutschland von 1600 bis 1900, Darmstadt 1984, pp. 139, 141

5 Hein Retter: Spielzeug. Handbuch zur Geschichte und Pädagogik der Spielmittel, Weinheim/Basel, 1979, p. 105

6 Günther G. Bauer, Manfred Zollinger, Regina Kaltenbrunner: Spielbücher und -graphik des 16.–18. Jahrhunderts. Exhibition Institut für Spielforschung und Spielpädagogik, Salzburg 1993

7 Gutsmuths [cf. note 1], pp 347f, p. 352

8 2nd unchanged edition, Schnepfenthal 1796; 3rd edition, Schnepfenthal 1802; 4th edition, edited by F.W. Klumpp, Stuttgart 1845; 6th edition, edited by O. Schettler, Hof 1884; 7th edition, revised by O. Schetler, Hof 1885; 8th edition, edited by J.C. Lion, Leipzig 1893; 9th edition, revised by Georg Thiele, Hof 1914.

9 Reprints by the pharmacist Dr. C.G. Flitner [pseudonym C.G.F. von Düben], Berlin 1816, 1819, 1831

10 This follows the subdivision on the Berlin edition of 1810: Spielalmanach für Karten-, Schach-, Bret-, Billard-, Kegel- und Ball-Spieler zum Selbstunterrichte von Julius Cäsar. Nach den gründlichen Regeln und Gesetzen durchaus verbessert und mit neuen Spielen vermehrt von G.W. v. Abenstein (Games Almanach for Card, Chess, Board, Billiards, Skittles and Ball Games Self-Taught, by Julius Cäsar. Augmented according to thorough rules and regulations and supplement with new games by G.W. v. Abenstein).

11 Walter Stengel: Zeitvertreib. Zehn Kapitel Berliner Kulturgeschichte, Berlin 1969, p.33

12 Das neue königliche l'Hombre, nebst einer gründlichen Anweisung, wie Piquet, Reversy, Tresett, Tarok, Casino, Connectionen, Whist, Boston, Patience, Kabale, Bouillotte, Jeu de Commerce, Pharao, Rapouse, Vingt un, Vive l'amour, Mariage, schwarzer Peter, Poch, Onze et demi, Drei Karten, Loup oder Wolf, Bester Bube, Ecarté; ferner: Trictrac, Verkehren, Billard, Kegel, Dame, Domino, Lange Poch, Schach, nach jetziger Art zu spielen sind, wobei die Ausdrücke, deren man sich bei diesen Spielen bedient, deutlich erklärt worden sind, Lüneburg 1837

13 Willi Geismeier: Biedermeier, Leipzig 1986, p. 60

14 Subtitled: Ein theoretisch-practisches Spielbuch aller bis jetzt bekannten, älteren und neuesten, ihrer Solidität wegen beliebten und erlaubten Kartenunterhaltungen, als: Piquet, l'Hombre, Alliance, Tarock, Whist, Ecarté, Boston, Reunion, Cabale, genug sechsundzwanzig an der Zahl. Nach den verschiedenen üblichen Arten, sowohl nach ihren Gesetzen und Regeln, als auch nach den ihnen eigenthümlichen Feinheiten, mit steter Berücksichtigung der wahren Raison, dann alle Bretspiele, Schach, Billard, Trictrac, Tokkategli, Dame, Domino etc. auf das gründlichste und in der kürzesten Zeit zu lernen; nebst einigen Winken zur Erkenntnis betrügerischer Mischungen der so genannten Grecs, für Jedermann faßlich vorgetragen.

15 Neuestes allgemeines Spielbuch. Enthaltend: Der vollkommene Kartenspieler, in allen bekannten, beliebten, erlaubten, auch mehreren noch nirgends beschriebenen Kartenspielen. Nebst warnenden Winken über die Mischungen listiger und unredlicher Spieler. Der allezeit fertige Brettspieler, oder Anweisung zur schnellsten practischen Erlernung sowohl, als auch der Regeln vom Schach-, Domino-, Dame-, Kegel-, Billard-, Ball-, Trictrac- und Toccategli-Spiel etc. Der willkommene Gesellschafter, oder Beyträge zur Unterhaltung froher Zirkel durch Gesang, Declamation, mimisch-plastische Tableaux,. Charadenaufgaben – Fragen und Antworten, Commerzspiele, Pfänderlösungen, Karten- und Taschenspielerkünste. Alles kurz und faßlich, auf Erfahrung gegründet dargestellt, und beschrieben für Jung und Alt, Vienna 1829, pp 36 f.

16 Verstand und Glück im Bunde[cf. note 14], p. VII f.

17 Neuester Spielalmanach für Karten-, Schach-, Brett-, Billard-, Kegel- und Ball-Spieler; zum Selbstunterrichte, nach den gründlichsten Regeln und Gesetzen. G.W. v Abenstein (Ed.), second revised edition supplemented by new games, Berlin 1820, p. XV

18 Die Kunst, stets mit Vortheil zu spielen und dadurch sein Glück zu machen, oder deutliche und gründliche Angabe der Mittel, durch Karten-, Würfel-, Billard und andere Spiele auf redliche Art seinen Wohlstand zu befördern und zu befestigen. Aus eignen Erfahrungen und den Mittheilungen der berühmtesten Spieler zusammengestellt von Ben Israel, Philadelphia's Enkel, Berlin 1834, p. 29

19 Bürgersinn und Aufbegehren. Biedermeier und Vormärz in Wien 1815–1848, exhibition Historisches Museum der Stadt Wien, Vienna 1987, p. 326

20 Ulla Heise: Kaffee und Kaffeehaus. Eine Kulturgeschichte, Leipzig 1987, pp. 150 f.

21 Joachim Petzold: Schach. Eine Kulturgeschichte, Leipzig 1986, pp. 193–196, 199, 211 f.

22 Der allezeit fertige Brettspieler, oder Anweisung zur schnellsten practischen Erlernung sowohl, als auch der Regeln vom Schach-, Domino-, Dame-, Kegel-, Billard-, Ball-, Trictrac- und Toccategli-Spiel, Vienna 1835, pp. 54-57

23 Günther G. Bauer: "Das Billardspiel liebte er leidenschaftlich". W.A. Mozart – der Billard- und Kegelspieler, in: Homo Ludens. Der spielende Mensch, vol 5, Munich/Salzburg 1995, pp. 167-230

24 Jean-Marie Lhôte: Dictionnaire des jeux de société, Paris 1996, p. 66

25 Previously, there had been other attempts at composing human figure from games and toy elements, e.g. the copperplate engravings "Habit de Tabletier" (An allegory of the cabinet maker), about 1700, by Nicholas de L'Armessin, as well as "Une Tourneuse" (Female Woodturner) and "Un Cartier" (Card Maker), about 1730 by Martin Engelbrecht.

26 Günther Böhmer: Die Welt des Biedermeier, Eltville 1981, p. 173

27 Hilarius Jocosus: Was fangen wir heute an? Oder: Unterhaltendes Gesellschafts-Panorama für heitere und lebensfrohe Cirkel. Enthaltend: Viele Scherz- und Pfänder-Spiele, Spiele im Freyen, Karten- und Würfel-Spiele, Nachsprech-Spiele, Taschenspieler-, Karten- und andere erheiternde Kunststücke, Räthseln, Charaden und Logogryphen, kurzweilige Histörchen und Anecdoten für Grillenfänger, Declamations-Stücke und eine Auswahl vortrefflicher Stammbuchs-Aufsätze. Für Freunde des Frohsinns und der Kurzweile geordnet und herausgegeben, Second edition. Vienna, no year stated [1839], pp. 33-35, 39 f.

28 Sigrid Metken: Komm spiel mit mir Blindekuh ... Ikonographie und Ausdeutung eines Fang- und Ratespiels, in: Kunst und Antiquitäten, 1/2 1991, pp. 52-61.

29 Golo Mann: Ludwig I. König von Bayern, Schaftlach 1989, p. 28

30 Ingeborg Weber-Kellermann: Die Kindheit. Kleidung und Wohnen, Arbeit und Spiel. Eine Kulturgeschichte, Frankfurt/Main 1979, pp. 222 f.

31 Jocosus [cf. note 27], pp. 15 f, 21 f, 55

32 Allgemeines und vollständiges Spielbuch. Eine Anleitung, alle bekannten Conversations-Spiele, als : Piquet, l'Hombre, Tresett, Alliance, Tarock, Casino, Whist, Boston etc. auf das Gründlichste zu erlernen. Nebst den Regeln und Gesetzen der Billard-, Kegel-, Ball- und Gesellschaftsspiele, und einigen nothwendigen Winken zur Erkenntniß betrügerischer Kartenmischungen, Vienna 1846, p. 480

33 Agnes von Aarau: Viel Vergnügen! Eine Original Sammlung von Gesellschaftsspielen aller Art, Vexier-, Reim- und schriftlichen Spielen. Pfänderspielen und Pfänderauslösungen, Orakelspielen, Zauber- und Kartenkunststücken, Aufführungen, heiteren Vorträgen, Rätseln und Charaden etc. etc. Nebst einem Vorwort: "Wie unterhalte ich meine Gäste" (Fingerzeig für Empfang, Bewirtung und Unterhaltung geladener Gäste), second unchanged edition, Stuttgart, no year stated [1892], pp. 11 f.

34 Subtitled: Unterhaltende Beschäftigungen und anregende Spiele für die Kinderstube. Zur Förderung des Schönheits-, Thätigkeits- und Ordnungssinnes sowie zur Gewöhnung an Arbeit und Ausdauer deutscher Kinder nach Fröbel'schen Grundsätzen bearbeitet, Leipzig 1874

35 Roger Kaysel: Pestalozzi – Fröbel – Montessori. Spielen – Gestalten – Lernen. Ein Beitrag zur Entwicklungs- und Wirkungsgeschichte des Lern- und Beschäftigungsspiels in Elternhaus, Kindergarten und Schule, Schweizer Kindermuseum, Baden 1996, p. 4

36 Subtitled: 1001 unterhaltende und anregende Belustigungen, Spiele und Beschäftigungen für Körper und Geist, im Freien sowie im Zimmer. Nebst einem Anhange: 500 Allerlei Kurzweil und kurzweiliges Allerlei für Jung und Alt. Zur geselligen Unterhaltung an langen Winterabenden, Leipzig 1865

37 Ibid. p. 176

38 Quoted from the 3rd edition, Illustrirtes Spielbuch für Knaben. 1001 unterhaltende und anregende Belustigungen, Spiele und Beschäftigungen für Körper und Geist, im Freien sowie im Zimmer, Leipzig 1870, p. V

39 Ibid. p. 249

40 Vater, Mutter, Kind. Bilder und Zeugnisse aus zwei Jahrhunderten, Exhibition Münchner Stadtmuseum, Munich 1987, pp. 14 f.

41 Neuestes Familien-Spielbuch. Leichtfaßliche Anleitung zur Erlernung der beliebtesten, interessantesten Brett-, Karten-, Hazard- und anderer Spiele. Reudnitz near Leipzig, no year given [1885]; Alban von Hahn: Buch der Spiele. Encyclopädie sämtlicher bekannten Spiele und Unterhaltungsweisen für alle Kreise, Leipzig 1894; Theodor Rulemann: Das große illustrierte Spielbuch. Enthaltend gegen 1000 neuere und ältere Spiele und Belustigungen. Berlin, no year given [1908].

42 Subtitled: Vorführung aller bekannteren Spiele und gebräuchlichen Unterhaltungsweisen für alle Kreise, zur körperlichen Erholung und geistig-gemüthlichen Erheiterung und Anregung im Freien wie im Zimmer, Leipzig/Berlin 1882. Jan Daniel Georgens also published: Neues Spielbuch für Knaben, Berlin 1887.

43 Ibid., p. V

44 J. Hesse: Das Spiel im häuslichen Kreise. Ein Rageber für die Familie, second unchanged edition, Stuttgart, no year given [1890], p. 4

Nuremberg – City of Games (pp. 24–41)

1 Georg Wenzel, Die Geschichte der Nürnberger Spielzeugindustrie, dissertation Erlangen-Nuremberg, 1967, pp. 27, 72-78

2 Georg Himmelheber: Spiele. Gesellschaftsspiele aus einem Jahrtausend, Munich/ Berlin 1972, pp. 57–115

3 Dorothea Rammensee: Bibliographie der Nürnberger Kinder- und Jugendbücher 1522–1914, Bamberg 1961, pp. 7 f.

4 Christine Pressler: Schöne alte Kinderbücher. Eine illustrierte Geschichte des deutschen Kinderbuchs aus fünf Jahrhunderten, Munich 1980, pp. 9 f.

5 Herbert Maas: Der Name Nürnberg in Sprichwörtern, Redensarten und Bezeichnungen, in: Mitteilungen des Vereins für Geschichte der Stadt Nürnberg, vol. 79, 1992, pp. 50-56

6 Johann Ferdinand Roth: Geschichte des Nürnbergischen Handels, Leipzig 1800–1802, vol. 2, pp. 291 f.

7 Verzeichniß von sämmtlichen Waaren so bey dem Kaufmann Peter Friedrich Catel wohnhaft in der Brüderstraße im Nürnberger Laden zu jeder Zeit um sehr billige Preise zu haben sind. (Complete directory of all wares presently available from the trader Peter Friedrich, resident in the Nuremberg Shop in Brüderstraße, at any time and at very cheap prices), Berlin 1785 (the author owes knowledge of this directory to a communication from Dr. Dieter Gebhardt, Nuremberg). Further directories were published in 1786, 1788, 1790 and 1792. The first catalogue, among others, contains 78 mathematical and magnetic games, Chinese puzzles and parlour games. An illustrated catalogue was to follow: Mathematisches und physikalisches Kunst-Cabinet, dem Unterrichte und der Belustigung der Jugend gewidmet (Cabinet of the mathematical and physical arts, dedicated to the education and entertainment of our young folk). With 216 illustrations on 9 copperplates, as well as a description of the various items and an indication of prices for which they may be bought from the author of this work, P.F. Catel in Berlin. Berlin/ Libau 1790. A second part with 50 illustrations on 4 copperplates was issued in Berlin in 1793. (This catalogue was first mentioned as an important source for research in toy history in Renate Müller-Krumbach: Kleine heile Welt. Eine Kulturgeschichte der Puppenstube. Leipzig 1992, pp. 59 f.).

8 Weitläufige Beschreibung des pädagogischen Kabinets, welches ich zur Erleichterung der Erziehung und zur lehrreichen Beschäftigung der Jugend angelegt habe. Nebst Anzeige der genauesten und billigsten Preise, für welche sie bey mir […] zu bekommen sind (Extensive description of the educational cabinet which I have established for the purpose of facilitating education and of entertaining young people in an instructive manner. In addition to giving the most accurate and inexpensive prices for which they may be bought from me), Nuremberg 1791. This book is to be found in the Nuremberg municipal library. It seems to be part eight of the above catalogue.

9 Manfred Bachmann: "Nürnberger Tand". Das Magazin des Georg Hieronimus Bestelmeier, in: Spielmittel, 1993, issue 1, pp. 30-35.

10 Pädagogisches Magazin zur lehrreichen und angenehmen Unterhaltung für die Jugend, es enthält solches eine Auswahl der schönsten Artikel, Städte, Dörfer, Palläste, Häußer, Gärten etc. aus einzelnen Bausteinen und Stüken zusammen gesezt: ferner phisikalisch-mathematische, hidraulische und magnetische Sachen, alles von denen besten Künstlern auf das schönste bearbeitet und nach der Natur genau abgebildet, in den billigsten Preißen, Nuremberg 1793; second instalment […] 1794; third instalment […] 1795; fourth instalment […] 1796, fifth instalment […] 1797. Nuremberg. 41 copperplates (668 illustrations) in total.

11 The copperplates shown in the Bestelmeier catalogue were mainly created by G. Roth, the first instalments were printed by the old-established Felsecker company. On the history of this Nuremberg publishing house, cf. Jakob Konrad: 333 Jahre Felsecker Sebald, Nuremberg 1990.

12 Systematisches Verzeichnis eines Magazins von verschiedenen Spiel-, Kunst- und andern nützlichen Sachen, Nuremberg, pp. 20-26.

13 This is most probably the earliest documented use of the Freischütz theme in a game. The games issued by Endter, Felsecker and Bieling in 1822/23 show how quickly the Nuremberg business world reacted to Weber's successful opera, as documented in Werner Schultheiß: Ein Nürnberger Freischützspiel; in: Mitteilungen des Vereins für Geschichte der Stadt Nürnberg, vol. 79, 1992, pp. 169–175.

14 Roth [cf. note 6] vol. 2, p. 291

15 Zweite Fortsezung meines Magazins von verschiedenen Sachen sowohl zum

gemeinnützlichen Gebrauche als auch lehrreichen und angenehmen Unterhaltung für die Jugend, Nuremberg 1794, p.3

16 Subtitled: *Zur lehrreichen und angenehmen Unterhaltung der Jugend, als auch für Liebhaber der Künste und Wissenschaften, welche Stücke meistens vorräthig zu finden. Neue verbesserte Auflage* (For the instructive and agreeable entertainment of our young people, as well as for all lovers of arts and sciences, which items are most often stocked. New and revised edition), Nuremberg 1803 (reprint Zurich, 1979)

17 Further editions in 1812 and 1823

18 Wittus Witt: *Zauberkästen. Entstehungs- und Entwicklungsgeschichte des Zauberkastens – Sammlung Wittus Witt*, Munich 1987, p. 11

19 Wenzel [cf. note 1], p.48; Jack Botermans, Jerry Slocum: *Geduldspiele der Welt. Wie man sie baut und wie man sie löst*, Munich 1987, pp. 104–107. Maas [cf. note 5] pp. 55 f also mentions a 70-page book on this subject: "Das Zankspiel, sonst Zankeisen und Nürnberger Tand genannt", Verlag Monath, Nuremberg 1803.

20 Horst-Dieter Beyerstedt: *Nürnberger Sesselgespräch 1802*, in: Nürnberg Archiv. Brunswick 1996, series 02.

21 Christian Gottlob Kayser: *Vollständiges Bücher-Lexikon*, Leipzig, 1834, part 1, p.242

22 City of Nuremberg Archives, C 7/II NL, No. 1808

23 Register of Births, Deaths and Marriages with the Regional Church Archives Nuremberg: In 1793, Georg Hieronimus B. married Catharina Christina Lotzbeck, his brother Johann Adam B., illustrator and later toy maker, married Margaretha Endter in 1799, and Johann Martin Christoph B.'s godfather (1796) was Johann Martin Felsecker.

24 Elisabeth Reynst: *Friedrich Campe und sein Bilderbogen-Verlag zu Nürnberg. Mit einer Schilderung des Nürnberger Kunstbetriebes im 18. und in der ersten Hälfte des 19. Jahrhunderts*, Nuremberg 1962, pp. 24 f.

25 Ruth Bach: *Der Stein als Anstoß. Die Lithographie und das Entstehen neuer Druckereiberufe*, in: Leute vom Fach. Nürnberger Handwerk im Industriezeitalter, published by Centrum Industriekultur Nuremberg, Nuremberg 1988, p. 131

26 Heiner Vogel: *Bilderbogen, Papiersoldat, Würfelspiel und Lebensrad. Volkstümliche Graphik für Kinder aus fünf Jahrhunderten*, Leipzig 1981, p. 66

27 Cf. Fritz Billmann: *Das lithographische Druckgewerbe in der alten Kunststadt Nürnberg. Eine historische Studie*, in: Graphische Presse, 35th year, 1922, no. 30, pp. 129–194

28 Otto Mackh: *Das Nürnberger Steindruckgewerbe*, dissertation Erlangen 1922, pp. 8 f.

29 Reynst, [cf. note 24], pp. 52 f.

30 The Nuremberg municipal library holds a list of 110 games: Parlour games and children's books available from G.P.J. Bieling, Nuremberg. Nuremberg, undated [about 1820]; on the history of the Bieling publishing house cf. Walter Gerlach (ed.): *Das Buch der alten Firmen der Stadt Nürnberg im Jahre 1930*, Leipzig undated [1930], p.126.

31 Manfred Bachmann: *Spielwarenbücher und -kataloge als Quellen zur Alltagsgeschichte*, in: Volkskultur in der Moderne. Probleme und Perspektiven empirischer Kulturforschung, Reinbek 1986, pp. 145–161

32 Bach [cf. note 25], p. 134

33 Hans Ries: *Illustration und Illustratoren des Kinder- und Jugendbuchs im deutschsprachigen Raum 1871–1914*, Osnabrück 1992, p. 279

34 Christa Pieske: *Das ABC des Luxuspapiers. Herstellung, Verarbeitung und Gebrauch 1860 bis 1930*, exhibition Museum für Deutsche Volkskunde, Berlin 1983, p. 11

35 Ries [cf. note 33], pp. 294–296

36 Julius Marfels: *Nürnberger Abziehbilder*, in: Wegweiser für die Spiel-, Galanterie- und Kurzwaren-Industrie, 1912, no. 622 [not paginated]

37 Nuremberg. Published by the City Council, Berlin 1927, pp. 428 f, 435, 510

38 On the history of the publishing house cf. Bruno Kestner: *Herr Geheimrat Theodor Löwensohn*, in: Deutsche Spielwaren-Zeitung, May 1931, p.28; Verona Jeuck, Werner Nostheide: 150 Jahre Pestalozzi-Verlag, Erlangen 1994.

39 Billmann [cf. note 27], p. 194

40 *Die Nürnberger Abziehbilderindustrie einst und jetzt*, in: Wegweiser [cf. note 36], 1919, no. 8, pp. 10–14

41 Helmut Beer, Maximilian Rosner: *Grüsse aus Nürnberg. Nürnberg in Ansichtskarten um 1900*, vols 1-2, Nuremberg 1992–1993

42 Commemorative publication on the occasion of the 40th general meeting of the Association of German Engineers in Nuremberg, 11th–15th June 1899, p. 561 (cf. Die Fabrikindustrie Nürnbergs). On Ernst Nister's biography (1842–1909), cf. B. Kaufmann, E. Hager: *Dem Andenken Ernst Nisters*. Published by Vereinigung für die Zollfragen der Papier verarbeitenden Industrie und des Papierhandels. Berlin 1909; City minister Schiller, Court preacher Kessler [two funeral orations] Altdorf 1909. With the beginning of the First World War, export figures for Nister products started decreasing. The London subsidiary was closed down in 1916, the Nuremberg publishing house given up in 1927.

43 Theodor Stroefer (1843–1927) was trained as a business man for four years (starting in 1858) with the art publishers Friedrich Bruckmann, and from 1868 on, was head of a New York sales agency for Bruckmann products, later on also for other German publishers. When the agency was established as an independent company in 1869 and Georg Kirchner was taken on as a partner in 1870, the publishing house of Stroefer & Kirchner was founded, with headquarters in New York and later on also premises in Munich. In 1877, the company was divided up: Kirchner took over the New York part, Stroefer took on the Munich part of the publishing business. The publishing house was completely destroyed during air raids in 1945, but was not completely removed from the register of companies until 1958 (according to documentation from the private archives of Stroefer's grand daughter Eva Klose-Eberth).

44 The "Verlagsverzeichnis von Theo. Stroefer's Kunstverlag in Nürnberg", 1911–1912 lists the puzzle "Aus dem Märchenlande" (From the World of Fairy Tales), consisting of 6 plates. A further puzzle documented is "Der Kinder Freude" (Children's Joy) from about 1894.

45 *Die deutsche Ausstellung in London*, in: Wegweiser [cf. note 36], 1891, no. 99, pp. 1231 f. The designation of origin "Made in Germany" introduced by Britain in 1887 was supposed to warn customers about the inferior quality of German merchandise.

46 *Die Geschmacksrichtung in der Spielwaaren-Industrie*, in: Wegweiser [cf. note 36], 1890, no. 87, pp. 1047 f.

47 Hildegard E. Krähé: *The Importance of Being Ernest Nister*, in: Phaedrus incorporating Die Schiefertafel. An International Annual, 1988, pp. 73-90; Ries [cf. note 33], pp. 52 f.

48 Ries [cf. note 33], p. 295

49 *Nürnberg*, in: Wegweiser [cf. note 36], 1907, no. 486, pp. 3632 f.

50 Julius Marfels: *Ball-, Fang- und Flugspiele*, in: Wegweiser [cf. note 36], 1909, no. 533, p. 5903

51 Eduard Butzmann: *Das Brettspiel*, in: Wegweiser [cf. note 36], 1913, no. 645, pp. 14, 16

52 ibid. p. 14

53 Bernhard Enzingmüller: *Alte und moderne Nürnberger Spielsachen*, in: Wegweiser [cf. note 36], 1910, no. 547 [not paginated]

54 This description is based on advertisement placed in the "Wegweiser" between 1890 and 1926, Deutsche Spielwaren-Zeitung, February 1937, p. 86 and on post-war issues of the magazine "Das Spielzeug".

55 This information was gathered from advertisements placed in the 1895, 1897, 1907 and 1910 issues of the "Wegweiser".

56 Carsten Hennig: 150 Jahre J.G. Schrödel, in : Das Spielzeug, March 1996, pp. 67-69

57 Walter Gerlach (ed.): Das Buch mit alten Firmen der Stadt Nürnberg im Jahre 1959, Prien 1959, p. 99

58 Julius Marfels: Die Landesausstellung zu Nürnberg, in: Wegweiser [cf. note 36], 1906, no. 465, p. 2628

59 Wegweiser [cf. note 36], 1910, no. 568, p. 13; 1913, no. 626, p. 10057; Deutsche Spielwaren-Zeitung, February 1931, p. 80

60 Wegweiser [cf. note 36], 1895, no. 194, p. 2888; 1899, no. 285, p. 5428

61 Gerlach [cf. note 57], p. 101

62 On the history of the Bing family cf.: Toni Eckert: Ignaz Bing – sein Leben in Streitberg. Published by Fränkische Schweiz-Verein, Streitberg 1995; R. Endres, M. Fleischmann: Nürnbergs Weg in die Moderne, Nuremberg 1996, pp. 127–131.

63 Julius Marfels: Bilder aus den Nürnberg-Fürther und anderen süddeutschen Industriebezirken, in: Wegweiser [cf. note 36], 1910, no. 568, pp. 11 f.

64 Wegweiser [cf. note 36], 1919, no. 1, p. 12; 1920, no. 19, pp. 22,24; 1921, no. 15, p. 27

65 Kurt Lebermann: Die Konzentration der Bingwerke, Leipzig/Erlangen 1924, pp. 53, 59 f, 63

66 The main dates of the company history were taken from some advertisements in the Wegweiser [cf. note 36], 1919, 1921, 1926, from advertisements in the Deutsche Spielwaren-Zeitung 1923, 1931, 1937–1941 and information provided by Klaus Borrmeister, Berlin

Games We Play, pp. 42–129

1 Hesse State Archives, Marburg: Records II Merzhausen 2; Records 16/III/14 No. 23

2 Ibid., Records 16/III/14 No. 23

3 Fürth Municipal Archives, sheet from Register of Citizens in the Town of Fürth – concerning Jacob Spear

4 Record of 1.4.1881. Fürth Municipal Archives, shelf 18 a, p. 1188

5 Wolfgang Helbich (ed.), "Amerika ist ein freies Land...". Emigrants write to Germany, Darmstadt 1985, p. 206 ff.

6 Spear Archives: Record of conversation regarding company history from 3.2.1974, p. 10

7 Record of 1.4.1881. Fürth Municipal Archives, shelf 18 a, p. 1188

8 Details from an inventory by Francis Spear, based on relevant documents, in: "Life History of Jacob Wolf Spear", in the Spear Archives.

9 Entry in the trade register for Sonneberg District, Section A No. CLXVII, company records fol. 227 vol IV (communication from Sonneberg District Council to J. W. Spear & Söhne of 4.7.1953)

10 Compare: (author unknown), "Die Geschichte der Firma Robert Hartwig. Holz- und Spielwarenfabrik zu Sonneberg in Thüringen", without place of publication, without date (presumably around 1950, a copy is to be found in the library of the German Toy Museum in Sonneberg).

11 Ibid., p. 3

12 Entries in the trade register for the Sonneberg district, section A No. CLXXXII (communication from Sonneberg District Council to J. W. Spear & Söhne of 4.7.1953)

13 Letter of 3rd April, 1884 from Fürth Municipal Authorities to the Royal State Home and Foreign Ministry. Fürth Municipal Archives, shelf 18a, p. 1888

14 Letter to Fürth Municipal Authorities of 20.6.1892. Building Administration Office Fürth, Building Records Office, Section VI, shelf 67, Vol. 1: Building and construction at property no. 26, Königswarter Straße

15 Wegweiser für die Keramische, Bronce-, Spiel-, Kurz-, Galanterie- etc. Waaren-Industrie, No. 14 (1887), p. 138 and 142 (in future referred to as "Wegweiser für die Spielwarenindustrie")

16 Letter to Fürth Municipal Authorities of 20.6.1892. Building Administration Office Fürth, property at Königswarter Straße 26

17 Ibid., report of 9.8.1892

18 Wegweiser für die Spielwarenindustrie, No. 131 (1892), p.1682

19 Letter to Fürth Municipal Authorities of 13.6.1892. Building Administration Office Fürth, property at Königswarter Straße 26

20 Fürth Municipal Archives, shelf 18a, p. 1452

21 Fürther Bürgerzeitung, 28.5.1892

22 Letter of 13.6.1892 to Fürth Municipal Authorities. Building Administration Office Fürth, property at Königswarter Straße 26

23 The following account is based on the building records at the Building Administration Office Fürth, property at Königswarter Straße 26.

24 Fürther Tagblatt, 5.9.1893, p. 2

25 Below from Fürth Municipal Archives, shelf 18a, p. 1188

26 Ibid., Engelbrecht´s letter to Fürth Municipal Council of 31.7.1882

27 Fürther Tagblatt, 5.9.1893, p. 2

28 Spear Archives: Excerpt from the Register of Companies of the Fürth Lower Court for J. W. Spear & Sohn. Sophie Spear left the company again on 6.1.1896.

29 Spear Archives: Land register for tax district Höfen Land 17, J. W. Spear & Söhne

30 Spear Archives: Excerpt from the Register of Companies of the Fürth Lower Court for J. W. Spear & Sohn

31 Spear Archives: Record of conversation regarding company history from 3.2.1974, p. 19 f.

32 Spear Archives: Richard Spear "J.W. Spear & Soehne, Nürnberg. Geschichtliches" (Typescript)

33 After a renumbering of the whole street the new address from around 1903 was "Höfener Straße 91".

34 Games. Richly illustrated price list published by J. W. Spear & Söhne Nuremberg-Doos, undated [1904]. This catalogue, printed in German, is incomplete, as a comparison with the English equivalent shows. The English catalogue ("J. W. Spear & Sons Manufacturers and Publishers of Indoor Games and Fancy Goods, Nuremberg-Doos") includes both sections and has 64 pages.

35 Spear Archives: New products index 1893–1910, 286 pages

36 Compare the list of registered trademarks in the appendix.

37 Wegweiser für die Spielwarenindustrie, No. 339 (1901), p. 7416

38 Price list 1904, foreword

39 Details of suppliers from the Spear Archives' new products index mentioned, and from Nuremberg company directories.

40 Compare the building records in City of Nuremberg Archives, C 20/V, No. 4190 and 21027.

41 Compare Parlour and Activity Games Price list published by J. W. Spear & Söhne, Games Factory Nuremberg-Doos. [1910]

42 Spear Archives: Copy of Order for Toy Department Xmas 1914

43 Wegweiser für die Spielwarenindustrie, No. 667/68 (1914), p. 6

44 Wegweiser für die Spielwarenindustrie, No. 679 (1915), p. 34

45 Company advertisement in: Wegweiser für die Spielwarenindustrie, No. 703 (1916), p. 15

46 Company advertisement in: Wegweiser für die Spielwarenindustrie, No. 729 (1917), p. 11

47 Exemplary in this respect was the rise of the Bing Works to a production and trade concern with many branches. Compare also: Kurt Lebermann, Die Konzentration der Bing-Werke Nürnberg, Leipzig/Erlangen 1924.

48 Max Welsch, "Die deutsche Spielwaren-Industrie auf dem Weltmarkt 1926", in: Deutsche Spielwaren-Zeitung, January 1927, p. 14 ff.

49 Compare also the very informative essay by Max Welsch, "Ist die deutsche Spiel-waren-Industrie für die bevorstehenden Existenzkämpfe auf dem Weltmarkt gerüstet?", in: Deutsche Spielwaren-Zeitung, September 1927, pp. 19 – 37 (quotation pp.31 and 33).

50 Spear Archives: Swabian Trust Joint Stock Company Stuttgart, Report … regarding the planned audit of accounts for business year 1931/32 for J.W. Spear & Söhne, Nuremberg, plus balance sheet, together with profit and loss calculation as at 30th June,1932, Stuttgart, 1933 (typescript), sheet 6.

51 These figures were cited by the Vereinigung der Deutschen Spielefabriken, whose headquarters were in Nuremberg. Ausschuß für Untersuchung der Erzeugungs-und Absatzbedingungen der deutschen Wirtschaft (ed.), Die Deutsche Spielwa-renindustrie. Verhandlungen und Berichte des Unterausschusses für allgemeine Wirtschaftsstruktur... Vol. 19, Berlin 1930, p. 10 f.

52 For comparison: The company census conducted by the Imperial Bureau for Statistics in 1925 revealed that 58,251 individuals were working in a total of 11,151 toy businesses. Only 18 concerns employed more than 200 people, among them one single concern in the paper toy branch, with 460 employees: Spear. Unterausschuß für allgemeine... (see above), p. 54.

53 Ibid., p. XI – XIV

54 City of Nuremberg Archives, C7/V, No. 6298

55 Ina Schabert (ed.), Shakespeare Handbuch, Stuttgart 1978, p. 489 ff.

56 Spear Archives: "Bilderbücher und Malbücher" Catalogue and Price List, 1923.

57 Wegweiser für die Spielwarenindustrie, 6 (1920), p. 73. Lettering and Spear figure were registered as trademarks on 21.1.1920.

58 Spear Archives: "Bilderbücher und Malbücher" Catalogue and Price List, 1925

59 Compare Georg Ramseger, "Ein Verlag und sein Gesicht", in: Otto Maier Verlag Ravensburg (ed.), 1883 – 1983. 100 Jahre Verlagsarbeit, Ravensburg 1983, p. 95 ff.

60 Prices from the price list for "Bilderbücher und Malbücher", valid from 15th August, 1925.

61 Compare Spear's Games main catalogue, 1926, p. 48 f.

62 Compare Illustrated Catalogue 1930 of Spear's Games. Home Amusements and Novelties. Manufactured by J.W. Spear & Sons, Nuremberg – Doos (Bava-ria), p. 59.

63 Compare Spear-Spiele. J.W. Spear & Söhne, Spielefabrik und Verlag, Nuremberg – Doos: second supplement to main catalogue (1931), p. 8.

64 Compare J.W. Spear & Söhne, Spielefabrik und Verlag, Nuremberg – Doos: 1924 price list with goods index for the C. Baudenbacher Section, p. 1 and Spear-Spiele main catalogue (1933), p. 23.

65 Spear's Archives, Record of conversation regarding company history from 3.2.1974, p. 29 f.

66 Spear-Spiele. Main catalogue (1933), p. 75

67 Advertising leaflet for "Annemarie" large loom, models 5 and 6, undated (around 1934). Almost all handwork gadgets were delivered, at an additional charge, with work already started (made by homeworkers commissioned by the factory).

68 "Kwiknit News" appeared from 1933/34 presumably on an irregular basis. It was illustrated with photographs and contained, for example, in the first num-ber detailed instructions on how to knit a shoulder scarf and a "smart blouse in modern Viennese knit" with the aid of a "Kwiknit" gadget. Editions of the custo-mer magazine are to be found in the Spear Archives.

69 Spear Archives: Record of conversation regarding company history from 3.2.1974, p. 24

70 In view of the fact that he also got married on 1st April, Richard Spear jokingly remarked during the festivities celebrating his 60 years of involvement in the firm: "I got married on 1st April – I did all the important things in my life on that date so that if I didn´t like them I could say it was a joke!" Spear Archives, "Name of game is Scrabble", undated newspaper clipping

71 All statistical information about the firm is taken from: Swabian Trust Joint Com-pany Stuttgart (Ed.), Report … on the company value of J.W. Spear & Söhne as of June and July 1938, Stuttgart 1938 (Typescript in Spear Archives)

72 Since in Porst's opinion the wages Spear paid were – "without any reason" – too high for the company to function profitably, after "Aryanization", the new owner reduced wages and dismissed numerous older workers. The compensation pay-ments made to these employees had to be born by the seller! Spear Archives: Purchasing contract between J.W. Spear & Söhne and Hanns Porst of 6.4.1939, § 5a

73 Interview with Lotte Stumpf of 5.5.1997

74 Interview with Betty Suthau of 12.5.1997

75 Interview with Lotte Stumpf of 5.5.1997

76 According to the assessment of the situation by Hanns Porst, who took over the Spear Company after "Aryanization" as of December 1938. Spear Archives: Memo by Hanns Porst, undated (presumably 1939)

77 Spear Archives: Letter by Friedrich Burr to the Deutsche Arbeitsfront, Fachabtei-lung Druck und Papier of 29.11.1938

78 Spear Archives: Minutes of the 10th meeting of the Works Council of 7.10.1938

79 "Der alte jüdische Dreh. Die Judenfirma Spear & Söhne und ihr Briefwechsel", in: Der Stürmer, Nr. 45, November 1938.

80 Interview with Herbert and Francis Spear of 10.12.1996

81 Nuremberg State Archives, State Police Department Nürnberg-Fürth, Aryani-zation Files, no. 265: Motorcar belonging to the Jew Hermann Spear

82 Ludwig Greck/ Karl Hermann Rühle, Der Photo-Porst Nürnberg. Der Welt größtes Photohaus, Leipzig 1939 (Deutsche Großbetriebe, Bd. 44)

83 Spear Archives: Memo by Hanns Porst, undated (presumably early 1939)

84 Remark by Hanns Porst to Else Spear. Spear Archives: Record of conversation regarding company history from 3.2.1974, p. 13

85 Spear Archives: Record of examination of Hanns Porst conducted by the Göring Special Commission of 8.3.1939

86 Spear Archives: Record of conversation regarding company history from 3.2.1974, p. 13

87 Spear Archives: Record of examination of Hanns Porst conducted by the Göring Special Commission of 8.3.1939

88 Spear Archives: Expert opinion on the company J.W. Spear & Söhne, Nuremberg, based on its status as of 9.12.1938

89 Spear Archives: Affidavit sworn by Richard Spear, New York, 16.12.1947, p. 3

90 Spear Archives: Letter from Hanns Porst to the Minister of Economics of 13.3.1940

91 Spear Archives: Warrant for arrest against Hanns Porst and others issued by the Special Court for the Judicial District of the Higher Regional Court of Nuremberg at the Nuremberg Regional Court on 26. 11. 1940

92 Spear Archives: Complaint against Hanns Porst on suspicion of imbezzlement filed by the State Criminal Investigation Department, CID Nuremberg-Fürth, on 21.1.1941

93 Curt Riess, Sie haben es noch einmal geschafft. Schicksale im Nachkriegs-deutschland, Berlin/Frankfurt 1955, p. 224

94 Spear Archives: Letter from Hanns Porst to the Chamber of Commerce of the Gau Franken of 17.4.1944

95 Spear Archives: Letter from Hanns Porst to Dr. Köhler of 18.4.1944

96 Letter from Hannsheinz Porst to Nuremberg Toy Museum of 7.4.1997

97 Interview with Herbert and Francis Spear of 10.12.1996

98 On Hermann Spear cf. Fürth's "Memorbuch": Komitee zum Gedenken der Für-ther Shoah-Opfer (Hg.), Gedenke – Remember, Fürth 1997, p. 406.

99 Spear-Spiele, Catalogue 1939, back cover

100 Spear Archives: Expert opinion on the company J.W. Spear & Söhne, Nuremberg, based on its status as of 9.12.1938

101 Spear Archives: Draft of speech by Hanns Porst, undated (April 1939). Porst presumably explained his programme to the Spear workforce in a general meeting after concluding the purchasing contract. One central point is missing, however: the planned dismissal of numerous members of staff, as determined in the purchasing contract of 6.4.1939.

102 Spear Archives: Record of conversation regarding company history from 3.2.1974, p. 14 f.

103 Porst prefaced his speech to the workforce in April 1939 (see note 101) with this Hitler quotation taken from "Mein Kampf".

104 Catalogue: Spear-Spiele, Neuheiten 1939/40, p. 12. Emphasis in the original.

105 All quotations from the new products catalogue 1939/40.

106 Spear Archives: Letter to the Ministry of Economics of 13.3.1940, p. 3 f.

107 Spear Archives: Record of a conversation regarding the company history, from 3.2.1974, p. 28

108 Ibid.

109 Curt Riess, 1955, p. 224 f. (cf. note 93)

110 Ibid. p. 17

111 Spear Archives: Restitution contract of 22.10.1948

112 Spear Archives: Letter to Elli Schulze, Berlin, of 18.1.1949

113 Spear Archives: Letter to the employees of 30.4.1954

114 Spear Archives: 1879 – 1954. Spear Spiele seit 75 Jahren (company brochure)

115 "Spear-Spiele: eine gute Partie", in: Spielzeugmarkt, March 1976

116 Regarding "Typ Dom", which has recently been brought back out by Spielverlag Piatnik, Vienna, compare "Neues Leben für einen Klassiker aus Österreich", in: Die Spielwiese, Issue 42 (July 1997), p. 9 ff. Also: Erwin Glonnegger, Das Spiele-Buch, Munich/Ravensburg 1988, p. 94 f.

117 The following account is based on internal company manuscripts "The History of Scrabble", "The Scrabble Game and J. W. Spear & Sons PLC. A Brief History 1954 to 1987" and "History of the Scrabble Game" from the Spear Archives. Also used: Derryn Hinch, The Scrabble Book, New York 1976 and Karin Spitzing, Alles über Scrabble. Regeln, Tips, Tricks, Informationen für Anfänger und Kenner, Wolfenbüttel 1981.

118 The history of the Schowanek company is based on information which Mr. Franz Aicher, managing director of A.P.S. Schowanek GmbH in Piding, kindly provided to the Nuremberg Toy Museum.

119 Spear-Spiegel. Company brochure on the occasion of its centenary, Nuremberg 1979, p. 6

120 "The A – Z of Scrabble" in: Daily Mail, 8.4.1993, p. 7

121 Das Spielzeug, February 1955, p. 183

122 Spear's Games Catalogue, 1963, p. 4

123 Ibid.

124 "Spear-Spiele: eine gute Partie", in: Spielzeugmarkt, March 1976

125 Das Spielzeug, March 1970, p. 737

126 "Spear-Spiele: Eine gute Partie", in: Spielzeugmarkt, March 1976

127 Staff figures according to the company's annual report.

128 Das Spielzeug, November 1979, pp. 1814 f.

129 Das Spielzeug, July 1979, p. 1291

130 The Guardian, 25th March, 1980

131 Francis Spear, "History of J.W. Spear & Sons", May 1997 (unpublished manuscript). The presentation of the company history during the company's last four decades is largely taken from this very precise document.

132 Das Spielzeug, April 1981, p. 793

133 The Times, 27th March, 1992

134 Playing to win, Spear's Games Catalogue, 1990

135 Staff numbers according to a compilation Francis Spear gathered from company statistics.

136 World Toy News, 31st May, 1994, p. 6

137 A very detailed description of events can be found in Martha Klein "The Games People Play", in: Legal Business, September, 1994, pp. 72-76.

138 Daily Telegraph, 4th June, 1994; Express, 4th June, 1994

139 Figures taken from UK Toy News, June 1994

140 "Spears chief is booted out" in: Enfield, Palmers Green, Southgate & Edmonton Gazette, 16th March, 1995

141 Enfield Independent, 13th December, 1995

142 Enfield Independent, 27th December, 1995

143 Letter to Nuremberg Toy Museum, 22nd August, 1997

Source of Illustrations

Bilderdienst Süddeutscher Verlag, Munich: 95
Klaus Borrmeister, Berlin: 40, 41
Building Records Office, Fürth: 48
City of Nuremberg Archives: 25
Fürth Municipal Archives: 46, 47, 79
German Toy Museum, Sonneberg: 45
Germanisches Nationalmuseum, Nuremberg (Graphic Arts Collection): 8, 17, 28 o., 29 u.
Herbert Kreppner, Fürth: 119
Nuremberg Municipal Museums, Centrum Industriekultur: 105, 107
Nuremberg Municipal Museums, Graphic Arts Collection: 32
Nuremberg Municipal Museums, Toy Museum:
5, 10–16, 19, 20, 22, 23, 27, 28 u., 29 o., 30, 31, 33 o., 36–41, 49, 51, 54, 55, 69, 71, 76, 85, 87, 130, 133, 135, 136, 138–142, 144–160, 163–174, 176–182, 184–186, 188–192, 195–203
Nürnberger Nachrichten: 80

A.P.S. Schowanek GmbH, Piding: 96–100
Spear Archives, Ware/England: 6, 42, 52, 53, 59, 61, 63, 65, 67, 73–75, 77, 83, 88, 90, 91–94, 101–103, 108, 109, 111–117, 120–127, 129, 204
Swiss Sports Museum, Basel: 57

The games depicted on plate 19, 21, 28 (Pfadfinder-Spiel), 38 (Katz und Maus), 60 (Feldpost), 65 (Briefmarken-Spiel, Naturgeschichtliches Lotto), 68 (Pferderennen), 80, 81 (Die fliegenden Hüte) and 85 come from the collection of Dieter Mensenkamp, Detmold. Rudolf Rühle, Bonn, made available the games on page 85 (Bomben auf England) and 87 as well as on plate 39 (Pünktchen und Anton) and 65 (Ansichts-Karten Spiel). The Nuremberg Toy Museum owns the games on plate 1 (Compendium, 1955), 3 (Halma), 7 (Die Windmühle), 37 (Der Weg zur Schule), 61 (Punch and Judy show, draft), 72 (Hexenkette, Wer kann's?), 74 (Weltreise-Quartett) und 78. All other games come from the Spear's Games Archive, Ware.

Index

The index consists of two parts: a general index (persons, firms, general terms) and a games index. Page and plate numbers of illustrations are given in **bold** type.

Index of Games